Blue Clay People

Blue Clay People

Seasons on Africa's Fragile Edge

William Powers

BLOOMSBURY

Published by Bloomsbury Publishing, New York and London
Distributed to the trade by Holtzbrinck Publishers

All papers used by Bloomsbury Publishing are natural, recyclable
products made from wood grown in well-managed forests. The
manufacturing processes conform to the environmental regulations
of the country of origin.

Library of Congress Cataloging-in-Publication Data

Powers, William D. (William Daniel), 1971–
Blue clay people : seasons on Africa's fragile edge / William D.
Powers.—1st U.S. ed.
p. cm.
ISBN 1-58234-532-5
1. Liberia—Social conditions—1980– 2. Powers, William D.
(William Daniel), 1971– 3. Americans—Liberia—Biography. I. Title.

HN835.A8P69 2004
306'.096662—dc22
2004012168

ISBN-13 9781582345321

First U.S. Edition 2005

1 3 5 7 9 10 8 6 4 2

Typeset by Palimpsest Book Production Ltd,
Polmont, Stirlingshire, Scotland

Printed in the United States of America
by Quebecor World Fairfield

To my parents,
for their love and their courage

And to A.

CONTENTS

We have lived by the assumption that what was good for us would be good for the world. We have been wrong. We must change our lives so that it will be possible to live by the contrary assumption that what is good for the world will be good for us. And that requires that we make the effort to know the world and to learn what is good for it. We must learn to cooperate in its processes, and to yield to its limits. But even more important, we must learn to acknowledge that the creation is full of mystery; we will never clearly understand it. We must abandon arrogance and stand in awe. We must recover the sense of the majesty of the creation, and the ability to be worshipful in its presence. For it is only on the condition of humility and reverence before the world that our species will be able to remain in it.

—Wendell Berry, *Recollected Essays*

AUTHOR'S NOTE

In the unpredictable arena of West African politics, even seemingly trivial things can trigger animosity. Though this is a work of nonfiction, I have disguised many friends' and colleagues' identities, including changing most names and relocating some events in place and time. In several cases it was necessary to use composites; that is, I grafted one or more traits from one actual person (e.g., mannerism, speech, nationality, job title, and gender) into another to more thoroughly camouflage identity. All of this, I hope, also serves in a more general sense to respect the privacy of those involved.

PROLOGUE

In the Beginning, God Sneezed

"THIS IS THE story of the blue clay people," Momo says. He's my driver, a six-foot-five-inch black man, the descendant of a Virginia slave named Milly who came to Liberia a century and a half ago. We're relaxing on the courtyard patio of a jazz joint in Liberia's capital, Monrovia (named after James Monroe), a fuzzy Miles Davis trumpet solo filtering out of some old phonograph speakers. Momo takes a sip from a bottle of beer wrapped in toilet paper. His graying, close-cropped Afro emerges from a deeply crevassed brow. The remarkable thing about Momo is his extremely large eyes, hooded by droopy lids and bordered by deep crow's-feet.

He clears his throat, and the light suffuses his eyes from somewhere within: "It all started when God came down off his mountain and got down to the business of making people." Momo spins out a tale in an accent etched with the lilting cadence of the American South: God, who plays sax and looks like John Coltrane in his *Love Supreme* period, molded the first six human beings out of blue clay—three men and three women. He sat by the river all day, humming jazz riffs while shaping his creations. By the time the sun was setting, they were almost perfect. All that was missing was a little spice. Pepper would do! But as God was grinding pepper with two stones, something happened that would change the entire course of history.

"God sneezed," Momo says. "It was a sneeze so mighty that even he could not stop it. It caused the pepper to swirl up and fall on the still-wet clay people! He had let loose a fire that would burn in their blood, making people destroy each other and all of nature. They would spoil his whole creation! . . . God sat down, his head in his hands. A miserable sit."

Here Momo pauses and sips his beer. The humid Monrovia night presses in on us. Several palm trees stretch upward into a black sky dotted with a million stars. "Finally God stood up and touched his blue clay people. He shrugged, saying, 'Well, if you grind pepper, you have to expect to sneeze! And one thing's for sure: You can *never* unsneeze a sneeze.'" ·

A well-known international aid agency sent me to the tropical West African country of Liberia in 1999 and told me to fight poverty and save the rainforest. At the time, I had just completed my graduate work at Georgetown with Dr. Carol Lancaster and others, focusing on the links between human poverty and environmental destruction in the global south (or what is often called the third world), so I was intrigued by the job. Liberia's seven-year civil war had ended in 1997, and I was to lead the transition from soup lines to sustainability. What I could not have known, then, was that Liberia's seven-year civil war would come to be known as her fourteen-year civil war; I had entered the eye of the storm.

The initial idea for this book was journalistic, or even academic. I was to use Liberia as a case study of conservation in what I term the "fourth world" the black holes in the international system, the sub–third world countries that are not just poor, but environmentally looted, violence scarred, and barely governed; the places where Pandora's box has been opened and cannot be closed. The book was to be an insider's analysis of the challenges of giving aid and conserving the environment within one of Robert Kaplan's "frontiers of anarchy."

That book was never written. It became obvious that it would be so technical as to be useful only to a handful of specialists: aid practitioners, policy makers, and scholars. I realized that Liberia, and the idea of the fourth world, could be best brought to life through speaking my own story in the form of a memoir. Far better to explore issues of rainforest politics and conflict diamonds while traveling Liberia by Jeep and surfboard; sipping mint juleps with Burkinabe mercenaries; inhaling the oxygen-rich air of a virgin rainforest.

Momo, who first told me the legend of the blue clay people, is missing. The most recent wave of fighting sent him running, along with hundreds of thousands of others. Momo is a bit actor in the global drama being played out in Liberia. It is a drama that involves arms trafficking, diamond smuggling, rainforest destruction, terrorist training camps, the spread of AIDS, and the global institutions that act—or fail to act— to contain these threats. A drama in which one man, Liberia's former president Charles Taylor, managed to destabilize West Africa using funds from diamonds and tropical timber sold to the West.

With Taylor's exile to Nigeria in the summer of 2003, the world's largest UN peacekeeping deployment now oversees a touchy Liberian peace. Meanwhile, the United States asks itself whether it has a special responsibility to the country;

Liberia was purchased in 1822 by the American Colonization Society (ACS) as a destination for American freed slaves and was the closest the United States ever came to taking a colony in Africa. In a larger sense, the world faces the question of what ethical responsibility wealthy nations have vis-à-vis poor nations when no strategic interest such as oil is at stake.

Beneath these and other questions lies a more fundamental one: Are we human beings made of blue clay? If the jazzy, deterministic Liberian God has it right, we are destined to make war on one another and destroy the environment until the end.

PART I
Rainy Season

Bossman Missy

The future is the only kind of property that the masters willingly concede to the slaves.

—Camus, *The Rebel*

CHAPTER 1

THIS IS THE world's most beautiful place.

There are many such places. As many, in fact, as there are people. For her it's the smooth-pebble beach of her childhood. For him it's the slick-rock canyons of southern Utah. For another it's a dreamscape: light, warmth, peace. As for me, the world's most beautiful place is Africa's Guinean rainforest, or, to be more precise, Liberia's Sapo National Park.

From the airplane I stare down upon this forest for the first time. Having flown over the coffee and cacao plantations of the Ivory Coast, we have just crossed the Cavalla River, which marks the border with Liberia. Below me is a block of peacock, kelly, and olive green stretching out to the horizon. I search for breaks in the canopy but find none. As far as my eyes can see, the earth is solid rainforest. According to Conservation International, this land is one of the world's twenty-five "hot spots" of biodiversity and has "the highest mammal species diversity of any region in the world." Liberia is one of the final niches on the planet for the pigmy hippopotamus, Diana monkey, viviparous toad, and zebra duiker. Their last stand. If this habitat disappears, they go the way of Miss Waldron's red colobus, into extinction.

I am already aware that the world below holds a secret that is whispered beneath this tree canopy. If one listens carefully, it can almost be heard—a single word, "utopia." Below, tribal people cup out a benign acre for agroforestry, hunt and gather, and exist in exquisite harmony with the biosphere. They leave a light footprint; live for the seventh generation; take nothing, not even pictures. In their world, your ancestor takes the shape of a screeching ibis; your own limb is that of an ironwood tree; and the stones you walk over feel your weight. This world is beautifully dimmed by a green canopy, the fleshy walls of the earth's lungs, which spew forth oxygen and regulate the planet's climate.

Flying over this mesmerizing rainforest canopy, I promise myself I will learn from the people who live there. While I am to direct a multimillion-dollar portfolio of agriculture, health, and food distribution programs out of an air-conditioned office in the capital, I vow to leave that comfort behind as often as possible. I sense already that only through understanding the people can I shape programs that might reduce infant mortality, enhance food security, and conserve the Liberian environment.

My heart feels as though it's slamming against my rib cage. In just twenty minutes I am to land in Monrovia. I squint down, trying to find the edge of the forests—there must be an edge!—but it's nothing less than a green sea of trees fanning out to the horizon.

It's been an incredible adventure, and I haven't even landed in Liberia.

"Abidjan, now boarding, gate ten."

My flight. I picked up my carry-on bag, walked over to the pay phone near my gate, and lifted the receiver. I held it for a long moment, as if considering its weight, but finally placed it back on the hook. The bustle of New York's JFK International Airport moved around me as my gaze drifted through the window to the Air Afrique jet. I took a deep breath and dialed the number I knew by heart.

"Hi, Jennifer."

"Hi, baby."

Jennifer was in Washington, D.C., where we met during graduate school. We had been dating for several years and were close to being engaged. As we talked, a tension tugged at the edges of our words. "I've got to go," I said. "They're boarding."

"Are you sure you want to do this?"

I flashed a sidelong look at the line of people handing over their tickets and disappearing into the gate. My last chance to back out. Jennifer continued, "I've always encouraged you to pursue your dreams. But this is more like pursuing a nightmare."

"Let's not exaggerate."

"*Liberia?* You've never even been to Africa and you're starting *there?* What can you hope to accomplish in a place like that? Liberia's not even a country; it's a war zone."

We'd been through this many times before. Almost everyone had boarded. I needed to go.

"I'm sorry," I heard Jennifer say. "It's just that I'm worried about you."

"Everything will be fine, Jennifer."

I could hear her breathing. She said, "I love you."

"Me too."

Air Afrique got us to Baltimore and no farther. There, a voice from the aircraft's loudspeaker asked us to "kindly deplane." At the desk inside, friendly West Africans told us the delay would be "less than eight hours" as they handed us each twenty-dollar vouchers for meals. "Twenty dollars! That's *chicken change*!" a Liberian woman shouted at the attendant as she snatched her voucher. "I can't even get me McDonald for that!"

Stuck in Baltimore, I called a lawyer friend to help me pass the time. When Diane arrived at the airport, I told her about the twenty-dollar voucher. She said, "Let me handle this." I watched her stride confidently over to the counter and ask to speak with the manager. She informed him about the severe inconvenience her client was experiencing and asked, "So what are you going to do for him?"

"We gave him a twenty-dollar voucher."

"That's a start, but I ask again: What are you going to do for him?"

First class. Diane had talked Air Afrique into the free upgrade. I sniffed the bouquet of my pretakeoff Chardonnay with more than a touch of guilt.

Our one stop, in Dakar, turned into two and then three as we took unscheduled detours to Conakry and then Lagos. "Lagos! Lagos, Nigeria?" exclaimed the Liberian woman who had called her voucher *chicken change*. "Nigeeeria. That's thousands of miles out of our way-o! Why don't we just fly to Timbuktu?"

"That's closer. It's in Mali."

"We have to put an end to this nonsense. Let's boycott!" someone else suggested.

"Let God's will be done!" said another.

"This isn't God's will. This is Satan's handiwork! And it is *hot* as all hell in this plane. In five minutes *I will be cooked like a bacon*!"

This lively banter lapsed into exhaustion as another two-hour flight south brought us to Lagos, followed by two hours north to Abidjan, where a fourteen-hour layover awaited us.

At each unplanned stopover, a voice apologized for "the inconveniences you have experienced on Air Afrique."

Finally arriving in the Côte d'Ivoire airport, we lined up at immigration. An American accent came from behind me: "Whew, rough flight." I turned to a man in a buttoned-up short-sleeve shirt, khaki pants, and immaculately white tennis shoes. "What brings you to West Africa?" he asked.

"I'm an aid worker," I said, testing out the new job title in my mouth. "Posted to Liberia."

"Hey, everyone! We've got an emergency cowboy in the house!" he announced to the people around us. "Whew-hoo! But *Liberia*!? Watch your back, buddy!"

I asked him what brought him to West Africa.

"Who, me? I'm preaching *the Word*. I've got teams of young people all over this continent, and I'm here to interface with them. Haven't put any young people in Liberia, of course. Waaay too hot there! *Ouch*!" He punched an invisible point in the air and snatched his finger away from it.

When we reached the immigration booth, an Ivorian official stamped my passport and then said something to me in French. We stared at each other for a moment, his look completely indecipherable. He finally let me through with an offhand nod. The American missionary shouldered toward me, thrust a sweaty hand in my direction, and said, "God bless you, man!"

Since I had the entire day in Abidjan, I checked my bags in the airport and took a taxi toward the Plateau district downtown. The taxi sped down the yawning autoroute past rawboned black women balancing baskets on their heads. I wandered beneath the Plateau's glass towers all morning. Coffee and cacao exports had lifted Côte d'Ivoire's economy to number three in sub-Saharan Africa, and the new wealth was obvious in the designer suits and shoes and smell of French perfume in the city streets. In one of the Plateau's coffee shops, I nibbled a brioche while listening to a pair of waiters argue as they towel-dried espresso cups.

Early that same afternoon, I climbed into a midsize plane operated by a company of which I'd never heard: Wesua. Inside, the exit signs were in Russian. The plane, an artifact of the Soviet empire, was gasping its final breaths in weekly flights from Côte d'Ivoire to Liberia. This was the only commercial flight into Liberia from anywhere in the world.

Two dozen of us sat in fraying seats, many of which were now permanently in the recline position. Several rows of seats had been removed and replaced by long wooden boxes covered by canvas. Wondering what was inside the boxes, I recalled that current Liberian president Charles Taylor had received training in Libyan terrorist camps before instigating the seven-year Liberian civil war on Christmas Eve 1989. While the war officially ended with the 1997 elections (which Taylor won by a landslide, campaigning under the promise that if not elected, he would restart the war), Taylor continued to sponsor Sierra Leone's Revolutionary United Front (RUF) rebels, who hacked off infants' hands to terrorize populations out of diamond-rich lands near the Liberian border.

Boiling hot, we sat in the plane, staring at the mysterious cargo, and everyone seemed too fatigued by the heat even to grumble. I was beginning to feel nostalgic for Air Afrique when two mustached Ukrainian pilots finally climbed into the cockpit. Sinister laughter could be heard in the cockpit right before the engine sputtered and then roared, and we were off to Liberia.

CHAPTER 2

*R*OBERTSFIELD INTERNATIONAL AIRPORT, *Monrovia.* As we taxi down the runway, soldiers in dark-blue-and-black uniforms flank either side of the plane. "Mother of Christ," a white South African whispers from the seat beside me. *"Where on God's earth are we?"* The soldiers pivot neat one-eighties as the nose of the plane passes each of them. Their disheveled uniforms suggest that they are fresh from the front. M-16s, tommy guns, and pistols hang from shoulders and belts, and one soldier shifts to balance an antiaircraft gun on his shoulder.

The plane slows to a halt where the airport's former control tower has crumbled onto the runway. We deplane into confusion. While customs agents are inspecting my World Health Organization booklet for yellow fever immunizations, soldiers scuffle with panicked passengers trying to get into the baggage area. I soon realize why: You need to get in before your bags disappear.

I spot one of the seventy-pound bags I have brought to Liberia. As I press against the crowd, a dozen airport employees shuffle the incoming luggage like Coney Island three-card monty sharks. Trying to keep my eye on the ace, I finally manage to squeeze between two soldiers and slip inside. But as I reach for my bag, another soldier pushes me back. "No!! You must stay there and wait. Wait!"

"Wait? *Wait for what?!*"

The soldier's jowled face tenses, and he squares his body

to mine, his M-16 across his chest. In that moment I hear a voice: "Mr. Power?" A big-chested woman who looks to be in her late thirties stands before me.

"Powers, yes," I say.

"You are the chief who brings many *powers* from America!" she booms out, her impossibly white teeth set against a face so dark, it is nearly black. She presses a few bills into the soldier's palm and the M-16 falls slack at his side. As we breeze through the crowds and round up my luggage, she explains that she is Amanda and that I am to replace her as Catholic Relief Services (CRS) director of projects for Liberia.

I trail Amanda through the airport door into another mad swarm of people outside. A gang of teenagers rushes to grab my luggage. One of them wrestles a bag away from me and drags it another few feet to a shiny white Jeep Cherokee emblazoned with a dark green CRS on the door. With sweaty gusto, the teen hoists my bags into the Jeep, and we push our way into its air-conditioned interior as desperate-looking faces press against the glass, demanding money. Amanda lowers her electric window in the front seat and hands a single bill to one of them and then growls at the others, "That boy carried this man's bag! What did *you* do?"

She laughs, saying, "Ah, Liberians, zay always back down in the end!" For the first time, I notice a touch of Amanda's native French: She is Congolese. Earning a graduate degree and successfully directing a prominent nonprofit in her own country helped her land a coveted CRS international staff position—permanent foreign service jobs paid on an American, rather than host-country, salary scale. I have been tipped off about her tragic experience in the Congo. It seems that she walked into her home one day after work several

14

years ago to find that rebels had captured her husband. Her two children's heads, severed from their bodies, were lying on the kitchen table.

As our driver shifts into higher gear, I glance back over my shoulder at the Russian Wesua plane sitting alone on the airstrip. As we race forward, it shrinks and finally disappears. We pass through a nearby village called Smell-No-Taste, and I ask about the name. The driver answers that Robertsfield Airport was originally built by Americans during World War II as a military base. "The people in this village near the Americans were hungry-o! They could smell their food but surely could not taste it!"

After Smell-No-Taste, the asphalt slices through a grassy savanna. Lamp poles lining the highway have been decapitated, and their multicolored wires toss in the wind. I ask the driver his name, and he tells me that he's Momo. He jives his way through various military checkpoints as the savanna gives way to increasing urbanization. Cinder-block buildings rise up along a white sand beach. Women and children hand-wash clothes in lagoons buffered from the Atlantic's waves. As we weave through the potholes downtown, I examine Monrovia's war-torn skyline. The highest building stands at ten stories and has been reduced to a windowless shell.

We slow to a crawl on the far side of downtown, where thousands of pedestrians choke the street. Shanties crowd the roadside. Orange rust covers the corrugated iron roofs. Sweat accumulates on my face, and I see a similar sleek of wetness covering everything outside, bleeding out of the vegetation that thrives in the gaps between shanties and slicking the road. My stomach tightens. It's been over forty-eight hours since I've slept. Out of the swirl of colors (the bobbing,

15

slapping, striding press of people) rises a pile of trash—smack in the middle of the street and blocking our way.

"The mountain!" Amanda exclaims.

Momo hits the brakes, steps out of the Jeep Cherokee into the crowd, and clicks the two front tires into four-wheel-drive position. He revs the engine and we begin to traverse a hill of decaying animal bones, rotten eggs, plastic bags, fruit and vegetable waste, and human excrement. The smell fills the Jeep, and I hold my breath to escape the noxious odor and peer out the window at the anomaly in the street. An old man climbs *the mountain,* his back doubled over, using a tree branch for a cane. To my left, children dig through the rubble, collecting pieces of scrap metal in a basket. Another young girl squats atop *the mountain,* relieving her bowels.

It takes us a full thirty seconds to traverse this apparently permanent landfill in the middle of a public market. Looking around at the people who live, breathe, raise their children, work, and play on and around *the mountain,* I wake up to where I am. This is a city of over a million people living on their own waste. When trash pails are put out on Wednesday mornings, no one picks them up. Nor are they picked up on Thursday, or any other day, because there is no trash collection anywhere in Monrovia.

There is no electricity in the nation's capital city, unless you happen to own a diesel generator. There is no pipe-borne water. There is no mail service to or within Liberia. The U.S. Postal Service does not deliver to Liberia because there is no one to receive and distribute the mail. Nearly all of the buildings appear to be collapsing into the roads. There are no streetlights. A telephone "system" covers only a few square blocks of downtown—the only phone service in the whole country. According to the United Nations, Liberia is the world's second poorest country, beaten out only by neighboring Sierra Leone. Monrovia is one million people, or half of Liberia's two million, living in darkness, on a mountain of trash.

After clearing *the mountain* and motoring out of Waterside Market and through a long string of connected slums, Momo turns left onto a dirt path barely wide enough for the Jeep. As we jolt over potholes, passing mud homes interspersed with minuscule corn, cassava, and rice plots, I shudder at the thought of the hovel I am likely to live in for the next two years but brace myself for the sight. After all, I am here not to be comfortable, but rather, in my supervisor's words, "to fight poverty while preserving the rainforest."

Amanda's cheeriness fills the car, challenging my dread. "I am so glad you are here!"

"Thanks," I choke out.

"Yes, so glad you are here, *mon bon ami.* Because you are my replacement, and now I am free to leave Liberia!"

Amanda bursts into a deep laugh, and Momo joins in with a throatier one. I am having trouble even forcing out a chuckle as Momo slows to a stop and slams on the horn. Before us rises an iron gate painted in white letters: CAROLINA FARM. The gate creaks open, each side pulled by a smiling guard, and I view my home for the next two years. A dozen white villas hug a gleaming bay. The sun shines over Carolina Farm, but dark clouds brew over the ocean beyond, and the quick lightning flashes of an electric storm animate the horizon. A squad of half a dozen black men stoop over, their backs slick with sweat as they cut the golf course–style lawn with machetes. A white couple peer lazily over at me from their wicker balcony chairs. Meanwhile, another white man races by on a four-wheeler, a chimpanzee in baby clothing hugging tightly to his waist.

The guards snap salutes as we pull in and then, sticking their heads in the window, pat me on the shoulder, saying, "Welcome to Carolina Farm, *bossman*!"

While exploring the Carolina Farm estate, I bump into my new neighbor Mona, a short British woman who works with the United Nations Development Program (UNDP). As we chat, I mention to her my initial shock over the army of gardeners, cooks, houseboys, and guards serving these dozen expatriates.

"Oh, you'll get used to it. I have six."

Six, I think. These are a half dozen of the people I saw collecting scrap metal in *the mountain* on the way in.

Noting my furrowed brow, Mona says, "I know what you're thinking: that it must get pricey. Nope. I spend less than a hundred British pounds a month on them all. One of them does the garden, another cooks, another cleans. Oh, and I need my own night guard since the Carolina Farm guards sleep on duty. It's bloody brilliant to come home from work, get out of your car, and have them right there serving your every need—carrying your briefcase inside, serving you a hot supper, and then doing your dishes and drawing you a nice bubble bath. One does foot massages. I really feel like they are my family."

A few days later, while exploring the estate, I bump into another neighbor, an Australian in his early thirties who works with the United Nations Children's Fund (UNICEF). Barrel-chested and grinning, he clutches a can of imported beer and says, "This sure ain't Europe, mate."

"Excuse me?" I say.

He gestures with his beer out across his vast lawn at two shirtless Liberian men, or "boys," cutting his lawn with cutlasses. The deep black skin of their backs glistens with sweat, and they work, doubled over, without speaking to one another.

"I could stand here watching them all day," he says with a chuckle.

The words take a moment to register, but when they do I turn and walk away. No ta-tas, just a turn of the back and a quick stride away. All my neighborliness disappears. I am too angry to speak. My neighbors are not living in the same country I saw coming in from the airport. Haven't they seen *the mountain*?

I had landed in a strange reconstruction of the southern antebellum plantation system, and I was unwittingly cast in the role of master.

Liberian history, from the settlement of the country by freed American slaves in 1822 until their overthrow in 1980, is about the domination of the country's vast majority by a minuscule elite.*

This is far from what Paul Cuffee had in mind when he began repatriating West Africa. A black Quaker and maritime entrepreneur from Massachusetts, Cuffee (whose father had purchased his own freedom) was an ardent abolitionist who joined with other freed northern blacks in abolitionist campaigns. In 1815, he captained a voyage to Sierra Leone,

---

*Before 1822, little is known about the area and its native peoples, as it was scantly explored. The Portuguese established contact with Liberia in the mid-fifteenth century, calling it the Grain Coast because of the abundance of Malegueta pepper grains. While the British installed trading posts along the Grain Coast in 1663, the Dutch destroyed the posts a year later. The next reports of settlement were the freed slaves of the early 1800s.

where he helped thirty-eight African Americans establish homes under an agreement with the British colonial authorities. Cuffee's dream: Ex-slaves use the skills they learned in captivity to help Africans develop their continent. They would also evangelize and work as watchdogs to cut off slavery at its source.

Cuffee died in 1817 with his dream only partially realized, but his initial success encouraged white southerners and slaveholders with a very different vision: a way to get rid of freed blacks. The American Colonization Society was chartered and given $100,000 by the U.S. Congress (this was seen by many as an extravagant sum at the time) and began searching for the right site along the African coast. In 1821, ACS representatives, accompanied by U.S. military officials, persuaded local chiefs at gunpoint to exchange the three-by-thirty-six-mile swath that would later include Monrovia for $300 of assorted goods, including a barrel of beads, ten iron pots, four umbrellas, and some biscuits. The first African Americans settled into a city that in their religious fervor they called Christopolis, but they soon changed it to Monrovia after American president James Monroe, an ACS member who championed a "little America destined to shine gem-like in the darkness of vast Africa."

All told, the ACS's accomplishments were modest: Fewer than twenty thousand freed slaves were repatriated to Liberia. From the very beginning, the society was an ideological battleground. Initially it was opposed by blacks, who, noting the ACS's white-only membership policy, feared forced deportation. In the 1830s, white abolitionists like William Garrison harshly attacked the ACS as a palliative to the real issue—slavery. (Until 1860, ships continued to bring African slaves to the United States.) However, other white liberals disagreed with

Garrison, feeling that American blacks would be happier in Africa, where they would be free from racial discrimination.

The blacks who chose to cross to the malaria-ridden coast of Liberia probably agreed with this latter group. Calling themselves "Americo-Liberians," they penned a declaration of independence similar to America's; adopted a red, white, and blue flag with eleven stripes and a single star; chose the Dixie square as the national dance; and approved a constitution written by a Harvard professor and codified at Cornell. Their first president, Joseph Jenkins Roberts, was born and raised in America. The Americos walked about their coastal settlements sporting bowler hats, white gloves, and morning coats; they lived in sprawling mansions, often with fireplaces (usually phony, since the tropical climate is much too hot for heating systems); and they came to rule the way the antebellum whites had ruled them: through domination.

Under the black colonial aristocracy that emerged, 99 percent of the population of indigenous Africans from sixteen tribes—including the Mano, Kpelle, Bassa, Mandingo, and Krahn—were disenfranchised and forced to labor on Americo plantations. As such, Americo-Liberian wealth was built on the backs of others. From their wraparound porches, the Americos referred to the tribal Africans as "savages" and "aborigines" right into the 1950s. In the 1930s, the League of Nations exposed the Americo penchant for selling their tribal compatriots into slavery in central African cacao plantations. While this scandal forced the resignation of a president and vice president, these leaders were followed by a string of similarly corrupt, smug, and downright racist leaders who all hailed from the same political party that ran Liberia for 133 years straight: the True Whigs.

The final Americo president, who governed Liberia from

1970 until its first coup in 1980, was William R. Tolbert Jr., grandson of a freed South Carolina slave and son of a wealthy rubber baron. Tolbert was a Baptist minister who lectured his people in grandiose homilies. "In a world of rising expectations and accelerated change," he said on one occasion, "the lofty goals of national destiny still require and demand that Liberians harness and channel all their resources . . . in order to achieve a sustained upward thrust for ever-escalating rounds of distinction—yea, higher heights."

As he moralized to public audiences, the Americo minister banked $200 million from public coffers. His son Adolphus B. Tolbert left a paper trail of his own corruption, including a note written to a European businessman who had recently been in Liberia: "I expect to meet you in London . . . to discuss the gold, diamond, and uranium project . . . Bring along the Rolls-Royce . . . Please transmit the balance on that amount given to me last night. Also send the papers for the two cars."

President Tolbert's government, and Americo rule of Liberia through the True Whig party, fell late one evening in April 1980 when an army sergeant, Samuel Doe (a country boy from the Krahn tribe), scaled the iron gates of Tolbert's home with nineteen others. Tolbert had just returned from a diplomatic reception in downtown Monrovia to his seven-story Israeli-built mansion overlooking the Atlantic, changed into his pajamas, and gone to sleep. Doe and his ragtag colleagues broke into Tolbert's penthouse suite, gouged out an eye, eviscerated him, and shot him several times in the head.

I feel shock and guilt over my position at the top of the Liberian social pyramid and express a tepid resistance by doing my own domestic work, including gardening. I am pruning the shrubs outside my villa when a Liberian man fumigating a termite mound near Mona's house puts down his sprayer and comes over to me.

"How'da'body?" he asks.

"Excuse me?"

"How'da'body? Body fine-o?"

I flash a confused look. He tries again. "I mean, y'all right, bossman? Body fine?"

"Oh! I'm great. You?"

"Body fine, body fine . . . But I say!" He shifts his weight from one foot to the other. "You need to get a *boy* to do that."

"I enjoy gardening."

"No, what you do is . . . *you get a boy*. Eeh? You pay him and he does that for you."

I try to protest, but he shakes his head and continues his explanation of the procedure. "After you pay the boy, you give your boy instructions. Then you can watch him from your porch while you sip a cool sof' drink!" He explodes with laughter and jogs back to his sprayer, shaking his head.

I recall a conversation I had in D.C. shortly before departing for Liberia. A Pakistani friend who had grown up with servants was insisting to me that I would have domestic help in Liberia.

"I won't have domestic help," I said. "It's *Catholic Relief Services*! You know, 'CRS—Giving hope to a world of need.'"

He smiled. "Trust me, my friend. You'll have help."

And then along comes Evans. When I am at work one day, he enters my house, does the dishes in the sink, and hand-washes all of my laundry. The next morning, I find a hot breakfast laid out for me in the dining room when I get up. I'm not exactly sure how he is getting in.

I ask my Congolese colleague, Amanda, about Evans, since he has worked as her houseboy for the past two years. "He eats my food. Not just bread, but good cheese." She shakes her head and continues, "*Oui,* and I'm not sure he washes his hands. I say to Evans when he comes inside, 'Evans! *Hands!*' and he always goes back to his boy's quarters and washes them. I know it sounds very colonial, but I need to think of my health since he prepares my food."

"What will Evans do when you leave?"

"Well, you can hire him if you want, but I don't trust Evans. I have some socks missing, and I suspect Evans. I have locked down most of my house for the last two weeks."

Despite my uneasiness about domestic help, Evans keeps coming to make my breakfast and wash my clothes, and I decide to hire him. I don't have the heart to put him out of a job. Or at least that's what I tell myself as I hesitantly get used to his excellent service.

CHAPTER 3

I'M ON A covert mission to give some lucky child a Beanie Babies stuffed toy. But I want to do it responsibly, so as not to encourage dependency.

If there is one thing that bothers me as much as the elitist attitudes of the expatriates, it's the parasitic posture of nearly everyone else. The begging irks me because it feeds and sustains the elitism. Nearly every evening, I take a walk through the Carolina Farm neighborhood outside of the estate where I live—the impoverished surrounding area has adopted the same name as the estate—where I am accosted by children demanding, "Bossman-gimmie-five-dolla!" Without exception every single child begs, as do many adults. I really want to give away the Beanie Baby that I have hidden in my shorts' pocket, but I don't want to reward begging.

It feels odd to have the Beanie Baby at all. My mother returned from Toys "R" Us shortly before my departure with two shopping bags full of toys destined for my suitcases. When I refused to bring the toys, she said, "Those poor children in Africa don't have anything!"

"Just giving people stuff creates dependency," I countered.

My mother and I argued for a while, and I finally broke down and agreed to bring one Beanie Baby. Just one. And now, in Liberia, I am going to give it to the first child who does not ask me for something. I stroll along footpaths under the palm and citrus trees of greater Carolina Farm, through clay earth clearings, all the while steeling myself against requests. A dozen children approach me, but each walks away empty-handed after asking for *their Christmas* or *their Saturday*.

Truth be told, in my first weeks in Liberia, absolutely everyone wants *their weekend*.

I became aware of the pattern when my driver, the tall, gravelly-voiced Momo, strode into my office during those first days at CRS. "Bossman!" he rasped. "My weekend on *you!*"

Uh-oh, I thought, *I've been tagged*. I had been receiving an average of a dozen requests for money daily in imaginative forms, such as "Where's my weekend?" or, alluding to the Liberian independence day holiday, "Where's my July twenty-sixth?" Others asked for a "sof' drink," soap, cold water, or transportation. Another form was simply asking to "be friends," which was a euphemism for "You are an ATM machine and my PIN is valid." While I did contribute to some folks, the ubiquitous need was beginning to have a numbing effect.

But how would I answer Momo? His *weekend* is on *me*? I knew that you never reply with an outright "No" in Liberia, since this is considered rude. So I chose to answer with a nondescript "Hmmmm." Momo stood in the doorway for a long moment, staring at me with his big eyes, and then exited.

The weekend came and went, and on Monday morning, Momo approached me in the hallway.

"Bossman!" he said, looking down at me.

"Momo! How are you?"

"I tryin' small. Hey! Remember when I told you m'weekend on you? What happened?"

I forced a laugh. "Momo! What do you mean, your weekend was on me?"

"You were supposed to take care of me!"

A much shorter driver who was with Momo chimed in, "Yeah! In Liberia when someone say 'My weekend on you,' you supposed to give them something small."

I stammered, "I really wasn't quite . . . clear on that." Then I offered a weak, "Next time?"

"Sure, man! No problem! Next time!" Momo said, slapping me on the shoulder.

The weekend drama was reenacted in a variety of ways with the police and military as well. The most common way was to be flagged down in your vehicle by an officer on foot, who would then affect a puffed-up anger over an invented traffic violation.

"Did you know that you were, uh . . . you were, hmmm . . . driving recklessly! You need to provide me with your valid Liberian license!" an officer demanded on one occasion. I handed over my license, and then the officer disappeared for a full ten minutes, letting me sit there as he examined it repeatedly with a ferocious scowl, all the while lamely directing traffic.

When he returned he threatened: "I am taking you to the station!"

I asked him why he didn't just issue me a ticket, to which he replied that we were going to the station!

"Bossman," I said to him, trying out my Liberian English, "if you wan' take me to the station, I not driving you there-o. You will need to impound my vehicle and take me there in a taxi."

He blinked in my direction a few times, poker-faced, and then said, as if out of a B movie, "Isn't there some way we could . . . handle this right here?"

I asked him if he could be more specific, to which he offered, "You got a sof' drink for me today?"

A few days later, another police officer was unusually direct. After hailing me for no reason whatsoever, he approached my window, rubbing his hands together, and with a toothy smile he exclaimed, "Time for some fine-looking *U.S. dollars*!"

By far the most common line from the police and military was either "We here-o!" or "It Saturday!" The best reply to this was "Thank you, boss. I coming back-o," or "On the way back," or even "You didn't come soon!"—which means that you already greased the palms of other police officers that day. But you never, ever, directly said "No."

As time went on, I was beginning to realize that I was rarely asked for money directly, with the exception of small children, who constantly delivered the command "Whiteman-gimmie-fi' dollar!" which comes out as a single, very cute word. On one occasion, a four-year-old approached me outside of my housing compound with a different spiel.

"Where-ma-Christmas?" she demanded, blinking up at me.

I looked down at her with a perplexed tilt of the head and said, "But, small girl . . . it's July!"

"Ma *weekend*?" she tried again.

"It's Tuesday," I replied. Looking puzzled, she walked away.

Yet another variant on the weekend theme played off of a seemingly harmless question, "How are you?" or, more commonly, "How-da-body?" Americans typically answer "Fine" or "Great, and you?" Not in Liberia. Instead, whether from war weariness, a hope for sympathy, or plain old honesty, the response is "Tryin'!" or "Tryin' small," or a dramatic "Thank God!" or "I here!" or "Well . . . we still here-o!" or "Bossman, I still breathin'." If someone replies "Well, hard times . . . ," this is a clear plea for a sof' drink.

One day, having been inundated by financial requests, I found myself savoring the thought of a quiet sundowner on my waterside porch. Finally home from work, I stepped out of my Jeep and found one of my housing compound's orange-shirted security guards strolling under my mango tree. The sun was setting behind him over the ocean. I waved across the lawn and made the mistake of asking the fatal question, "How's it going?"

He shrugged dramatically and said, "Well, boss, it's all up to *you*."

Just walk away, I told myself. But I couldn't. Filled with indignation, I strode toward him at a quick clip, saying, "We are responsible for our own happiness, right?! Why would how *you* are doing be up to *me*? Huh?"

He blinked a few times, lips pursed. "Weekend here, hard times! No money for sof' drink!"

"So it's my responsibility?! For you? For hundreds of others? For saving the Liberian rainforest, too? Where does it end? *Where does my responsibility end?!*"

My irritation flowed right over him. He wiped sweat from his brow and head with a white handkerchief, smiled, and spoke to me patiently, as if he were explaining something to a willful child. "No money . . . boss . . . means no fine times," he said, drawing out the words. "My weekend . . . *is on you.*"

My walks with the Beanie Babies toy continue until it finally happens. Someone does not ask for *their weekend*.

A five-year-old girl approaches me shyly and asks, "Whayo' name?"

I tell her, and she says, "Oh," turns, and walks away.

One, two, three, I count to myself. *She is not turning back to ask for her Saturday.* "Wait!" I say, chasing her down. "What's your name?"

"I'm Precious," she says, a puzzled look on her face.

"How would you like this, Precious?" I display the floppy toy puppy and hand it to her. She strokes its ear, runs her finger along the shiny tag, and then looks up at me as if I am God. "Yes, it's for you. A gift from my mother in America."

I walk home at a clip. My mind races back at the joy of directly giving to that little girl, one human being to another. That Beanie Baby is probably the first toy Precious ever had! There is a gaping hole of need in the larger Carolina Farm slum, and I had filled a tiny corner of it with that doll. Alas, a nagging thought hits me: *It's not sustainable. It creates dependency. You did something bad.* I walk on, picking up the pace even more, wrestling with what I have done.

Thunder crackles and a misty drizzle begins, but the weekend requests continue from my left and right, and I have no Beanie Babies left. And even if I had a truckload of Beanie Babies, or a thousand truckloads to give away, it would not be enough.

Suddenly an idea hits me, and I know exactly what I must do: I must distribute guinea pigs.

CHAPTER 4

I'M BACK AT Carolina Farm, peering into a hole full of half-starved guinea pigs, the chimpanzee Nicky clinging tightly to my waist. A stench of urine rises from the hole.

"Nicky!" my neighbor's houseboy says as he rushes over and peels the chimp off me. Nicky sports a blue sailor's suit over her diaper. Her perfume lingers on my shirt. Carolina Farm gossip has it that my neighbor, the head of Greater Diamond's Liberia operation, sleeps next to his pet chimpanzee every night.

"Nicky came to my house to visit again," I say. "She pulled down my mosquito net!"

"I will surely beat her."

"No, that won't be necessary. No problem whatsoever." I stare into the hole and ask, "Why do you have guinea pigs in there?"

"We feed those rats to *da'snay*." He leads me over to a glass tank under a thatched covering where a python sleeps. Beyond the snake tank graze four dwarf antelope.

"It's like a zoo over here."

"Bossman likes animals."

"I want to ask you something," I say, leading him back to the hole. "Could I buy two of these guinea pigs from you?"

"I will ask the bossman. You got *snay*?"

"No, I want to multiply them. I'll spread the offspring around greater Carolina Farm."

He laughs. "Enh?"

"Each family that receives a pair will have to pass two pairs on to other families. And so on, until all of Monrovia has a sustainable supply of protein."

He stares at me blankly.

"Anyway, I have my eye on that brown one there and that white one. I'll call them Fred and Minnie."

"You already named them-o!"

"Long ago."

When I was growing up, there was a tension in my house between progressive intellectualism and liberal Christianity. The religious dimension found earthly form in *Cavia porcellus,* aka the common guinea pig.

You might say it all started one Christmas morning, when I woke up my little sister, Amy, at daybreak and we both raced down the stairs of our Long Island home to retrieve our stockings. We sat on Amy's bed, playing with the Snoopy Pez dispensers and *Star Wars* cards from the stockings until we were bored stiff and couldn't wait a second longer. We burst into our parents' room.

"Can we look for the baby Jesus!?" my sister shouted.

Amy and I knew the rules. You could get your stocking but couldn't open a single present until two conditions were met: First, our parents had to be awake; and second, we had to find the hidden wooden statuette of Jesus. He was born today and could now join Mary, Joseph, the wise men, and an assortment of Fisher-Price barnyard animals that we had been placing one by one into the stable each day of Advent.

"Wait just a minute, honey!"

Mom left for a few moments and then returned and gave the green light. Amy and I began the search. We looked in the oven, my mother's den, my father's office, and the other office my parents rented to a psychoanalyst friend. We searched all the bedrooms, the basement, and the laundry room. No Jesus! Finally my sister suggested the garden.

We ran out into the cold, and I peeked behind the St. Francis of Assisi statue. I was *sure* Jesus would be there. But he wasn't! Our backyard was a maze of paths, birdbaths, and hundreds of oaks, birches, and pines. We would never find Jesus and never get to open our presents!

"Kids! Come inside, you'll freeze." We moped in, dejected. "Here's a hint: If you want to find Jesus, you need to listen. *Listen*."

We did listen, and we heard! The silence of our suburban home was broken by squeaky chattering. *Dweeet dwweeet*. I led the way, with Amy stalking behind me and my mom right on Amy's heels. The whistling and squeaking led us to a shoebox behind the love seat in the solarium. Inside was the Jesus statuette, and cuddled against him on either side were two other, fuzzier babies.

"Guinea pigs!" I shouted.

"Piggies!!" my sister said.

We tossed Jesus into the manger and, forgetting about the other gifts, shredded the previous day's *New York Times* to line a fish tank, placing a salt lick, water bottle, and food pellets inside. "And whenever we make a salad," our mom explained, "you take the celery and carrot scrapings up here to the tank.

"So . . . what are you going to name them?"

"Fred Flintstone!" I yelled, picking up the white-, black-, and coffee-colored male.

"Mine's Minnie!" Amy said, cuddling the pure white female. Amy and I continued to grow up, along with Fred and

Minnie, in the comforts of suburbia. One day I came home from my second-grade classroom, sulked into the living room where my parents were reading, and pouted, "We're the poorest people I know."

"What do you mean, we're *poor*?"

"We don't have anything! Everyone has a pool, but we don't."

"Not *everyone* has a pool."

"Yes, they do."

Unbeknownst to me, my parents began scheming that very evening. They would take Amy and me away to "someplace poor" for a few months so that we would see more of the real world. That "someplace poor" would turn out to be Wilson, North Carolina.

But in the meantime, I continued to *feel* poor. Our neighbors were the sons and daughters of Grumman engineers and tax attorneys, while my parents were plain old college professors. Not only that, but they had been a priest and a nun before entering academia.

My dad was writing his sociology Ph.D. dissertation on Malcolm X while still a priest, and an older priest shook a finger at him and growled, "The social sciences will lead you away from the church!" But in the end it wasn't Weber and Durkheim that did it, but rather a beautiful young nun. Their eyes met over a communion wafer. My father bowed out of the priesthood and wrote her enough love poetry to lubricate the path out of the convent and into marriage.

I came first and then my sister. My father baptized us both in our own house, surrounded by dozens of friends, all of them liberal-intellectual Catholics. At my sister's baptism, just as my father was about to pour water over her infant head, I rose from my mother's lap and launched into a clear-eyed speech—in a completely unknown language. Then I resumed my place in my mother's lap, and my sister was baptized. For years, I would hear the story repeated by my parents' still puzzled friends about the time when I spoke in tongues.

Every Sunday, my parents took Amy and me to mass at the University Parish's Old Chemistry Building, where Father Vinny Rush wore jeans and sat on the floor with the rest of us. We prayed and sang together in a classroom next to the Happening Lounge, a graduate student bar. Sermons were sprinkled with references to Aquinas and Kant, and we chanted Latin Taizé prayers while Bonnie Paysen and her husband, Steve, played guitars and spoons and clapped, the last of which they called "the world's oldest percussion instrument."

Meals in our home began with a prayer, followed by discussion of a clipping from the *New York Times*. I could never figure out which was holier, the Bible or the *Times*. Our prayer would start with my dad saying, "Let us remember that we are in the presence of God," and my mom merging in with, "And let us adore *Her*!" We often had the guinea pigs right there with us beside the table, and during the prayer they were always strangely silent. After the prayer, my dad would begin the dinner conversation with something like this:

"So, there is an article in the *Times* today that says that only 1.2 percent of new Ph.D.s in the social sciences last year went to blacks." Spoons clicked against china serving dishes. "One percent is pitiful, since blacks make up over thirteen percent of the country."

"It's terrible, isn't it!" my mom would exclaim. "You see, kids, first we enslaved Africans, and now we still don't give them half a chance. We need more affirmative action!"

At this point, my sister (four) would be showing me (six) a mouthful of chewed London broil and string beans.

"Do you always have to be so reflexively liberal, Ann? Children, don't have bad dreams about slavery. It's been over for one hundred forty years. Way back in the 1820s, freed slaves were already making their way back to Africa, to Liberia, where they formed their own country! The *New York Times* just ran a fascinating article on Liberia— Don't you remember last Wednesday's dinner topic?"

"You can analyze everything to death, Bill, but there is still horrible racism in this society. It's heartbreaking that we can't share the goods of the earth," my mom said, a disturbed look on her face.

"Kids, there's no need to get frantic like your mother does. The African American community needs to examine its own cultural norms to see what's holding them back. Now, do you know what 'cultural norms' are?"

My sister answered the question by spitting a mouthful of chewed London broil onto her plate.

One day Minnie gave birth. The pink sacks gushed out one by one from Minnie's womb and lay amid the *Times* shreddings. Minnie ate the skin coverings right off her babies as my sister shielded her eyes, sneaking a peek every once in a while. Out of the sacks came five perfect miniature guinea pigs. One was smooth haired and the rest cowlicked, each its own distinctive blend of white, cream, black, tan, coffee, and rust.

Amy and I begged to hold them, but my mother said, "You can hold them all you want later. Right now they're too fragile. But look! Look at their eyes!" We stared into the fish tank. Unlike other rodents' eyes, which are shut at birth, the guinea pigs' eyes were wide open right out of the skin sack, exploring their cage and their mother. "Kids . . . later in life, you'll remember this moment. You'll remember the joy you felt at the birth of precious new life! These new guinea babies are proof of God's love in our home."

We looked up at our mom and then back at Minnie and her litter.

"They are divine, unselfish bundles of love!" my mother said, folding Amy and me into a warm hug.

My parents did take us to Wilson, North Carolina, where we lived in an African American community for four months. We then spent a year on sabbatical in rural Texas, working with Mexican Americans. And so on. The trips were motivated in equal parts by the curiosity of the social scientist and a feeling of universal love. In the end, these journeys exposed me to the rich diversity that lay beyond our sheltered Long Island suburb and began the path that would eventually lead me to Liberia.

But as for Fred Flintstone, the years went by on Long Island, and his aging body shriveled up and he lost all interest in Minnie. But Fred had lived well; he and Minnie became Long Island's most prolific guinea pigs, bringing dozens of offspring into the world. After the first litter, my mother suggested we "spread the love around Long Island," and cream-, chocolate-, and rust-colored guinea pigs began to fill the homes of our neighbors in the Storybook subdivision next to ours. If today you walk down Cinderella or Mark Twain Lane, or along the streets called Camelot and Lancelot, or take a swing through the cul-de-sac King Arthur's Court, you will probably find Fred and Minnie's fuzzy descendants.

One Easter morning, we found Fred's stone-cold body. Fred had undertaken a small odyssey, climbing out of his fish tank upstairs, carrying his crippled body down a dozen stairs, across the living room and piano room, and into the solarium. There he chewed on the red ribbon of our New Testament, which lay open to the Easter readings under a cross. He died right there on the Bible, on the story of the Resurrection.

I dug a hole amid the pachysandra, placed Fred in the ground, and covered him with dirt as my parents and sister looked on. With help from my mother, I hand-wrote this eulogy on a wooden plank: "Here lies Fred the sacred guinea pig: Proof of a loving God."

CHAPTER 5

M ORE THAN TWO decades later, I'm in Liberia cuddling the reincarnation of Fred Flintstone.

He looks remarkably similar to the original Fred: a coffee-colored base with splotches of black, tan, and auburn. Minnie, the next generation, chews carrot scrapings in her pen. In these pioneering guinea pigs, I see a future for Liberia. Their offspring will not only fill the cages and stomachs of the hundreds of people in the Carolina Farm slums, but could reproduce to fill the nation with a quickly multiplying source of protein. *It's sustainable. It won't create dependency.*

I look at Fred and I see purity. As the original Fred filled Storybook with little bundles of love and then died selflessly under the cross, so too would this Fred give of himself to increase Liberia's food security.

But guinea pigs began as a hobby. Most of my hours were spent learning the ropes at CRS.

"Your desk!" Amanda announced on my first day in the office. She lifted her chin and extended an arm as if presenting a royal throne. "You sit here, and I will be on the sofa, on the sidelines. You, *mon ami,* are at the helm."

I sat. And then just kept on sitting. The swirl of activity each day revolved around the "sidelined" sofa, where Amanda wrote memos on her laptop and received coffee from her secretary, who called her "bossman missy."

Meanwhile, I had very little to do besides watching her work.

One morning, Amanda said from her position on the sofa, "Starting next week, you are the chairman of Liberia's Seeds and Tools Committee!"

"The what?"

"Come! We have a meeting now, which *I* will chair for the last time."

Amanda strode into our conference room with me in tow and announced to a group of a dozen well-dressed Liberians, "Gentlemen, my replacement!"

"Hey!" the men said, leaping up with smiles, patting me on the back, and shaking my hand. *"He doesn't know the snap!"* one man said, laughing, and tried to show me the hand-shake I had been seeing everywhere, which is a normal grip followed by both parties trailing their middle fingers together and flourishing with a mutual snapping sound. The room was full of exclamations and laughter as I repeatedly failed to execute the Liberian handshake. The men introduced them-selves as representatives of various UN organizations, foreign governments, and nongovernmental organizations (NGOs).

Everyone sat, and Amanda's secretary entered with a tray full of cold drinks and sweet cakes. Amanda called the meet-ing to order, saying that her replacement could not yet snap but would make an outstanding chairman of the Seeds and Tools Committee. "Now, who will read the minutes?"

There were no minutes. The next half hour was devoted to the topic Why Not? Cakes were consumed over impas-sioned statements about why the Seeds and Tools Committee must have minutes. In the flurry of overlapping Liberian English, I understood only phrases here and there, but the meaning emerged. Finally, a Liberian representative of the European Union (EU) said, "Gentlemen! Seeds and tools distributions ended two years ago! *Why do we continue to meet?*"

This question silenced the group. Someone sipped his Coke to the bottom. The Liberian EU representative continued, "I am but forced to demand we bring this process to an end. Millions of tools and bags of seed, and seed protection rations, were distributed. Why? To rehabilitate the agricultural sector-o! Is this accomplished? *Gentlemen?*"

"Yes!" someone cried out.

"Yes, it is! Cassava is what? Cassava back to hundred percent of prewar levels, and rice is almost there, too."

"We need an *independent evaluation* of seeds and tools distributions!"

"Yes!"

The next half hour was dedicated to this topic, with everyone agreeing that the evaluation was needed, but with equal consensus that there were no funds budgeted to pay for it. The meeting adjourned after the following week's meeting was scheduled. No minutes had been taken.

The Seeds and Tools Committee is a total enigma. I am beginning to feel lost at work when Amanda arrives one morning with a pile of maps.

"*Mon ami,* I have a very special gift for you!" She hands me several maps, which we unroll on my desk. My heart quickens as we page through from one map of Liberia to the next. One shows the original coastal settlements of Monrovia, Buchanan, and Greenville, another the Liberia of the *Victoria Atlas,* another Liberia during the war. "This is your orientation to Liberia. It was passed down to me two years ago, and now I pass it to you." She places on top of the stack a current map of the country with green dots showing the CRS

Monrovia offices and rural outposts. "You, *ami,* are now in control of the second biggest pipeline of food aid into Liberia."[*]

I was to supervise a department with 150 Liberians and 1 Irish national. My staff were located in two Monrovia offices and four field offices, which Amanda shows me on the map: Gbarnga, Kakata, Buchanan, and Greenville. I ask Amanda how long it takes to get to Greenville, which appears to be the farthest from the capital.

"They say it's eight hours in the dry season, and maybe fourteen hours in the early rainy season. And it's shut off for two or three months in the middle rains."

"*They say* it takes that long?"

"I never made it to Greenville," Amanda says, picking a piece of lint off her pressed sleeve. "My team of independent monitors make that awful trip and report back to me. I am not very fanatical about mud."

During the coming weeks, I pore over my inherited map collection. Through the maps I begin to make sense of the baffling context of my work, including its place in Liberian history. Three of the maps particularly interest me.

The first is from the 1930s, similar to the one Graham Greene saw in England before leaving for Liberia in 1935. He wrote, "I examined the usual blank map upon the wall, a few towns along the coast, a few villages along the border." The rest of the map of Liberia that Greene looked at was

[*] After that of the UN's World Food Program. During my two years in-country, CRS was Liberia's largest NGO. It formed part of a constellation of NGOs, first-world government aid programs, and multilateral agencies (such as the UN and World Bank) that performed many of the functions that a national government and private sector would under normal conditions: Provide education and health care, construct basic infrastructure, and protect the environment.

blank. In some of the unexplored areas were only the words *Cannibals here.* Greene called his book *Journey Without Maps,* traveling into those blank spaces with only his imagination and a team of porters. The area was thinly administered, nearly anarchic. The British and French implored the Liberian administration to survey and take control of the interior; if they did not, the Europeans threatened to carve up Liberia and add it on to their bordering Sierra Leone, Guinea, and Ivory Coast colonies.

While the Americo-Liberian elites made enough inroads into administering the interior to placate the French and English, they still lived in their own cozy coastal world. The map tells it all. The coastal settlements of Greenville, Harper, Buchanan, Monrovia, and Robertsport *are* Liberia. The rest is blank. The coast was the extent of the consciousness of the black aristocrats.

I look at the second map. It is from the mid-1990s, sketched by a hurried pencil, showing a fractured Liberia. The area right around Monrovia is labeled "Liberia," whereas the rest of the country is carved up in the territories of half a dozen warlords, the Liberian Peace Council (LPC) in the southeast, and one faction of the United Liberation Movement of Liberia for Democracy (ULIMO), the ULIMO-K, in the west. The biggest chunk belongs to warlord Charles Taylor's National Patriotic Front of Liberia (NPFL). This part is labeled "Greater Liberia" and encompasses the heart of the country's interior.

This dismembered Liberia is the result of the fall of the Americo-Liberian aristocracy.

When Master Sergeant Samuel Doe killed and disemboweled Americo-Liberian president Tolbert in his bed in 1980, he ended 150 years of Americo rule over the 99 percent native population but ushered in an era of turmoil. The way the Doe era began is telling. After Doe murdered Tolbert, he rounded up most of Tolbert's cabinet (other wealthy Americos) and marched them to the beach in their boxer shorts to be killed by firing squad. British journalist David Lamb witnessed the event:

> The soldiers taunted and tickled them during the twenty minutes it took the firing squad to get organized. The officer in charge cursed as he tried to unjam his rifle . . . "Squad, fire!" the commander ordered, his rifle finally functioning properly. For three minutes the executioners unleashed volley after volley. Bullets smacked into Phillips' [the finance minister] arms and shoulders before one struck his forehead . . . Denis [the foreign affairs minister] continued to stand upright, eyes closed, as one bullet after another zinged harmlessly by. Finally a soldier stepped out of the ranks and killed him with a burst of machine gun fire. A great shout of joy rose from the mob: "Freedom. We got our freedom at last!"

Their joy was premature. The firing squad debacle was followed by ten years of buffoonery and savagery. Doe promoted himself to His Excellency the President Doctor Doe, made his birthday a national holiday, and mass-minted "Doe dollars." Each morning, an expensive hairdresser came to the executive mansion to soften up his Afro. Meanwhile, Doe stirred up tribal hatreds through widespread killing, torture, and humiliation of non-Krahn people in the interior. Washington turned a blind eye and supported Doe with $500 million per year ($100 million more in aid than in the accumulated history of Liberia up to that time). In exchange for mouthing anti-Communist sentiments, Doe was rewarded with a state visit to the White House, where President Reagan famously called the Liberian leader "Chairman Moe," apparently mistaking Doe for Chinese Communist chairman Mao Tsetung.

On Christmas Eve 1989, Charles Taylor and a small group of mercenaries trained in Libya invaded Liberia from a base in the Ivory Coast. They tapped into the rage of certain tribes over years of persecution by Doe and quickly captured much of the nation's interior. Meanwhile, others rose against Doe as well, including one faction leader named Prince Johnson, who successfully captured Doe, slowly chopping him to pieces on videotape. On video, "Johnson bangs on the desk and orders one of his men to cut off Doe's ear. The camera jerks to show the president being held down by several men while one of them takes a knife first to one ear and then the other." Johnson then eats Doe's ear as the president slowly dies from loss of blood. Johnson puts on Doe's trademark glasses and displays the former president's body publicly to show that he has killed the Big Man.

The seven years after Doe's death were anarchic. War raged among factions fighting for control of territories that held diamonds and timber. All ideology vanished. The war had little to do with overthrowing corrupt Americos or installing democracy, Communism, or any other system. It was a naked struggle for power: the power to get wealthy off diamond and timber resources. Meanwhile, CRS staff crossed into these dangerous warlord-controlled territories and delivered food to hungry civilians. Finally, in 1997 Liberians voted the strongest of the warlords, Charles Taylor, into the presidency in a 75 percent landslide. They were wise enough to know that the only way to stop the war was to put Taylor on the throne.

Now it is 1999, two years after Taylor was elected president. The map has changed, and I examine it. It displays a solid integrated Liberia unbroken by factional domains. It shows not only the coastal towns, but those of the interior: Gbarnga, Kakata, Voinjama.

I get up and hang it on the wall next to my desk and stare at it for a long while. In the two years since the war has ended, Liberians have enjoyed relative security. Agricultural production, education, and health care are gradually returning. And now CRS wants me to lead the charge toward sustainability; lead the transition from free food distributions to sustainable development; teach people to fish, rather than giving them a fish.

But Amanda's handover training speaks otherwise. Our lesson on how to execute the monthly food distributions goes like this: "I like to put my feet up on the desk when I do this each month," the large Congolese woman says, propping her feet up and pressing the repeater button on her radio. "Tibet Five, Tibet Five, Tibet One." Tibet Five is our logistics officer, and Amanda is Tibet One. When she leaves I will take her place as Tibet One.

The response comes back, "Good afternoon, bossman missy. Go ahead with your traffic."

Amanda pauses and says into the radio: "Do it."

"Done."

Done. Amanda keeps her feet up on the desk, a smug grin spreading over her round face. Through the window behind her, the crumbling shells of Monrovia's buildings, gutted in the war, are set against the crashing Atlantic Ocean. After a lingering moment, Amanda puts down her radio and says, just above a whisper, "Hundreds of trucks will now leave the port, following my command. They will deliver food to thousands of starving souls who would otherwise perish. In a few weeks, this will be you."

CHAPTER 6

AMANDA INVITED ME to her house for a number of "working" breakfasts and dinners. Evans laid out delicious meals for us, refilling our coffee and clearing and washing the dishes. On one of these occasions, the Carolina Farm landlord's son stopped by with a going-away card for Amanda. He stared at his feet as Amanda read the card and then told her he was jealous that she had other boyfriends. He was correct. Amanda and I were eating breakfast together the next day when a different boy, who also looked to be around twenty, came out of her bedroom shirtless, yawned, and went into the bathroom. He joined Amanda and me in the Jeep Cherokee as we left for the office, and we dropped him off at the end of the dirt road. Amanda said as we drove away, "Amazing, *mon ami*. His brother used to come to me, and now he does. I do not know why they changed."

Amanda also introduced me to her Rwandan friend, who invited the two of us to his apartment for dinner. A Liberian woman, who turned out to be his girlfriend, met us at the door. She worked in the kitchen along with a servant while we three drank Scotches until dinner was ready. We joked and enjoyed potato greens (a Liberian dish that combines the leaves of the sweet-potato plant with oil, spices, and meat) until we were ready to head out to Bacardi's Discotheque. Alone with Amanda on the way out to the car, I asked her about her Rwandan friend and his Liberian girlfriend.

"They have a unique relationship."

"How so?"

"Well, he will be leaving soon, and not taking her, of course. He pays for her typing classes and gives her a place to stay, and she . . . well, she finds inexpensive help to cook and finds good deals on food in the market. They both gain."

In Bacardi's, I danced a couple of songs with a young woman Amanda knew, and then we joined the others in leather sofa seats around a glass table. She was a secretary at the UN. I asked her what kind of music she liked.

"I like mellow music," she said.

"What exactly is mellow music?"

"Mellow music."

"Is it jazz? Easy listening? What type of music?"

"Mellow music."

The next day she told Amanda, "I tried to get da whiteman, but whiteman did not want me."

Amanda initiates me into the norms of being a bossman not only at work, but also at play. This includes the two-country rule: If at least one country lies between you and your spouse, adultery is permitted. I'm not married (*not yet,* anyway), but I am in love with Jennifer and have no interest in anyone else.

I'm not only in love with Jennifer, but also increasingly enchanted with life in general. I have a touch of "the third-world glow": a sense of buoyancy over being in an exotic place. Glad to be alive and in the tropics, I awaken each morning and ritually listen to Cat Stevens's "Morning Has Broken." My alarm sounds at seven sharp, and I push aside my wall-length curtains as the first acoustic notes emerge, a world of wetness outside. I dance past Fred and Minnie's cage, singing along with Cat Stevens.

When it's not raining during those first moments of the day, I often walk into the thick wet grass and watch the first shafts of clear light peek over the compound wall. Drops of rain blow down from banana, mango, plum, and palm trees, falling onto my strawberry blond hair and freckled shoulders. I breathe deeply and give thanks for the new day.

In the evenings, I type letters to Jennifer to e-mail the next day at work. I write of Nicky the perfumed chimp, the next generation of Fred and Minnie, and the logging, mining, and humanitarian aid *bossmen* and servants who populate Carolina Farm. I write about how shocked I was initially by both the domination of the expatriates and the obsequiousness of many Liberians. I hint that it is becoming frighteningly normal with time.

Jennifer's reply warns me not to lose hold of my idealism, and she sends along a telling quote from Mike Tidwell's *The Ponds of Kalambayi*:

> Like most people who go overseas to do development work, I did so expecting to find out what it's like to be poor . . . That's not what happens. Instead you learn what it's like to be rich, to be fabulously, incomprehensibly, bloated with wealth.

I'm sending off an e-mail to Jennifer one morning when an attractive young woman strides into my office and lays a report in my in-tray. It's the first time anyone has delivered something directly to me and not Amanda. I pick up the report, the sole item in my tray. As I thumb through it, she says, "It's my field report on your swamp rice projects in Greenville. I just got back from the bush. Name's Ciatta."

"Bill," I say, shaking her hand firmly but fumbling on the snap finish. I take note of Ciatta's hair, which is tied into one hundred tight braids that cascade over her shoulders. The braids are black but dyed with hints of light and dark blue.

"Welcome to Liberia. You better work on your snap."

"I'm trying-o."

"Now that sounds Liberian! I hope I'm not interrupting anything."

"No, please." I'm listening to her voice. She speaks fairly standard American English, with only suggestions of Liberian English. "You're a field monitor?"

"Yup, one of your spies! I'm stationed in Greenville, but travel a lot to projects around the country and report back to you."

"How long have you been with CRS?"

"A year. But I'm actually an engineer. Work is giving us all a hard time, so you take what you can get."

"You look young to be an engineer."

"I'm twenty-four. Hey, your office . . . do you need any interior decorating? I do that, too."

I look around my office. The sofa's floral pattern clashes with the maroon paisley curtains. "Not at the moment," I say.

Ciatta stands up. "I'm going to get Ghana food for lunch if you care to join me." She seems to be choosing her words carefully to avoid Liberian colloquialisms. "Joint's called Kind of Blue."

It still hasn't sunk in that Momo and the Jeep Cherokee are always at my disposal, so I hail a cab to carry Ciatta and me to lunch. Like many Monrovia taxis, this one seems to crawl sidewise, crablike, through the city's decaying streets. Ciatta climbs into the front seat, and I join two others in the back. We stop a block up Randall Street, assumedly to drop off one of the passengers. Instead a woman in an orange-and-green African gown and head wrap opens my door to get in. She lands in my lap, her perfume filling my lungs.

Everyone in the taxi seems slightly embarrassed, until an Americo-Liberian gentleman to my left says, "Pardon me, but you are sitting wrong."

"Sitting wrong?"

"Yes, you put your left arm here," he said, demonstrating, "and then cross your legs like this, and then your right arm straddles her shoulder . . ." I execute these Twister-style moves and—voila!—she slides right into place beside me.

An incredible seven human beings now sit snuggly in the tiny Nissan Sunny as we putter down Randall, across Main, and over the bridge to Bushrod Island, stopping again for *another* passenger! A twelve-year-old boy in his school uniform gets in to the *left* of the driver, wedged in between the driver's side and door and bringing the economy car's capacity to eight people.

Ciatta finally asks the driver to stop. I follow her on foot down a dirt road. Not wanting to lose her in the swarm of people, I keep my eyes glued to her blue braids, which hang over a white tank-top-style blouse. She ducks between some wooden shacks and into a courtyard.

It's a simple place, a few wooden tables in the courtyard and several others under a low overhang. A dented saxophone leans against a table that holds an old-fashioned phonograph playing jazz. The tune is John Coltrane's "A Love Supreme."

"How'da body, sis Ciatta?" the waitress asks.

"Body fine, y'all right, ma'?" Ciatta says, switching seamlessly into Liberian English.

"I tryin' small!"

"What y'all got today?"

"Got goat meat. Got cow meat."

"Y'all got dumboy?"

"Got dumboy. Got ri'. Groundnut-pepper-soup-o."

"Bring me one dumboy with goat meat in groundnut soup. Plenty skin-o!"

Both women turn to look at me. A rhythm of solid thuds emerges from the screened-in kitchen. Through the screens I spot two silhouettes of teenagers thrusting six-foot poles into a hollowed log. I slap at a fly on my sweaty arm and notice the source of the flies—three goats tethered to a stake beside the kitchen. Ciatta and I sit a few feet from the goats, and the waitress wipes our table with a filthy rag, asking, "What you want, *whiteman,* goat meat or cow meat?"

I glance at the chomping trio beside us. "Beef."

"One cow meat for da whiteman, ma'," Ciatta translates to the waitress, and then asks me, "Would you like rice or dumboy?"

"Rice."

"Pepper soup or groundnut soup?"

"The same as you."

As the waitress calls the order into the kitchen, Ciatta smiles in my direction. "You embarrassed to eat goat meat in front of the goats?"

I try to force a chuckle. Flies make frequent round trips between the goats' bodies and mine, with brief layovers on a trash heap. As the waitress emerges with our food, I know there could be no source of clean water flowing into that kitchen.

"This is dumboy," Ciatta says, digging her tablespoon into a blob of off-white dough smothered in a brown gravy. "It's from Ghana, but the same as what we call *fufu* here in Liberia. It's cassava and yam pounded together with water into this form."

"Cassava?"

"It's the most common root crop in the world. Here, try some."

She thrusts a spoon toward me, and I slide the contents into my mouth, chewing the gelatinous cassava-yam mix. Ciatta laughs. "You don't *chew* dumboy! You *swallow* it-o!"

I stick to my rice dish, which is smothered in a spicy peanut sauce. As Ciatta rips the skin off a chunk of goat meat, she says, "There's money in the bush. I'm bringing charcoal into Monrovia on the weekends. Hiring a taxi, and then selling it in Dualla and Waterside."

I brush the flies away from my food, but more return from the direction of the goats. The jazz plays on in the background. Ciatta continues, "A million people in Monrovia cook with charcoal. People in the bush burn wood in pits for three days to make it. My dream is to supply the transport to Monrovia, to have the trucks and everything. Big money."

"It must be difficult to do business in this context."

"That war's been over *two years*! People need to get on their feet and rebuild. Everyone's so used to asking 'Where's *my weekend,* bossman?' Nobody's my bossman."

We eat without talking for a long moment, and eventually I say, "I like the name of this place, Kind of Blue. After the Miles Davis album."

"You like jazz?" she asks. I nod that I do. "I'll bring you here some evening. Sometimes these old guys come in and play sax, trumpet."

"Okay, Ciatta, what's this tune?"

She listens for a moment and says, "'Song of Praise.' Track four on Coltrane's *Spiritual.*"

"You're good."

"I know."

She swallows a spoonful of dumboy. I notice that the pounding of cassava in the kitchen has fallen into sync with "Song of Praise." Ciatta says, "Nothing bothers Liberians more than this: We know everything about America, but you all don't know a damn thing about us. We Liberians came over here from America. Our flag is red, white, and blue! We are America in Africa . . . But it goes so much deeper than all that."

Dozens of Ciatta's braids fall around the wooden bowl as her long fingers bring a chunk of goat meat to her mouth. Her large eyes are absorbed in the meat and bone, and she eventually says, "I got plenty dreams, *plenty* dreams . . ." Her voice trails off, and our eyes lock for a long moment. I close mine to yank myself out of the trance and fixate on a mental image of my angel, Jennifer.

As we leave Kind of Blue, I resolve to keep my distance from Ciatta.

CHAPTER 7

"WELCOME TO PARADISE."

I look up from my hammock to see CRS's security and logistics boss, a blond American in his late thirties. In the Liberia program pecking order, he falls at exactly my level, right below the country director. His name is the Jacket, but I still haven't learned why people call him that. "Hey, Jacket," I say, sitting up to shake his hand.

"Keep close to that hammock and the beaches and you'll love Liberia." He surveys the waterfront view of Carolina Farm and adds, "People in the States work their entire lives hoping to get a spread like this. I just took a job with CRS!"

The shrill cry of my neighbor's chimpanzee, Nicky, rings out. We look over to see Nicky ripping off the shirt of her sailor suit, throwing it on the ground, and stomping on it.

"Nicky's a total trip. I bet she'd make a killer surfer," the Jacket says.

"I just hate to see a wild animal kept in captivity."

"Hmpf! That's the least of Greater Diamond's evils. Your neighbors are keeping Charles Taylor on the throne."

I'd already picked up the story in bits and pieces. My neighbors headed up Greater Diamond, a South African company that gave Taylor a significant cut of the diamonds they found in exchange for exploration rights.* Recently,

---

* The Hoge Road Voor Diamant (or High Diamond Council) estimates Liberia's prewar annual diamond take at 100,000 to 150,000 carats per year. However,

some of Taylor's elite Antiterrorist Unit (ATU) troops have been stationed full-time at Carolina Farm, evidently keeping their eye on Greater Diamond, suspecting that they've been smuggling diamonds on small boats from my neighbor's dock. This, of course, without giving Taylor his share.

I stand up from the hammock and stretch. The ocean disappears from view as a heavy fog rolls across the bay and onto our estate. It has been raining so much recently that the palms and succulents and broad-leafed plants around my villa appear ready to burst. You can practically watch them transpire. My eyes wander from the Greater Diamond house to that of the director of Caterpillar Liberia, the heavy equipment and engine manufacturer that was supplying the logging industry.

I finally say to the Jacket, "I've got diamond-smuggling neighbors on one side and timber barons on the other."

"Bingo. Lesson number one about Liberia. It's a commodities-based economy run by a complete wacko: His Excellency Dahkpannah Dr. Charles Ghankay Taylor . . . Maybe you've heard the term *vampire state*? Taylor's sucking the blood out of this country. Our neighbors are helping him do it."

"And what about us?"

"That's an easy one. We aid workers exist to ease the conscience of the world's rich . . . But the important news at this moment is that the surf's up in Robertsport! Why don't you join the Liberian Surf Buddha Club tomorrow?"

"I don't surf very well."

"You'll learn. R-port is the third best surfing in the continent

---

between 1994 and 1998, Liberia averaged 6 million carats per year, far beyond its mining capacity. This discrepancy is explained by Liberia's role as a conduit for Sierra Leonean "conflict diamonds," which are exchanged for cash or arms that continue to fund the RUF insurgency in Sierra Leone.

after Mozambique and South Africa. There's a limestone floor, so the waves break in the same spot every time."

Nicky lets out another shrill cry and is scampering toward us. She leaps onto one of my palm trees and scrambles up. Two Greater Diamond houseboys chase her down, gasping for breath underneath the tree. Nicky tears off her disposable diaper, hurling it down at them, chattering hysterically.

"I'm going to make Nicky an honorary Surf Buddha," the Jacket says, shaking his head. "But what do you say? You in?"

I look at the now naked chimpanzee in my palm tree and then at the Jacket. "But it's the rainy season."

"Better waves. Everyone's going: EU, Save, ACF, the Lebanese. *All* the Buddhas."

"Slow down, douche-wad!" the Jacket shouts into his handset radio. He and Amanda, who has her hair tied back and wears a bikini top and wraparound skirt, burst out laughing. We trail the European Union Land Rover in a caravan of four white SUVs heading to Robertsport.

"Okay, Jacket. We will surely slow down," comes a Lebanese voice over the radio from the Land Rover, and the vehicle speeds up.

"Gun it, Momo, let's get 'em," the Jacket exclaims, and I notice the speedometer climb to eighty-five miles an hour. Our sleek convoy races past overgrown cassava farms and abandoned palava huts, broken by savannah and low bush. For many miles I don't see a single sign of habitation.

"This place was a no-man's-land during the war. All the way from here to the Sierra Leone border," the Jacket says.

"Still is," Amanda says, and then turns to me. "Do you know why they call this man the Jacket?" I shake my head.

"I will tell you why. He showed no fear at the SBU checkpoints up in Gbarnga. The Small Boys Unit, Charles Taylor's most loyal soldiers, a bunch of drugged-out eleven-year-olds with Soviet AK-47s. Unpredictable!"

Amanda goes on, "I was with this man who we now call the Jacket. We were in the lead truck of a food convoy when we came to an SBU checkpoint. Jacket jumps down and shouts, 'Attention!' Before we could blink our eyes, he had half a dozen small boys lined up and saluting him! He barked at them that we had 'bulgur wheat to deliver to some hungry people ba'dare' and that they must let us pass. As we rolled through the checkpoint, he promised to bring them each the gift of a jacket the next time he passed through."

"I never brought them the jackets, of course," the Jacket says. "It was just psychological. Child soldiers respond to firm resolve. I would just play the commander role, and they fell for it every time. As commander you always promise gifts. After that, when I came through those little boys would salute me and say, 'Don't forget dat jacke', boss jacke'.' 'Boss Jacket' was my name. It stuck."

I ask what it was like behind the checkpoints during the war. "Nasty, but we got used to it. The worst was the elderly and those who couldn't walk, you know, the handicapped or folks with broken legs. We'd pull into these empty villages and everyone would have fled except for these few. They'd be wasting away, just skin and bones . . ."

"Darwinistic," Amanda says, "but the Jacket was their white savior, pulling up in a truck full of food."

"I can never tell when you're kidding, Amanda. You are one of the most demented women I've met, and I've met a few." Amanda laughs, and Jacket continues. "Look, I won't deny that aid work isn't a head rush. The adrenaline flows.

But I'm not on some kind of power trip over here. My philosophy is simple: People should sleep on a mattress."

As the Jacket says this, we reach a checkpoint. Since we are a convoy of official diplomatic vehicles, the soldiers wave us through. Just beyond the checkpoint is a sign: SIERRA LEONE—20 MILES. I am relieved when we turn in the opposite direction, away from Sierra Leone, where civil war is still in full swing. We drive along the shore of Lake Piso, glistening on our right while mangrove swamps crowd our left, and again there is not a soul, not a home, in sight.

We are silent for a while, looking out over this incredible lake, when the Jacket continues. "The mattress theory of international development."

"Go on," I say, intrigued. I'd not heard of this one during my time at the World Bank or at Georgetown.

"International aid work is about one thing: giving all six billion people on the planet a mattress. I'm not talking about saving the world. I'm not talking about stopping evildoers like Charles Taylor. Fuck that, it's goddamn impossible! But there is one thing I can do. I can go into a country—and I'll go anywhere that's screwed-up and not landlocked—and make sure people get food and water. Beyond that, there's only one thing that gets me. People sleeping right on the ground like everyone has to do here. Christ, is a *goddamn mattress* too much to ask for?"

Beyond Lake Piso, the first structures of Robertsport come into view: the shells of the former weekend homes of Firestone rubber employees. We race through abandoned Robertsport and down a sandy road toward the beach. As we sweep through the reeds and grasses, children leap onto the back bumpers. We come to a jolting halt right on the beach, and Amanda shouts, "To Loco!"

The Jacket echoes her cry: "To *Looocooo!*"

The Liberian boys from our bumpers clamor to carry as many of our surfboards, body boards, fins, and coolers as they can. While we whistle along empty-handed, a line of bare-chested boys lug our equipment along a half-hour stretch of rocky coastline hugged by rainforest.

At Loco, the dozen Surf Buddhas wax up boards and jog down to the water. Most have surfboards, but one Frenchman and I use body boards.

"I guess we're the wimps," I say to him as we both pull on our fins, the waves crashing against our legs. "Where do you work?"

"Logging company. You?"

"For an NGO."

"Ah yes, zee NGO, yes. I sometimes envy you."

"Why?"

"You have an income, very, *very* small . . . but *constant*. But I? It is—how do you say?—feast or famine. OTC is getting all the forest concessions, and the little people like me are good-bye."

"OTC?"

"Oriental Timber Company. Malaysians, I think, or maybe Indonesians. Huge timber company that just arrived in Buchanan."

The French logger and I paddle out together, ducking under the waves, until we are floating with the others out beyond the break. "Turtle!!" the Jacket shouts. Sure enough, less than twenty meters from us, the head and leathery shell of a sea turtle have surfaced.

The surfing goes on for hours. Intimidated by the size of the swells, I hold back beyond the break for long stretches. Floating, I scan the horizon for turtles and dolphins, chatting with whichever Buddha floats by. The Jacket and Amanda are the most daring of the club, executing crisp 360-degree turns. I survey the vibrant green forest westward, trying to discern where Liberia ends and Sierra Leone begins, but the one country bleeds right into the other.

In the late afternoon, lightning begins to flash in the thickening sky. When it starts to drizzle, the French logger and I paddle back to the beach, but the other Buddhas keep surfing. When the drizzle turns to rain, most of the other Buddhas paddle to shore, but the Jacket and Amanda don't quit. Coolers and gear are finally packed up and being hauled back along the coast by our teenage helpers, and I am about to follow them when I see the Jacket and Amanda surf straight in, their final wave of the day. As they pump the last bits out of the wave and beach in sync, they howl with laughter under the thunder.

CHAPTER 8

OMO AND EVANS load the last of Amanda's baggage into the Land Cruiser. "Good-bye, Evans," Amanda says, ending Evans's two years of houseboy service with a cool nod. She then turns to face me. "You are now ready to lead CRS's projects."

"Thanks for everything, Amanda."

"A test! What do you say when you want the trucks of food to roll out each month?"

"'Do it!'"

"Yes, and he says, 'Done.' Nothing more. Those two words and a nation is fed." She looks out over the water and then obliquely toward me. "In my first six months, I packed to leave Liberia twice, both times with bad malaria. I missed home. *The Congo.*"

Momo looks over at us, ready to go to the airport.

She continues, "You are full of energy. And now, with the war over for two years, I sense possibilities here. To use the word *renaissance* would be ridiculous, of course. But in the people here I think I sense something like . . ." And she pauses, staring out at the bay again, before saying, "Something like hope. Maybe not. But you brought some hope from America, *mon ami.*"

Evans and I stand in Amanda's driveway, watching the Land Cruiser roll away and disappear through the compound gates. I think of Amanda's family being butchered in the

Congo. What happens to a person's soul when she comes home from work and finds her children hacked to pieces in the kitchen? I think about what Amanda may have been like before her tragedy: warmer, gentler, more compassionate. What's more, I am living in a nation of people similarly traumatized. Some two hundred thousand Liberians perished in the civil war, many of them in the same brutal way as Amanda's family. Liberian rebels, for example, had a game when they came across an obviously pregnant woman. "Boy or girl?" one would ask. Bets were laid down, and out came the knife to find out who won.

My mandate (Reduce poverty and dependency while conserving the rainforest) seemed more quixotic each day. I remembered what Jennifer had said to me when I was at JFK Airport, about to board the plane: "What can you hope to accomplish in a place like that? Liberia's not even a country; it's a war zone."

My call sign comes over my two-way radio on a Sunday morning. I press the rubber transmitter and say, "This is Tibet One, go ahead."

"Emergency! Regional crisis has boiled over. We need you at Oscar Bravo right away. Over."

"Roger. Twenty Mikes. Out."

I grab my keys and dash out to the Jeep, motoring through the rains over Bushrod Island toward CRS. When I enter John's office, the first word I hear is "hostages." John, the executive director of CRS Liberia, and the Jacket huddle around a rattan table along with representatives from the United Nations High Commission for Refugees (UNHCR) and Medical Emergency Relief International (MERLIN). All of their faces look grave.

"We've got a hostage situation in the north," John says as I sit at the table. "Rebel elements based in Guinea have taken a few dozen hostages, including six British staff from MERLIN." I know the MERLIN hostages, three of whom are young English nurses known as "the Merlinettes."

"What are they demanding?" I ask.

"The rebels are cornered by Taylor's troops and want safe passage back into Guinea."

We discuss the crisis but can do little at the moment since this is a military situation between Liberian government forces and a particular faction. The conversation turns to evacuation protocol in emergencies. The Jacket lays out the procedures. "First, United Nations and foreign government personnel are evacuated, then international nongovernmental aid workers, and finally Liberian nationals, time and resources willing."

"Wait a minute!" I say. "You mean UN staff are evacuated *before* NGO staff, even if both are foreign nationals and doing similar work?"

"Let me put it to you this way," the Jacket says, fully in his element, leaning toward us with a flash of urgency in his blue eyes. "If there's room for only one more person in the helicopter—and hell is breaking loose everywhere around you—*he* gets in . . . ," the Jacket says, pointing to the UN staffer. His finger then turns to me, and he says, "And *you* do not."

A pleased smirk spreads over the UN representative's face as a look of horror covers mine. "So *he's* helicoptered out, but what do *I* do?"

"The helicopter pilot will try to return for you. In cases where this is not possible, you either hunker down, or if necessary you bushwhack your way through to the nearest international border. And remember to always pack Fansidol in your grab bag because the malaria'll hunt you down quicker than rebels."

Back in my house, I begin to experience fear for the first time in Liberia. The Merlinettes are my friends. I know the color of their eyes, how they laugh, and some of what is in their hearts. Over beers at the embassy happy hour just a week ago, one of them opened up to me about why she came. She wanted to share her skills as a nurse with the world's most vulnerable children, not (as she put it) "just heal rich kids' acne." I picture her now, her dirty blond hair caked with mud, on a cement floor as the rain pelts down in the jungle beyond. Has she been raped? Is she even still alive?

The rain falls. I take Fred out of his cage and hold him against my stomach. Minnie *dweets* and I toss a handful of potato greens into the pen for her. She is now pregnant. When our first litter of guinea pigs was born back on Long Island, my mother said, "These guinea pigs are proof of God's love in our home." Petting Fred, I try to hold on to the feeling I had as a child. When I used to hold a guinea pig, I felt that they were a piece of God, a God that loved us and took an active interest in our well-being. We didn't need to fear anything.

I sit down at my computer, Fred in my lap, and type, "Dear Jennifer . . ." But the words fail to flow. I want to tell her I'm scared. That what happened to the British nurses could have happened to me. That I miss her. That I'm feeling some regret at having come to Liberia. Why *did* I come?

No one forced me to get on that plane. I was offered another position in the U.S. presidential management program, which gives fast promotions up through the U.S.

Agency for International Development (USAID) or the State Department. Comfy, safe jobs. I would have swooped into third world countries for a few days, advised foreign governments from a Sheraton conference room, and returned to Jennifer's arms. We would have raised a family and collected our pensions together. We would have been happy.

I wrestled with the decision for several weeks. Should I accept the CRS Liberia post or take the government job? I was leaning toward the latter when the former CRS Liberia country director called me from Monrovia. His voice squeezed through a gauze of static: "Your job will be the brains behind the transition from emergency to development. The war is over and we need to jack up program quality. You'll be in charge of eliminating dependency. Our vision: empowered Liberians taking charge of their own development while securing the rainforests for the future."

He must be joking, I thought.

"But before we go into any more detail about the position, I want to be sure you are accurately picturing the reality on the ground here. Fighting can explode at any time, and with no forewarning. We all carry handheld radios for 24-7 communication since phones are scarce. We will probably have to evacuate you at some point, and death—in a manner of speaking—will be your constant companion. How does this sound to you?"

This was no advertisement for the job. All reason pointed away from Liberia, and even the very people trying to recruit me seemed bent on talking me out of it.

The CRS director repeated through the static from Monrovia: "Are you okay with the conditions I've described?"

I heard myself reply, "Yes, I am."

* * *

The hostage crisis drags on.

We keep contact late into the night with MERLIN's London headquarters and a communication post across the border in Guinea. To let off steam, we sometimes end up at one of the few social events in Monrovia: happy hour and movie night at the United States embassy.

One such evening, we are sitting outside around a table above the swimming pool and tennis courts. An American in his fortes named Dave (who liked to call himself a "military attache," though I always wondered) says, "Yeah, those crazy young cultural dancers who performed for the ambassador . . . I did three of those chicks at the *same time* after the show!"

"How much did it cost you?" cracks the embassy doctor.

Dave's face assumes a pink hue as he gropes for a comeback. It becomes obvious to the half dozen of us sitting around the table that Dave paid. "Yeah, pretty funny. Hey, man, it's the African way, right? You know, like multiple wives . . ."

"Sure, but not usually at the same time!" the doctor says. "And the dowry is a onetime fee for life!"

"Hmm," grunts Dave, opening his leather wallet and removing a small plastic envelope. He pulls out a steel needle and uses it to mine vigorously between his teeth for pieces of chicken wing. His serpentine face assumes an unblinking fixation, and blood flows from his gums.

We all stare at him. After a long moment, Dave snaps out of his trance and says, "Well, boys, do we head to the Marine House?!" As he says this he slaps the Jacket, who is sitting next to him, on the shoulder. A good-natured slap, but he evidently forgot about his steel toothpick.

"Ouch! You freakin' stabbed me!" the Jacket says, leaping up from his seat and grasping his shoulder.

Dave also stands up and begins to apologize. "My bad. Sorry, Jacket. Definitely won't happen again."

"Better start popping AZT quick, my friend," says a U.S. Marine at the table. Nervous giggles.

"Look . . . ," Dave stammers, backing away with his hands up in the air. "An *accident*. Okay? Sorry. See you all at movie night in a few." He winks and disappears around the other side of the swimming pool.

The tables on the patio around us resume their conversations as Jacket and the marines express further incredulity over the toothpick incident. I lapse into a muse: *I can't believe these are my friends.* For expats, the American embassy is the hub of social activity—happy hours, movie nights, the annual Marine Ball, and regular Sunday brunches where missionaries and aid cowboys come for their Jimmy Dean sausage fix.

After finishing our beers, we walk across the oceanside embassy compound toward the Marine House, where the film will be shown. We pass the pool and tennis courts and climb a few dozen steps. White condos hug the cliffs. The ambassador's three-story mansion towers behind the condos. Though I've visited the embassy compound many times, I am again struck by its opulence and insularity. The two dozen Americans working here are said to share thirty-two generators, each of which could serve a hundred Liberians. The cliffside fortress has been essentially annexed from the heart of Monrovia and is home to just over twenty single people, each inhabiting an enormous air-conditioned house or apartment. I think of it as a Hanseatic city-state from medieval Europe: a walled-in island of wealth, with thousands of half-starved serfs just beyond the moat.

As we climb the stairs toward the Marine House, Liberian

Intercon security guards flank us left and right, staring stoically into the night. The embassy compound contains hundreds of these guards. Climbing the stairs, I say to the Jacket, "You really should think about AZT."

"Why?"

"Dave was saying he'd slept with three cultural dancers at once. Just before stabbing you with a bloody needle."

The Jacket says, "I'm an atheist, Bill. I don't believe in God, never having met Him. But you know what? I've met the guy down below. I've seen hell, and you will too if you ever leave this city and go behind the lines."

We keep climbing toward the Marine House. The Jacket goes on, "That's why I love surfing and would never live anywhere landlocked. The devil will get you if you're land-locked. When you surf . . . you *riiide*." He stops and pantomimes a surfing posture. Then he places his hand on my shoulder. "Surfing so fast and smooth, soaked with sun, how's the devil going to get you? Don't try to save the world, because it's useless. The best you can do is ride. Flow with the world."

"You've risked your life to save other people, Jacket. You're an aid worker."

"That's because the only thing as good as surfing is spit-ting in the devil's face. Each mattress I slip under somebody is a way of saying 'Fuck you' to him. That mattress means he's one more foot above hell."

The Marine House comes into sight, a white colonial revival with fluted columns, and the Jacket and I go inside and find the theater. The film has just started. We take our seats among a few dozen other expats. Free popcorn circu-lates in straw baskets, and the bar offers Red Dog and Budweiser for one U.S. dollar a can.

When the film ends, I feel suddenly awkward. *Now what do I do?* People are getting up from their seats and heading to the pool table and bar. While I recognize almost everyone—marines, UN and USAID staff, NGO folks, some private businesspeople—I have only superficial relationships with them.

I hand a crumpled bill to a marine behind the bar and ask for a Red Dog. As he hands me the cold can, a voice comes from behind me: "New York!" I turn to see Bob, a flat-topped marine.

"Hi, Bob," I say.

"I don't do so good with names, but I always remember where people are from!" he says. "So I call them Philadelphia, Orleans, whatever!" He stands an inch or two taller than my six-foot frame. Drunk on another occasion, Bob had divulged his life story. He experienced physical and emotional abuse growing up as his convict-on-the-run dad moved his family from one trailer park to the next throughout the American Bible Belt.

Bob notices me staring at the machine guns mounted as decorations on the wall. "I love guns," he says. "I really want to kill some fucking rebels."

A bit jolted, I try to shift the conversation in a more constructive direction by asking, "So, what do you marines actually do here in Liberia?"

"We protect the ambassador," Bob replies, wiping his nose with his forearm. We both sip our beer. "But really what I do is kill people. That's what they trained me to do. While you were in college, I learned different ways of killing people." He takes another sip and stares at the guns on the wall. "I can feel it. They're going to attack. They've taken the Merlinettes hostage and nobody will let us do a damn thing about it. Those chicks are my friends. I want to kill some black rebels."

Another flat-topped and tattooed marine has joined us. "Where are you from?" I ask him.

"Grew up in East L.A., but I was born on Parris Island."

"This boy is sick, dude!" Bob says. "He actually believes he was born on Parris Island. You know, it's where we all go to become U.S. Marines."

"Eat me, bitch. I *was born on Parris Island*."

The Jacket comes over to us with a tray of flaming shots. After handing them around to the marines and me, he raises his shot glass, his blue eyes alight, and says, "A toast to all of us. To all of humanity!"

"Not to them hostage-taking motherfuckers," Bob says.

"This, my friend, is a toast to *all* of us! All six billion souls crowded onto this small planet." I look into the flame arising from my shot glass as the Jacket continues, "You see, God goofed by sneezing pepper all over us when we were still made of wet blue clay. That pepper is so deep in us that we're destined to screw up for eternity. It's our fate to be fuck-ups, so let's *riiide* it for all it's worth. A toast! To all of us. To the blue clay people!"

A cheer goes up from our small circle, and we tuck away the flaming shots.

CHAPTER 9

W E GET A proof-of-life on the Merlinettes: their fright-ened voices over a satellite phone from up in the Lofa jungles near Guinea. At least we know they are alive. Meanwhile, hostage-taking child soldiers visit me in my dreams nearly every night. They've come for me, too. In my dream I wake up and it's pouring rain. Lightning flashes every few seconds, an electric storm that illuminates the whites of their eyes, the steel of their AK-47s. They are kept out of my house only by the bars on the windows. Behind the bars I know I'm safe.

We continue the evening solidarity ritual of monitoring the status of the Merlinettes by radio and often eventually end up at the Anchor, a fishing club outside of Carolina Farm. I show up there one night with my boss, John. We park, greet the guards outside the fifteen-foot fence surround-ing the bar, and go inside. A dozen or so other expatriates huddle over their mugs. On the walls, bullet-scarred signs announce the presence of embassies that shut down during the war and never returned: AMBASSADE FRANÇAISE, EMBAIX-ADA PORTUGUESA, CONSOLATO ITALIANO. Marlin and sail-fish trophies decorate the walls as well, and a wooden sign hangs over a door to a back room: DO NOT ENTER, FISH-ING CLUB MEMBERS ONLY!

John and I sit down and a waitress places a mug of Club beer in front of each of us.

"It's funny how they don't even ask you what you want here," I say to John.

"They only serve beer."

We each take long pulls on our beer, and I say, "John, I want to go to Greenville."

John practically chokes on his drink. "Greenville!? We're in the middle of a hostage crisis and you want to go into the bush!"

I think for a moment before answering. In some senses, the hostage crisis feels like the backdrop to the exotic adventure I'm living. But it has been largely an armchair adventure, something like what I pictured my life would have been as a Washington-based desk officer, flying into African capitals and working via laptop from my five-star hotel. And more than anywhere else, I feel a tug toward Greenville, for two contradictory reasons. On the one hand, the name of the place evokes familiarity: the verdant village, an ecological paradise only gently "civilized" by Americos from Mississippi in the early 1800s. On the other hand, I am lured by a conversation I had with an intrepid Dutch missionary. He made it to Greenville by boat recently and told me the town has been "swallowed up by the bush" and is a "power vacuum." I want to experience that kind of anarchy.

"Greenville is far from the hostage area," I finally say to John.

"And what about the rains?"

"The rainy season's almost over. The Greenville road is drying out, and I think the Jeep can make it."

"I don't think so. I kind of like having you here. There's a mountain of administrative details . . ."

I look at John, who seems to be lost in thought. John arrived at the same time I did a few months back. He is a short African American man with glasses who got off the plane with an array of empowerment techniques straight out of his last job in the private sector. Not long ago, I caught him trying to apply one of his techniques on my driver, Momo.

He had asked Momo, "How are you?" as they passed in the CRS hallway.

Momo replied in typical Liberian English, "I tryin' small."

John stopped in his tracks and said, "Okay, Momo, let's try that again! When I ask 'How are you?' you don't say 'Trying.' That isn't *empowering language*! What would be a better reply?"

"'Still breathin'?'" Momo suggested.

"No, Momo, that's even worse. Instead of 'Trying small,' you say 'Succeeding'! Okay. So! How are you doing today, Momo?"

"Succeeding small!" Momo said.

John empties his mug and nods to the waitress for another. He is about to say something to me when some friends from Save the Children come into the Anchor.

"Save the Children, but *kill the parents*!" someone calls out from the bar.

"Hey, that's a new one," the Save employee answers, and then he says to John and me, "And what does 'CRS' stand for, anyway? Is it 'Can't Refuse Sex' or 'Can't Remember Shit'?"

The Save group orders beers, and jokes some more in British English, one of them referring to the evangelical NGO World Vision as "Blurred Vision." Another who has just arrived in the country says to me, "Whenever I come into a country on travel, I'm amazed by the expatriate scene. You know, places like this. It used to be Stanley and

Livingstone and Cecil Rhodes, now it's the NGOs."

I let her words sink in. "You're saying that the NGOs have taken the place of the colonialists in Africa."

"Yes," she says, savoring the idea. "We've filled their shoes. We're living in their homes!"

A few days later, the rebels free the Merlinettes. A helicopter evacuates the young nurses to Guinea, where MERLIN colleagues put them on the first plane to London. I imagine the relief of their families when they hug them in the London airport. Back in Monrovia, we hold an impromptu celebration at the Anchor, toasting to the Merlinettes but knowing full well that they will not join us again in Liberia.

Meanwhile, the sun breaks through the clouds for a few hours each day, and I relish the time outdoors walking, playing tennis, and paddling to the ocean in my yellow inflatable kayak, which I shipped over from the States. I delight in these first moments of dryness, having made it through my first rainy season.

I am pressing my hand against Minnie's belly on a Saturday morning when I notice that Evans is standing silently behind me, his eyes on the ground.

"What's up, Evans?"

"Bossman," he says, "I got dreams. I've been cleaning floors all my life, and I want something more. I want to open a second shop. Base One earning small! I want to start a store on the main road."

I stroke Minnie a few times and look at Evans as he gathers his thoughts. He is a hard man to look at until you get used to him. His sinewy, hirsute body is about average height for a Liberian (around five feet ten), and he is missing all of his upper front teeth. During the war, one of Taylor's rebel fighters bashed in Evans's teeth with a rifle butt.

Evans finally says, "I thought you could . . . advance me a few months' pay."

I point to Minnie's belly and say, "One source of funds for you is going to be right here. You get the first litter and can make a business selling guinea pigs after giving away the first two pairs."

"I know. Thank you!"

"And sure, I can advance you your salary. But only after we sit down together and analyze the potential of the new shop. We'll do a mini business plan."

Evans lavishes thanks on me and then returns to cutting my lawn with his machete. I place Minnie back next to Fred in their cage and toss in a heap of potato greens. I look over at Evans in the middle of my enormous lawn—*swish, swish, swish*—with bits of grass flying up and sticking to his sweaty arms. It will take him an entire day to cut the lawn by hand. Maybe two days. *Swish, swish, swish.* The palm trees rustle above, and three simple words percolate up into my consciousness and nearly make it out of my lips.

Three words that startle me to my very core.

I snatch up my kayak, beat a path across the lawn to the bay, and row toward the ocean, wanting to purge myself of that phrase. I plunge the oar deep, making it out to the Atlantic in no time. Thoughts race through my mind as I row. What happened to my ideals? When I looked down from the airplane at Liberia for the first time, I saw a potential utopia. Under that endless block of virgin rainforest were indigenous people who had something to teach me. I would become their student and learn about living lightly on the planet. At the same time, I would give a gentle nudge toward more profitable agricultural production and meaningful education.

Like the proverbial frog being slowly boiled to death, I have been sucked into the expatriate bubble colony and lost sight of why I came. I dreamed of seeing the real Africa but have been lulled into another mug at the Anchor, another day of surfing. I dreamed of projects that reduce dependency and empower people but have ended up as a desk jockey shipping out freebies. Just this morning I put my feet up on my desk, pressed the transmitter on my handheld radio, and said, "Tibet Five, this is Tibet One."

The voice of my logistics officer came back, "Good to hear your voice, bossman! Go ahead with your traffic."

"Do it," I said.

"Done." Hundreds of trucks left the port filled with food to be dolled out to people. Bossman missy had taught me well.

I have to get out of Monrovia. Many embassy and NGO expatriates never leave the capital, where there is movie night, the anchor, and e-mail; where an airport stands ready for quick evacuation; where we live in compounds with servants and drive enormous SUVs like maharishis on their elephants. I must go into the places where all comforts are left behind and I too am exposed: exposed to war, to insecurity, to what it feels like to be a regular person in Liberia.

I must leave Monrovia to purge myself of the thoughts that are bubbling in my brain, unwanted.

No, I was not the one who looked at Evans and thought that. It was bossman missy Amanda's francophone accent. Or perhaps it was the Jacket or another Surf Buddha. Or it could have been that Save the Children consultant, or John, or my neighbors from UNICEF and UNDP. Maybe it was the spirit of President Tolbert or one of the former Americo-Liberian aristocrats who entered my thoughts and whispered those words.

Because it surely wasn't me who watched my houseboy's sweaty back, heard the slicing of grass, and thought: *Evans, my slave.*

PART II
Dry Season

Bushmeat

West Africa is reverting to the Africa of the Victorian atlas. It now consists of a series of coastal trading posts . . . and the interior that, owing to violence, volatility and disease, is again "unexplored."

—Robert Kaplan, *The Ends of the Earth*

CHAPTER 10

THE MERLINETTES FREE and the rainy season over, John has finally cleared me to travel to Greenville. I find myself riding shotgun next to Momo, who drives our Land Rover down the highway into a sun-soaked savanna. Distant hills grow larger as we race toward them. I savor the vibration of rubber on asphalt, knowing that the pavement will end soon.

Momo eases our passage through a string of checkpoints. At one of them, a lanky Armed Forces of Liberia soldier with a frayed AFL insignia on his shirt comes to my side of the car and asks me, "Where's my weekend?"

I mentally dial back to the Jacket's advice about checkpoints: *Always let the driver answer*. I feign incomprehension, and Momo takes my cue: "We coming back-o."

The soldier ignores Momo and says to me, "The *heat*! Ya got my sof' drink?"

"On the way back," Momo insists.

The soldier glares at Momo and me and then peers into the backseat, where two CRS field officers sit, similarly unbending. He takes one final look at me before lifting his head to let us pass.

At the next checkpoint, another soldier says, "We are here-o!" to which Momo replies: "Thank you, boss, but you didn't come soon!"

At a third checkpoint, a uniformed teenager with a tommy gun strapped over his shoulder lowers a chain to let us pass.

As we roll by him, he struggles to read the green CRS insignia emblazoned on the side of our truck. "A . . . C . . . F!" he forces out.

The scrub bush turns to a shady row of trees as we cross the threshold into Firestone's rubber concession at Harbel, past a sign proclaiming it to be THE WORLD'S LARGEST RUBBER ESTATE. The Liberian government leased Harbel's thirty-five thousand acres to Firestone in 1923 at the rock-bottom price of $1 million. As the miles click past, the precise rows of the monoculture hypnotize me. Each of the towering rubber trees is sliced with downward-pointing incisions (one for each year it was tapped) and has a steel cup under the most recent incision to capture a white liquid that oozes out of the tree. Barefoot men remove the cups from each tree, pouring the contents into larger buckets.

The plantation gives way to Firestone's housing and processing area. The company's half-dozen expatriate employees and dozens of Liberian managers live in 1950s-era brick ranches clustered together in a leafy subdivision. Beyond the housing, we pass a fenced-in compound of windowless warehouses. Here the cups of white liquid find their form as two-hundred-pound blocks of rubber to be loaded onto U.S.-bound ships.

Just beyond the Firestone operation, we stop at a checkpoint in the town of Cotton Tree, where small boys press in around our Land Rover, selling cold Cokes. Beyond Cotton Tree, the highway deteriorates into deep potholes, and our spinal cords are forced to absorb one jarring mile after the next. Tiny plots of cassava, rice, oil palm, and pineapple break the monotony of abandoned farmland. We pass through Bassa villages where naked teenage girls are shellacked with white paint from belly to forehead.

"*Sande* bush school!" Momo said, explaining that these were initiates into secret societies. The others explain that bush school for boys is known as *poro* and for girls *sande*. It is a way of transmitting traditional culture from one generation to the next.

We finally reach Buchanan (population thirty thousand), Liberia's second largest town, after Monrovia. Before the war it was a lively weekend getaway from the capital, but it is now an assortment of tumbledown cinder-block houses, mud huts, and empty outdoor markets. People wade through a layer of roadside trash, and no one seems to be working. "They waiting for LAMCO to come back," Momo says, referring to the Liberian-Swedish-American Mineral Company, which had abandoned its iron ore operations during the war a half-dozen years back.

Waiting for LAMCO to come back. LAMCO would not be coming back to Buchanan, not for a long time, at least. I look out the window at their former infrastructure around the Buchanan port. It's a multimillion-dollar production platform collapsing into a heap, rusting away, beyond repair. Yet the people of Buchanan are waiting for them to return instead of taking their own initiative, meanwhile surviving on CRS food shipments. Waiting for *their weekend.*

Momo stops at Sis' Rita Spot for lunch. The bamboo chop shop is the only functioning business I've seen in Buchanan. "Y'all right?" Momo says to Rita as we stoop through the low doorway. Sheets of textured linoleum cover part of the dirt floor.

We flop into rattan chairs, and one of the CRS field officers asks, "What kind of food y'all got?"

"Got palm butter with *fufu.*"

I ask, "What kind of meat is in the palm butter?"

"Dat bushmeat," Rita answers.

"Okay, but what kind of animal is it?"

"Bushmeat."

"Right, *bush*meat, but what was it *before* it died?"

"Meat."

"No, I mean what kind of creature was it? Did it climb trees? It dig holes? It fly?" I flapped my arms like wings.

"It bushmeat."

"You got goat meat or cow meat?"

"Jeh' bushmeat."

"How about chicken?" She shakes her head.

"What about a sandwich? Turkey sandwich?"

"Bushmeat."

We share bushmeat out of a single bowl. The *fufu*, which is pounded, gelatinous cassava, glistens with the orange butter of the palm nut. My spoon is less adventuresome than those of Momo and the two field officers. I avoid the mystery meat, going for the *fufu* instead and letting it slide down my throat without chewing it, as Ciatta taught me during our lunch at Kind of Blue.

"I say," Momo points out between mouthfuls, "bossman not eating any meat-o!"

"*Why?!*" one of the others exclaims. "It sweet!"

My companions insist that I share the bushmeat, so I brace myself and scoop up a small bone covered with . . . *meat*. My incisors slice into a bit of the skin. Then, everyone looking on, I grab the end of the bone and suck off the meat. The others laugh as I lick it clean. "Yum!" I say unconvincingly, examining the bone. It's not a chicken bone, nor is it duck. Not pork. Not beef. The bone is a miniature archer's bow, with another thin bone running through the middle like the bow's string. I hope it's cane rat or possum and not something on the endangered species list. I pray it's not roadkill.

We roll on, with another five hours left to Greenville. Buchanan falls behind us, and oil palm, cassava, rice, and pineapple farms line the road. Bassa villages of a dozen mud thatch huts appear occasionally along the dirt road, which is getting muddier by the mile. The pavement ended completely back in Buchanan.

"We are entering the *high* forest. You will not see any people for two hours!" Momo says as we pass a final Bassa village. The road narrows to barely more than the width of our Land Rover. Secondary forest and low bush give way to a towering canopy of trees. What we have just entered, without signage, is the enormous Krahn-Bassa National Forest. This area's mahogany and makere, its lacewood and ironwood, shelter the highest concentration of mammals in the world, including pigmy hippos, dwarf elephants, chimpanzees, forest buffalo, bush buck, and leopards. Eagles and ibis soar up near the top of the canopy. Our thin road, a humble incision, gently slices the forest.

Suddenly, a bright yellow bird thuds against the windshield. Momo hits the brakes, unclicks his seat belt, and jumps down into the mud, coming back to the driver's seat a moment later with the sparrow-size bird. A field officer asks from the back, "Momo, you gonna nurse that baby?"

The bird's head pivots lifelessly on its neck, and Momo replies, "It for my soup!"

As we lurch forward through the mud, a lively conversation emerges about the merits of eating small birds. Is there really enough meat? "No!" insists one. "But the meat sweet-o!" counters another. Momo talks about a childhood of hunting birds like this one with a slingshot and his mom cooking them with the daily palm butter or potato greens. The conversation then turns to using CRS vehicles as weapons. CRS drivers traveling after dark sometimes catch a startled duiker in their headlights. They run it down with the vehicle and load it into the back for the evening meal. Momo surprises me by saying, "But it not right. Some of those are *zebra duiker*. Those antelopes endangered!"

One of the field officers says, "It's all meat, my man," and chuckles. I notice Momo doesn't join in the laughter.

After hours of pure jungle we finally hit a town, followed by two notoriously hard-to-pass places along the road: Face-to-Face and Palm Butter Hill. Both are steep and mud choked, and numerous vehicles appear stranded. My statistical information on Liberia indicated that the rainy season was officially over, but the Greenville road tells a far different story. As we cheer him on, Momo miraculously gets us through both Face-to-Face and Palm Butter Hill, but we become stuck in an especially tricky spot near Theresaville. Our wheels spin in the mud soup. We will have to spend the night in Theresaville and work our way to Greenville in the morning.

I am not crazy about the idea of sleeping in Theresaville. The hamlet consists only of Theresa, her two sisters, and three scrawny chickens. I picture the Merlinettes having been held hostage in this kind of lost place. Theresa offers me her best bed, a straw mattress on planks, but as I lie there I feel anxious and cannot sleep. My first day in the bush was perhaps a little too thrilling, and here I am stranded in a jungle outpost. Momo snores contentedly on the floor next to my bed, and I envy him for falling asleep so easily. What's more, I haven't even brushed my teeth, and a piece of the stringy bushmeat I had for lunch is stuck between two molars.

As I fish it out with my fingernail, I get an unwelcome second taste of the gamy meat.

I listen to the sounds of Theresaville, a symphony of insects, the rustle of trees, and the low call of a chimpanzee. When I finally fall into the beginnings of sleep, I dream of bones. I am gnawing on unidentifiable animal parts and pull from my mouth the bow-shaped bone that I'd licked clean at lunch, tossing it in a pile with other unusual bones. Splinters pierce my tongue, and I feel foreign, feline, wild. The mound of bones grows, and I look down at the kill before me. What I see there are no longer my familiar human hands, but large paws with sharp claws. Blood drips down my furry jowl as I hunch possessively over my kill.

CHAPTER 11

A DEEP ORANGE SUN melts into the churning waves as Ciatta and I stroll along Greenville's beachfront. Ciatta's braids, with their hints of blue, blow back over her shoulders. The tropical paradise we're walking through (a white strip of sand lined with palm trees, deep lungfuls of sea air) is disturbed only by the human excrement underfoot. It's tough to enjoy the scenery when you are concentrated on sidestepping fecal land mines. Moreover, we have to stop every few minutes to let squatting Greenvillites finish their business and wipe themselves with banana leaves.

I've seen little of Ciatta since our dumboy-and-goat-meat lunch in Kind of Blue. She has been spending most of her time in Greenville monitoring projects. I had kept my resolution to stay away from her after sensing a spark between us. In these first few days in Greenville, however, we've been getting along nicely as friends. Until she abruptly asks me on the beach, "You don't want me?"

I stop, and so does she. She looks at her feet. "Ciatta, I have a girlfriend in the States."

"Humpf! What can she do for you on that side?"

That's a mighty utilitarian way of looking at it, I think to myself. Ciatta looks away from me and out over the water. Her light and dark blue braids blow back, revealing her bare shoulders, the strap of a tank top. Her wraparound skirt picks up the colors in her hair. I find her to be incredibly beautiful and want to reach out and stroke her shoulder, her cheek. Instead I say, "Jennifer and I are engaged."

"You getting married!"

"We decided to make it official a week ago. Over the phone. We don't have a date set, but we plan to figure that out when I'm back there on vacation."

"Well, congratulations. Really, that's great." Then she mumbles, "Wish you had told me before I embarrassed myself."

"Sorry. But I think you and I will do great as friends."

Ciatta gives me the silent treatment for a while, but we soon find ourselves chatting again. As the sun's lower edge meets the ocean, we leave the beach and head through town. I feel buoyed by the dramatic change from Monrovia. People laze in rattan-vine chairs and hammocks on their porches, men hunch over hands of cards under a mango tree, and a woman in a head wrap and *lappa*-style skirt pushes rice seedlings into a swamp. As Ciatta and I cross Mechlin Street and amble along Mississippi Street, my limbs swing to the rhythm of her voice, which has switched into a singsong Liberian English. The last of the day's light softens the edges of the town's antebellum Mississippi plantation houses and churches. Greenville is beginning to charm me.

We arrive at Dickson's house. He stands grinning on the front porch. Dickson, who manages CRS's field office in Greenville, has not stopped smiling since I first met him a few days back. The toothy grin seems a permanent fixture on his face.

"Hi, y'all!" he says to us. "My wife made some *fine* palm butter with fish for y'all!"

Ciatta and I join him on rattan chairs around a candlelit table. We listen to the waves crashing as we dig into our bowls of palm butter with tablespoons. No grinding generators or noisy vehicles break the peace of the place.

When we finish eating Dickson sighs and says, "Well! My wife is waiting for me, so I'd better go." Then his trademark smile vanishes and his brow wrinkles with what looks like worry. "Besides, we sure got a lot of work ahead of us tomorrow."

Greenville is CRS Liberia's most remote outstation. While it lies only 150 miles southeast of Monrovia as the bird flies, bad roads make it into an eight-hour drive in the dries and completely inaccessible during the middle rains. The CRS office is a two-story building on the corner of Sinoe and Mechlin streets. The bottom floor serves as a warehouse for U.S. government surplus food—bulgur wheat, corn-soy blend, and vegetable oil. The USAID logo, depicting a solid handshake over an American flag, is emblazoned on the warehouse's iron doors. The building's second floor is office space for the twenty full-time CRS employees stationed here.

Our security guards salute me as I climb into the Land Rover in front of the office. In the vehicle I immediately sense an edginess in Dickson and the two field officers who will be coming along with me to inspect CRS projects. They wonder why I am taking a much greater interest in them than their former boss, Amanda, had. Perhaps they see me as a threat because I have come to evaluate the results of millions of dollars of investment. They know I am going to write a report that could affect their employment. Jobs, *any* jobs, but particularly those with an international agency like CRS, are rare and precious.

As we roll out of Greenville toward the projects, I recall

some of the books and articles I'd read on emergency and postcrisis relief programs such as this one, which are infamous for haphazard planning and sloppy implementation. A classic blunder occurred during the 1985 famine in Ethiopia, when a well-intentioned agency shipped Slim-Fast diet products to people on the brink of starvation. The image of emaciated nomads trying to shed yet a few more pounds with Slim-Fast sounds outrageous, but in the heat of a crisis, aid officials often make bad decisions. So it is with low expectations that I head out to evaluate three types of postemergency reconstruction projects: infrastructure, agriculture, and primary education.

We start with a visit to an open-air market building intended to rekindle trade between the Kruu and Sapo tribes, who had been bitter enemies during the war.

"Where is the nearest town?" I ask Dickson as we survey work on the imposing structure. It cost $50,000 in U.S. taxpayer money channeled to CRS through USAID.

"By car it's thirty minutes."

"Do people have cars?"

"Nooobody got car!"

"By foot, how far are the people from here?"

"Four or five hours."

"Was there any kind of spontaneously occurring market here when you chose this location?"

He is silent and then shakes his head. In my subsequent trips to Greenville, I would see the useless structure progressively smothered by bush until only the roof was visible.

I ask Dickson if we could visit one of the seven small bridges that CRS constructed in the Greenville area. The bridges were built so that farmers could transport their goods to market. To my dismay, when we arrive at the site, the

Atakai Timber Company (ATI) is tearing down the bridge we had built just a few months before.

I track down the ATI crew boss and say, "We put thousands of dollars into that bridge! Why are you tearing it down?"

"CRS can build *decent* bridges," he says. "But we need to get tons of logs over these creeks. So we are rebuilding your bridges."

"How long have you known you'd do this?"

"For over a year."

Neither Dickson, the Jacket, nor anyone else in CRS asked ATI about their plans before building the bridges, though it was common knowledge that ATI would be logging in their forest concession in that area. One hundred thousand dollars flow down the drain as the logging company tears down all seven bridges.

That afternoon, we shift our focus from infrastructure to agriculture. I hope to find paddies thick with fresh rice shoots. Dickson first takes me to his best site, the Sawehstown Farmers Group. As Momo guides the Land Rover along a narrow road, half a dozen shirtless men come into view. They shovel earth from the swamp into a border that will hold water in place to irrigate the rice. If implemented correctly, swamp rice is beneficial for both people and the environment. After an area of forest is cleared just one time, that same area continues to produce year after year, thereby avoiding shifting cultivation (slash and burn). Additionally, once the labor-intensive setup is complete, up to three times the amount of rice can be produced in a given acre, increasing a farmer's food security.

To encourage farmers to leave the uplands and complete the difficult initial setup in the swamps, CRS gives them an incentive—a daily hot meal at the site plus a monthly ration of bulgur wheat and vegetable oil to take home to their families. The incentive was intended to be temporary, lasting only until the farmers experienced the wonders of swamp rice.

In a brief meeting with the rice farmers beside the site, I ask, "Are you going to keep farming here in your swamp when the CRS food is gone?"

"Yes! We will stay ri' here in the swamp, bossman."

We visit a number of other sites, each of which has been cleared of mature secondary or primary rainforest. After clear-cutting the forests in exchange for CRS bulgur wheat and vegetable oil, the farmers abandoned the sites and continued to slash and burn in the upland. They left the sites because the CRS technician had selected areas that were floodplains and not swamps. The areas dried up when the rain stopped and were useless. The few sites that were properly selected were abandoned anyway since the European Union had upped the ante with a juicier cash-for-work incentive elsewhere.

The final series of projects I am to visit before composing my much-dreaded report are CRS's so-called institutional feeding centers. The idea is simple: We provide hot meals to schoolchildren to encourage attendance. We also feed the teachers so they will come to work. This is necessary because in the nearly four hundred Liberian primary schools that CRS feeds, an average of one out of every two teachers does not receive the government salary of $20 per month, and most of those who do receive their payments get them irregularly, sometimes up to a year late.

Dickson takes me to the Demonstration School in downtown Greenville, an enormous structure built by the American NGO CARE in the 1980s with USAID funds. The interior smells of mildew, and the ceiling panels are either rotting away or have already fallen out. Children run wild. I stick my head into the boy's restroom but shrink back from the stench. It lacks running water. When we enter the sixth-grade classroom, the students jump up from their seats, which are large rocks collected from outside, and chant in unison, "Welcome, visitors!"

"Thank you!" I say as they sit back down on their rocks. Their teacher has written sentences on the remnants of a chalkboard, and the students dutifully copy them into their notebooks: "The United States is the capital of _____," and "France is the capital of _____."

For our benefit, the teacher asks his students to do an example aloud: "Children! Please! Okay, let us begin . . . 'The capital of Washington, D.C., is . . .'"

The students shout, "America!"

"And what is the capital of Paris?"

"France!"

In another classroom, two dozen first graders squirm on their rocks as they squint in the dim room to copy their teacher's lesson from the board. The lesson is about dangling participles.

I whisper to Dickson, *"Dangling participles?* These are six-year-olds!"

The teacher is barely literate himself and has apparently just copied the lesson out of an advanced grammar book without considering that such a topic is inappropriate for such young children. Teacher education came to a grinding halt during the long civil war. CRS's bulgur wheat and vegetable oil are successfully attracting students and teachers to the Greenville Demonstration School each day. But are the benefits of the nutrition they receive outweighed by the risks of disease-vector bathrooms and incorrect or confusing knowledge?

I walk along Greenville's beach that evening to reflect on the day. Avoiding the excrement underfoot, I take in the vivid sunset. It occurs to me that the Greenville program I have inherited is one giant shipment of Slim-Fast to Ethiopia. *It isn't sustainable. It has created dependency.*

The core of the problem has to do with relationships. The CRS Greenville program is Carolina Farm writ large, with Amanda, the Jacket, and Dickson as the bossmen dolling out *weekends*. These are not horizontal relationships; they are completely vertical, patron-client ones. The bridges, rice paddies, market buildings, and education programs were driven as much by a need to spend the money and meet monthly food quotas as by concern for people's economic and social development. The activities were designed by people in Monrovia and imposed upon the local people, instead of rising from the ground up.

But herein lies the challenge! I will start by writing a report to shake things up within CRS. I will make the grueling trip to Greenville as often as possible to help shape better programs: projects that promote self-reliance and eschew dependency; projects that foster environmental stewardship, not the destruction of virgin forests; projects that grow from the bottom up, not from the top down. As the red and orange hues wash the sky, I vow to make right my piece of international development.

In the midst of these noble thoughts, the diarrhea that has been plaguing me violently kicks in, and—lacking facilities anywhere nearby—I am forced to yank down my jeans and squat right there on the beach. Momentarily relieved, I look to my right and my heart jumps. Another person is squatting not fifteen feet away. He grins and nods in my direction, and I nod back, my relief having turned to dread.

It's a guy I'd seen a few times at the local Greenville bar, Mississippi Street Blues. As we both nod at each other, he with a grin and me with a frown, things get worse. I realize that I have no toilet paper and will have to ask this guy to share some of his banana leaf.

My squatting neighbor is still grinning. "Y'all right?" he calls over to me.

"I'm tryin' small," I answer.

CHAPTER 12

"I CALL THIS MEETING to order! This is not only my first, but also my last time as the Liberia Seeds and Tools Committee chairman," I say to the dozen Liberian UN, NGO, and government officials seated around a CRS conference table in Monrovia.

"If not you, who will chair!" one of the men cries out.

"No one will ever chair again! Because this is the *last* Seeds and Tools meeting."

Everyone begins talking at once. *Impossible!* General confusion and dismay.

"Please! Come to order!" I say. "Now look. The emergency period is over. The Seeds and Tools Committee is a fossil from the war period. One of you described it to me as an 'old boys' club' where you get together every week or two for sof' drinks."

A bit of knowing snickering. I continue, "This is not an ending, but rather a beginning. We are coming to an end of the era of free handouts and embarking on a journey toward sustainable development!"

"Well, I surely hope we at least have sof' drinks *today*!" someone grumbles.

The Jacket bursts through my office door, clutching a copy of my report on Greenville. "You want to blame Dickson for the bridges!"

I sit there stunned for a moment. "Jacket, that was one hundred grand down the drain. All that someone had to do was talk with the logging company about their plans."

"What, talk with Atakai Timber? Oh, and they're trustworthy. And then you have this recommendation about doing 'participatory rural appraisal' to determine 'a community's vision for their own development.' If you do that, you'll just create hopes that can't be satisfied! And then"—he flips through—"*then* you talk about the swamp rice projects being 'environmentally unsound.'"

"They cleared virgin rainforests in areas that weren't even viable for swamp rice."

"That's the kind of naïve shit that comes from people fresh off the plane. Were you here in the war? Do you think we had time to go around hugging goddamn trees?" He storms out of my office and heads straight for John's.

A half hour later, John calls me into his office. "The Jacket is pissed."

I look at my lap, and John continues, "He's the third person in here this morning complaining about your report. But you know what I told them? That this is exactly what we need more of. We need to shake things up a bit around here."

I experience a surge of relief. If John had sided with the Jacket, I'd probably be searching for a new job. We discuss my observations, and John gives me the green light to go forward with the changes. As I get up to leave, he says, "Good work, but in the next report drop the comparisons between our projects and shipments of Slim-Fast to Ethiopian famine victims."

Meanwhile the middle dries begin, which means more kayaking at Carolina Farm after work each day. I love to unwind at sunset with a strong row across the St. Paul estuary into the ocean, letting the kayak fill with seawater as I ride the waves into a sand spit. There I collapse exhausted onto the sand before heading back home.

Hoisting the kayak from the water onto my Carolina Farm lawn one afternoon, I sense a silence hanging over the Greater Diamond house. As I drag my kayak the long way right past their house, I notice their boat is missing. After peeking inside and finding the house empty, I walk around back. The python and duikers have vanished. I peer down into the guinea pig pit to see if there are any stragglers in need of rescue. Empty. While I shed no tears over the departure of my diamond-smuggling neighbors, I know I am going to miss the mischievous chimp Nicky.

I mope back to my house, put the inflatable kayak in the garage, and lament to Evans about Nicky.

"Nicky was a *fine* baboon," Evans says.

"Well, she was actually a chimpanzee," I point out.

"Yeah," Evans says, returning to the dishes he was washing.

A few days later, I get home from work and Evans jogs over to the Jeep. "Minnie gave birth!" I jump down and run over to Fred and Minnie's cage.

"Where are the babies!?"

"There only one. But it dead!"

"No, they always have four or five! And they can't be dead."

"Small-small pig dead-o."

"Let me stop by my old ma's to drop off money for Yeanue's food," Ciatta says. We are headed to do a food inventory at the Monrovia port, and I prefer not to make the detour. But she flashes me a pleading look, so I shrug and turn into New Georgia Estates, where her mother lives. It turns out to be neither new, nor resembling Georgia, nor consisting of estates. Instead it is a cluster of box homes erected in the 1980s. We park and climb a few steps to Unit 73.

"Mama!" an adorable four-year-old squeals, and runs for Ciatta's arms. Her daughter's hair is a Christmas tree of plastic hair ties.

"Yeanue! You thin!" Ciatta says, hugging her daughter, and then shoots a slicing glance over the little girl's shoulder at her own mother. Wearing a white dress and red high-heeled shoes, the stocky woman stands above her two seated teenage daughters, Ciatta's sisters. Her tiny living room is immaculately clean. One of the few decorations on the wall is a crucifix beside a weekly planning calendar with the hand-written caption "No visitor shall interrupt our daily family prayer hour."

"Well, daughter, we just heading off to the Kingdom Hall," she says.

"I just stopped by to bring something for Yeanue. Has she been eating? This is Bill from work."

I exchange pleasantries with Ciatta's mother, and then she abruptly asks me if I am "a God-fearing Christian."

Before I can respond, Ciatta jumps in. "Why you always gotta be harassing people-o? Not everybody Jehovah Witness like y'all!"

Her mother adopts an innocent look. "I just asking a question."

"We're leaving. Y'all need a ride, or what?"

Ciatta's mother, daughter, and two younger sisters pile into the Jeep, and we drop them off at the Jehovah's Witnesses' Kingdom Hall. Continuing toward the port, Ciatta is choked with anger: "My mother's a hypocrite! I gave her money to buy milk for Yeanue, and what did she do? She bought material to reupholster her sofa and chairs. I found out from my sister that Yeanue is not getting any milk, only rice, rice, rice. She doesn't look normal! As soon as I can, I'm taking Yeanue back."

"What about Yeanue's father?"

"That man in the States-o! He abandoned his daughter."

"He's Liberian?"

"Yeah, he's Liberian. He was a big bossman in the government. When I was a teenager, he paid my school fees, helped out my family. Well, after a few years I grew to really love him." She looks out the car window and then continues, "We lived together, and then I had Yeanue. I drove around in my own Mercedes and had money to do whatever I wanted. He always promised me we'd be married . . ."

Ciatta and I reach the Monrovia port. I flash my CRS ID card at the gate and am waved through. We park in front of the CRS port office, where we meet the two CRS food officers who will lead us through a food commodities inspection. As we pass an inventory clerk guarding the entrance to the first of our many warehouses, I draw in a quick breath. Before me sprawls an area bigger than a football field, covered with neat rows of fifty-pound bags of U.S. surplus bulgur wheat stacked twenty feet high. Ciatta notices me gawking and says, "If you think this is a lot of wheat, you should have seen what CRS did during the war. We had a dozen warehouses this size and were feeding a million people."

Walking down the rows with the food officers, who check off boxes and jot down figures on their forms, I feel the weight of a paradox. On the one hand, the food is beautiful. The people of America sharing the surplus of their bountiful fields. A freely given gift to the other side of the world. A way of saying "We have enough, so this is for you." But there is a darker side to these stacks of food. It says "Here's your weekend" rather than teaching somebody to make his own weekend. CRS continues to pump food into the economy years after the war, which is delaying the inevitable need for the country to find ways of feeding itself.

"This is why Liberians love CRS," Ciatta said, flipping back one of her blue braids. "They think CRS stand for 'Come Receive Small' or 'Catholic Rice Sweet.' CRS been feeding us for ten years now."

The next time I issue the order to ship out the food, it is with much less resolve. I don't even put my feet up on the desk as Amanda taught me.

"Tibet Five, Tibet One," I say into the radio.

"Good to hear your voice, bossman Tibet One," comes the reply.

"Do it . . . *I guess*," I say, swallowing.

"Done," he says after a pause.

CRS Liberia employs a small army of laborers who receive $4 a day, or four times the minimum daily wage of $1. Known as "casuals," these workers are not counted among our three hundred full-time employees who receive health insurance, sick leave, and severance pay. They are selected in a biweekly lottery—the lucky two hundred among thousands of names. I picture them now in their bright red CRS CASUAL WORKER vests, snapping into action based on my command, loading the trucks that will fan out to all corners of the country. These casuals come down from *the mountain,* that hill of trash that continues to grow daily in

Monrovia, grateful for the precious $4 they will receive at the end of the day. Any decision I make about the pipeline of food I oversee, be it to slow the flow of food or stop it all together, will affect their livelihoods.

CHAPTER 13

A BENT-OVER VILLAGER grunts to carry and then deposit
CRS field officer Boimah in the canoe right next to me.
Boimah then hands the man a five-liberty bill.* I say,
"Boimah, you must be joking."

He laughs, teeth flashing, and says, "I can't swim!"

The two of us are crossing the waters meet outside of
Buchanan in order to inspect several remote CRS feeding
sites. The motorcycles we will use to get to them, once we
cross, are strapped into a second canoe. As we skirt sand
dunes to our left, a phosphorescent tropical Atlantic opens
before us. The waters toss our canoe as we enter the estuary where the Mechlin, John, and Benson rivers spill into
the ocean.

In twenty minutes we reach the beach landing in Edina. A
few villagers scramble down the sandy bank to help our oars-
man unload the motorbikes. I follow Boimah up to the town
plaza and get the sensation that I am no longer in Africa but
have suddenly entered small-town Virginia, circa 1867.

Dilapidated manor houses with gabled roofs and dormer
windows line the wide streets around the plaza. The houses'
twin parlors straddle central hallways. People lazing on their
porches fan themselves and swat flies. Plots of grass in front

* Liberia's official currency is the Liberian dollar, commonly known as "liberty."
Between 1999 and 2001, the exchange rate was approximately forty liberty to
one U.S. dollar.

of some of the houses have been macheted down into what resemble lawns, and orange blossoms move ever so slightly in the breeze. I examine the headstones in the cemetery of the town's 1834 Methodist church—names like Johnson, Morris, Browne, and Coleman. They were among Liberia's ex-slave pioneers from the previous century.

"Good morning, gentlemen! I'm Reverend Ephraim Bacon!" an old man says, shaking our hands with a snap. Ephraim Bacon needs a cane to keep his back straight, but his eyes are alight. I can easily picture his grandparents strolling Edina's streets in the nineteenth century, his grandfather in top hat and morning coat ambling beside his grandmother fanning herself beneath a white lace parasol.

Ephraim leads us through Edina, on the way to the school and clinic that CRS feeds, but the old man is much more interested in showing off the history of his town than in school feeding. "That, of course, is the former home of President Jenkins—what a pity it's being smothered by the bush!—and *this* building is one of Liberia's oldest churches! Shall we take a quick peek inside?"

We step inside the church, which is all dust and scaffolding. The single remaining stained-glass window casts an iridescent pool of light on the altar. Ephraim makes a pitch: "We are trying to obtain . . . *support* for the restoration of this most historical landmark."

"Couldn't others from here who are now in the States help with the restoration of the church?" I asked. After all, I consider, Edina is one of the hubs of the former ruling class Americo-Liberians.

"Yes, I know, I know," Ephraim says as we leave the church and walk toward the school. "Everyone thinks that since two Liberian presidents came from Edina, and because we talk in high English and have these nice old buildings, that we must have rich connections in the U.S."

He looks at me and continues. "Well, in any case it sure is ironic that we Americo-Liberians migrated here from the U.S. long ago, and now—with all this war business—we find ourselves back on that side again. So, it's true, Edinans are over there, but they're struggling like the rest. You really think they have money to send to restore our town?"

We arrive at the schoolyard. *Recess.* No matter what time of day I inspect a school, it is inevitably recess. Moreover, though it is barely ten-thirty in the morning, some of the kids are already wolfing down their CRS-provided bulgur-wheat-and-bean lunch. I scan the schoolyard for signs of privilege among these Americo-Liberian youth. Were there Nike shoes, oversize backpacks, or kids playing with Power Rangers? No, none of these things. Just the usual bare feet kicking a deflated ball amid howls of delight. As Ephraim suggested, Liberians with resources—usually Americos—fled to the United States during the war, swelling the Liberian population there to around two hundred thousand according to Liberian immigration activists. These Liberians settled in pockets around the country, especially Massachusetts, Pennsylvania, Rhode Island, and Minnesota. Those Americos who remained at home seemed to have been knocked down to the same level as Liberians of other ethnic groups.

Boimah and I finish inspecting the Edina school feeding program, shake hands with Ephraim Bacon, and are about to mount our motorcycles to leave for the next village when I notice a girl skipping home with a container of bulgur and beans from the school lunch. I ask Ephraim about this.

"Their mothers tell them not to eat *all* of their CRS lunch, but to bring home half to share with their brothers and sisters who are not yet in school." He leans more heavily on his cane and adds, "Every bean here . . . is precious."

Edina is a good hour behind us when we motor into the next town, a dozen mud huts around a clearing. I take off my helmet and brush some of the red dust off my jeans. The town chief comes out to greet us, ushers us into a palava hut, offers us kola nuts, and then just sits there waiting, surrounded by a dozen other men. His expectant look is laid squarely on me until I realize that he is hoping for a *dash*—or gift—in return for the kola. But I am not going to budge, our project support being *dash* enough.

The silence eventually works to my advantage. The chief realizes he will not be *dash*ed and leads us toward the swamp rice site. Two men hack back undergrowth along the path. I note to myself that it's a bad sign that the path to the site is not brushed. Any slim hopes I may have had of surveying a fertile breast of paddy rice disappear when we arrive. There is a swamp, yes, but without rice. The site has been cleared of undergrowth, but only a fraction of the area has been dug into the appropriate water control structures.

"What's the delay?" I say to the chief, who looks to Boimah for assistance. Boimah translates from English into Bassa, and the chief responds in Bassa, shaking a finger at me.

"He says," translates Boimah, "that everyone is in the bush school, so there is *noooo* farming here now."

I direct my next question to Boimah. "But your plans, as the field officer in charge, show that the site should be planted by now."

"The bush school was a constraint."

"Is this the first time they've had bush school this time of year?" I know quite well it isn't; the bush school is the mysterious tribal initiation process that takes place in one way or another in nearly all Liberian rural communities each year.

"No! It always exactly this time of year!"

"So is it a *constraint*, as you say, or an *excuse*?"

"It's not an excuse-o . . . they have bush school!"

"But you knew it would happen?"

"Yes."

"So why didn't you factor the bush school into the plans?"

Boimah is seriously confused at this point. In a culture where time is a fluid notion, the idea of planning ahead, of being able to regiment time into controllable chunks, is only dimly grasped.

"Another thing," I say. "This is supposed to be a food-for-*work* exchange. Your records show that the food was eaten, but there has been no work done."

Boimah translates this and then relays the chief's response to me. "The chief would like to thank CRS for the delicious food, but unfortunately the annual bush school destroyed their hopes."

We follow the chief to a cluster of huts bordering the future rice farm. Children pluck oranges from a tree and hand them to us. I stuff slices into my mouth, savoring the sweet juice. Eventually, I ask how many families live here.

"One," comes the translation.

"One? But there are five huts!"

An animated discussion breaks out in Bassa, and Boimah finally says, "The huts are for the chief's five wives and twenty-three children."

I look at the chief, who is smiling proudly, and then back at Boimah.

"The five wives," Boimah explains, "they work and give him children, and he gives them a house and food."

"Don't they get jealous?" I ask.

"Yes!" Boimah grins. "My ol'pa had three wives! But it works small-small. Like this chief. He sleeps three nights with one wife, three with the next, like that, until he comes back to the first wife. So then *nooo*body will get jealous."

In Buchanan's nightclub Jazz 2000, you take one step down into an airy room filled with comfortable sofas. I'm on one of those sofas, two beers into a mellow evening after returning from the field, when Boimah suggests some meat. He beckons the "meat lady" and says, "Please bring us one cow meat and one feesh."

When she returns she says, "One hundred and sixty dollars!" I bill out the liberty and we dig into spicy cassava fish with our tablespoons. Theresa, whom Boimah described as his "deputy wife," is enjoying the beef platter along with her friend Kuku, who showed up when the food did.

As we finish our snack, Kuku asks me, "Wa'a dance?"

We head over to the dance floor. The DJ spins a currently popular tune from South Africa, and we move to the beat along with a few other couples. As the song changes, I ask her, "How old are you, Kuku?"

"I twenty-one."

"Are you a student?"

She nods.

"What are you studying?"

"Seventh grade."

Kuku and I are both sweating when we return to the group, and Momo and Boimah are ready to go. We climb into the Jeep, Momo at the wheel and Boimah next to him. I find myself sandwiched between Theresa and Kuku.

When we arrive at the office-guesthouse to drop me off,

Kuku jumps out as well. As she trails me up to my room, it finally dawns on me that she is offering herself to me. I unclick the lock to my room, and she follows me inside. A hot sweat covers my forehead and I flip on the fan. To buy time, I push my *Collins Guide to African Wildlife* into her hands.

Kuku flips through the glossy color photos of elephants, rhinos, and chimpanzees. She eventually points to a photo of an okoai and asks, "What kind of *meat* is that?"

I sit next to her on the bed. Her skirt is hitched way up her thigh, which rubs against mine. "An okoai? An okoai is more than just meat. It's kind of like a giraffe . . ." Kuku shifts and her arm presses against mine; I catch the scent of her perfume.

"An okoai is like a giraffe," I repeat.

Kuku looks up at me, blinks once, and then bursts out giggling. I laugh as well. Our eyes meet and hold, and she leans her head back and then presses herself closer against me, ready to be kissed. I am more tempted than I have yet been in Africa, though dozens of other girls have shown similarly obvious interest. I have come to realize that there are few women, married or unmarried, who are not available to a bossman, a bwana.

I want to just let my instincts take over, and I feel myself leaning toward her slowly, see her lips part, and just as ours are about to touch I blurt out, "Kuku! I can't do this."

She blinks and looks at me. It's a completely indecipherable look. I get up and search around for my keys, my head and hormones swirling. Kuku sighs, shrugs, and follows me down to the Land Rover.

We drive together through the Buchanan night, at five miles an hour through a moonscape of potholes. Fires illuminate some windows, but nearly everyone is asleep. Inside me a debate rages. Why can't I just go with the flow of Africa? Am I a slave to my own cultural norms of fidelity and monogamy? When I was about to kiss Kuku, I suddenly pictured Jennifer sitting in the corner, arms crossed, watching me, and was swept with a wave of guilt.

Everybody wants me to kiss Kuku. Just as it is the path of least resistance to slip into the fancy expatriate lifestyle, so too is it painless and fully accepted to take multiple girlfriends. In fact, monogamy is so countercultural in Liberia that I feel *stingy*. The other men at CRS have begun looking at me as if I'm a tightwad, so wealthy and yet refusing to support my share of young Liberian women. They may also view me as a snob, preferring only white women, which is far from the truth.

The traditional practice of polygamy in Liberia did not stop in the villages. Every Liberian man in the CRS field stations, without a single exception, has his local girlfriend in addition to his wife in Monrovia. The CRS drivers have many, one in each of the villages in which they work. Momo has perhaps half a dozen *deputies*. Liberians claim that these relationships do not affect their love for their primary wife and would tell me that having girlfriends here would do nothing to affect my love for Jennifer.

The wives, too, are in on it. Every woman knows that her partner has *deputies,* but it is a taboo topic. Also not discussed is the fact that the whole thing has an economic basis; it is an accommodation polygamy makes to modern life. Momo, for example, provides food, clothing, and education for his several *deputies*.

By paying excellent salaries by local standards, the aid NGOs and UN unwittingly fund sexual tourism all around the country. Without our salaries and work in the field, hundreds of teenage villagers might still be virgins, might not be sleeping with drivers like Momo! I think of the southern African highway where AIDS is spread at lightning speed between truck drivers and the roadside brothels. While HIV-AIDS in West Africa is much lower than in eastern and southern parts of the continent (less than 4 percent of Liberians as compared to 35 percent in Botswana), it is on the rise here, and I imagine our drivers contributing to the spread of AIDS.

When we get to Kuku's parents' house, she sits there for a long moment and then asks me if CRS has any jobs available. I tell her we don't have anything full-time right now but that she could probably do some part-time work. I will let the Buchanan manager know she'll be by to apply on Monday. She thanks me and gets out of the car, and as I pull away I see her still standing there in the doorway, looking at me as if maybe there'd been some mistake.

CHAPTER 14

THE FIRST TIME I see Gabriel Ballayan, he seems to irradiate the area around him with a vibrant light. Below his close-cropped Afro lie facial features that are chiseled into a near-perfect harmony. Mesmerized community members in a village near Greenville gather around him and tilt their heads up to the tall man's face as he talks about the importance of protecting the environment.

I wait for the group to disperse so that I can finally meet this legend. I've heard two general opinions about Gabriel. One side sees him as a quixotic dreamer, refusing to accept the reality of human nature: that we are made of blue clay. The other uses words like "saint" to describe him. They see him as a conservation missionary who has recruited thousands by his mere presence (including his physical attractiveness) and the depth of his belief in a higher cause. As an expatriate colleague put it, "Jesus Christ was just the warmup act. Gabriel's the real God-made-flesh."

When the group disperses, I approach Gabriel. In a quiet, confident voice he introduces the stumpy man beside him: "Meet Boss Hog." Three deep scars mar Boss Hog's face and neck. After we shake hands, he leaves me alone with Gabriel. Noticing my puzzled expression, Gabriel explains, "Boss Hog was a feared warlord with one of the rebel factions, and for a while ruled over much of the rural area around Greenville."

Gabriel smiles broadly, his straight white teeth standing out against his face.

"So he's a friend of yours?"

"You could say that! You see, Boss Hog didn't know what to do when the war ended, so he turned his guns against the elephants in the park, profiting off the ivory and meat. Anyway, we bought him off. We pay him more than he made hunting."

I flash a puzzled look.

"Boss Hog is an environmental activist now. He and his former fighters guard the wildlife. We just upped the ante! Desperate times call for creative solutions."

Gabriel's eloquence intrigues me. I ask him about his accent, and he explains that he is Ghanaian. He lived in England for several years, studying at Cambridge and marrying a British woman. After their divorce he returned to West Africa to work among his own people.

Before we part ways, he invites me to see one of his projects. "We'll be showing a film on Friday evening from Sierra Leonean refugees. Have you ever been to a refugee camp?"

Gabriel's voice crackles over my two-way radio: "Tibet Five, Tibet Five, Ecoforest."

"Go ahead, Ecoforest," I reply.

"I'll be in front of CRS in five mikes."

"Good copy, standing by."

"Roger, Ecoforest standing by."

It's a Friday night, and viewing environmental films in a refugee camp sounds like work. I had thought about refusing Gabriel's invitation in order to have the weekend night free. But you don't refuse Gabriel. I mentioned the idea to my colleague Susan, another American aid worker, and when she heard I was going with Gabriel, she begged to come along as well, saying, "He's the sexiest man I've ever laid eyes on."

Minutes later, she and I climb into Gabriel's pickup and roll through Monrovia. He eventually steers the truck off the pavement onto a dirt road. "This is an environmental classroom on wheels," he says. As he speaks I glance at Susan, who hangs on his every word.

Gabriel is president and founder of Africa Environment Action (AEA), a small NGO operating in Liberia under several grants, including one from the United Nations High Commissioner for Refugees, to ensure environmental quality in refugee camps. He explains to us that refugees have an enormous impact on natural resources around their camps. "Where there was originally forest, there are suddenly thousands of people in need of wood for building makeshift homes and cooking, which leads to deforestation and soil erosion."

As he speaks, I try to decipher the secret of Gabriel's charm, that captivating effect he has on everyone he meets. He is a tall Ghanaian man in his late fifties but with the vigor of someone much younger. I watch the way his mouth moves, listen to the music in his voice. Susan asks him if he works like this every weekend, and he replies, "What's work? I love everything I do. It's all part of a seamless expression of care. Gandhi told us that we should be the change we want to see in the world, and I take that to heart."

We turn onto another dirt road. It is now completely dark, and the stars shine with exceptional clarity. The mud-and-wood huts slide past the pickup in the darkness, candles burning inside. There is no gate into the camp, and suddenly we've come to a stop in an open dirt plaza in front of a large tin-roofed, open-air structure. This is where the film will be shown.

When we first rolled into the plaza it seemed sleepy, with only a few souls walking around. Within a minute the open-air structure filled with people, and a bubbling crowd now surrounds our pickup. When we get out, children in tattered clothing shout, "Hello!" and shake our hands. Since guests are rare, our arrival is a major event. Six thousand Sierra Leoneans live in this camp, and it seems that most of them are gathered around the truck.

Gabriel's crew unloads the pickup—video projector, speakers, a screen. While they set up, Susan and I are swarmed by bodies in the dark wanting to touch us, shake our hands, exchange words. "Excuse me, but what is the film about?" one older man asks.

"Uh . . . ," I say, stalling. "One is about women's issues in refugee camps, and the other about environmental issues. But they will explain before the film. I am seeing the films for the first time."

"Ah, you are most welcome here!"

"Thank you."

Lots of children ask our names. We ask their names. Then I question one teenager about how long he had been in the camp.

"Since 1994," he answers.

Amazed, I ask others. Many have been there for six, seven years or more. Most people say they are from Freetown. A few are internally displaced persons (IDPs) from other parts of Liberia.

The first film is about to start. They prepare a bench for Susan and me in the middle of a thick, noisy crowd. It's the seat of honor. Everyone else stands except for the children, who crouch in the dirt in front of us. The film begins with images of women in different camps around Africa. The women explain how they never expected to become refugees, losing everything. Many have been raped. Scenes from various camps are shown—Sudan, Ethiopia, a Liberian camp in Ghana—and then a gasp rises from the crowd when a Sierra Leonean camp in Liberia appears on the screen. The film then focuses on various projects within camps that attempt to help women: images of women learning soap-making, tie-dying, and baking skills or receiving microcredit loans.

Throughout the film, a tremendous background noise of talking surrounds us. The crowd is too big for the speakers Gabriel brought, and he doesn't have a microphone to encourage order. People yell for quiet. In vain. The crowd is just too big. During the second film the roar of the crowd continues, making it impossible to hear the sound track. It's difficult to breathe with so many bodies pressed together. The odor of unwashed bodies grows around me. I begin to feel nauseated. A sense of anarchy creeps up my spine. This is so close to being wild.

At the end, Gabriel tries to reinforce a point made by the film, and he shouts into the roar of the audience, "Refugees have lost many things, but what is *one thing* they have not *lost?*"

A few people in the front chant the correct answer: "*Their dignity.*" The rest can't hear a thing.

After the film, the need, hurt, and loss press in around us again. A swarm of children and teens. I ask one small boy, "What's your name?"

"Jonathan." As he says his name, I notice that his face is covered with four or five open sores.

"Did you like the film?"

"Yes!"

"What's one thing you learned from the film?" I ask, teacherlike, thinking of the various themes presented.

He is silent, thinking about my question, and I see his eyes well up, about to burst out in tears . . .

In the pause, my mind flashes back to another Sierra Leonean I'd recently met at a workshop in Monrovia. She was an old, wise-looking woman of about eighty, and it was her birthday. We—her fellow workshop participants— surprised her by singing "Happy Birthday" that morning. At the end of the song, she stood and addressed us pensively: "Why is it that you wish me a happy birthday? Is it that you are happy that I am born? Or is it because I do not bring you pain?"

"So . . . what is something you learned from the films?" I ask the boy again. "Anything at all?"

"I learned . . . that I want to go home," he replies, tears falling into and around the large sores on his cheeks.

I do not bring you pain.

The truck is now packed up and Gabriel comes over to tell me it's time to go. He notices the small boy sobbing in front of me, looks at him for a moment, and then lifts him off the ground. The boy grabs on to Gabriel's shoulders. Gabriel hugs Jonathan, patting his back and speaking comforting words. He touches the boy's facial sores. The boy's body stops hiccuping and calms. Meanwhile, the crowd directly encircling us has become quiet, entranced by this moment between Gabriel and the refugee child.

Gabriel places the now remarkably serene boy back on the dusty ground and leads me through the crowd toward his truck. I steal a glance back toward Jonathan. Not only are his tears dried up and his expression calm, but I sense that his sores have visibly begun to heal. The crowd splits to let us through, and Gabriel seems to float millimeters above the ground, a tiny bit above our world.

Driving away in silence, I look out into all the white eyes in the dark night, and the only lights are the piercing stars and earthbound candles.

CHAPTER 15

"FIGHT POVERTY AND dependency while saving the rain-forest." I've come to see it not as a job description, but rather as a riddle.

I am not certain if Gabriel has been helping me solve the riddle or adding layers of complexity to it. After our visit to the refugee camp, we've spent a lot of time together, wrestling with the social, economic, political, and ethical issues under-lying our work. There are certain things that he does not talk about with me, but I begin to discern that he is secretly involved in efforts to undermine the growing deforestation of the country.

Meanwhile, everything in Liberia becomes muted by a hazy tinge as the Sahara's red sands blow over. It's an annual dry season phenomenon called "*harmatan,*" where sand clouds blanket tropical West Africa. What was crisp green against clear blue sky is now blurred, softened. I feel my own inner state blurring as well, particularly after a luncheon with the American ambassador and a work trip to Liberia's anarchic interior. As if I were peeling the layers of an artichoke one by one, I'm going deeper into the entrenched connections between poverty and environmental degradation.

John pressed the doorbell to the U.S. ambassador's mansion as I reluctantly tightened my tie more snugly against my neck. A servant in a starched tuxedo shirt and black bow tie ushered us up a carpeted stairway to a cool parlor, where the ambassador greeted us.

"Gentlemen!" he said, striding across the thick carpet to shake our hands. "Lunch is served!"

As we made our way into the dining room, he asked me how the tennis was coming along.

"I haven't played since our last match," I said. We had played doubles once. My partner was "Jim" from "embassy administration" ("administration" was sometimes a euphemism for CIA), and the ambassador had been joined by the embassy doctor. They whipped us.

The ambassador glanced at John. "Would you care to say grace?"

John squirmed. "I really wouldn't know what to say."

"Oh! I just assumed you were Catholic."

"Well, actually I'm agnostic. Can't really say whether there's a Big Guy up there or not. *Eh-hem*. I come at it from a secular humanist point of view. And CRS . . . it's aid *based on need, not creed.*"

The ambassador gave a thin smile and then bowed his head and led a quick prayer. Then he lifted a golden bell that sat beside his plate and rang it. Two white-gloved servants strode through a swinging door and began to ladle mushroom soup into our bowls. John seized the moment to show off our programs to our big donor. "CRS implements U.S. Title Two school feeding programs in four hundred and twelve schools in the Monrovia-Buchanan-Greenville corridor. We used to feed refugees in what I call the 'tristate area'—Guinea, Sierra Leone, and Liberia—but we pulled out when the rebels sacked Voinjama . . ."

The ambassador nodded at all the right times, yet I sensed he was grasping little of John's ten-minute speech. At one point he rang the golden bell again, and the servants exchanged our empty soup bowls for plates of roast duck in a raspberry sauce. Finally the ambassador asked, "What are you doing to help *poor people?*"

John practically choked on his duck over the simplicity of the question. "Well [cough] Ambassador [cough-cough], our food security analysis indicates . . ."

Over dessert, the ambassador shared some thoughts about his embassy. "I'm trying to get the Americans here more out in the community. Many of them rarely leave the embassy, preferring to enjoy the many creature comforts it offers. Would you believe that some of us leave without getting to know a single Liberian person?" He spooned some flan out of his bowl, but before putting it into his mouth, he added, "Except their servants, perhaps."

The conversation eventually turned to logging. All of Monrovia was talking about OTC, the gigantic Malaysian company that, having finished clear-cutting an Indonesian island, had now set up shop in Liberia. I mentioned that a fledgling resistance movement seemed to be growing.

"You mean the famous Gabriel Ballayan, dashing hero of the rainforest? Off the record, he is on Taylor's hit list. You can't directly oppose Taylor's interests and not get burned." The ambassador then added in balanced tones, "But the OTC issue is complex. We need jobs here, naturally. Hopefully the timber industry will employ Liberians." He tilted his empty espresso cup toward himself, studying the inside of it. "But I'm really wondering if they will exercise . . . *restraint* . . . in their logging."

A half-dozen logging trucks raced past us on the road between Buchanan and Greenville, creating a minor dust storm.

Coughing, Momo and I rolled up our windows as we jerked to a halt on the side of the road.

"Look at the size of those logs!" I said to Momo. "North America hasn't seen diameters like that for fifty years."

As the last of the yellow trucks with their doors sporting black OTC lettering sped by, I said, "And can you believe the road! This all happened in the last few months!" The former road through the rainforest, barely the width of a car, had been widened into a dirt highway. OTC had razed everything in its way—trees, people's huts, and cassava patches—to smooth its passage to the Buchanan port.

"You know what OTC stand for?" Momo said. "Only Taylor's Children. It Taylor's pepper bush! All that money for him and the Malaysians. The drivers, managers, everyone Malaysian! They bring two thousand workers, and don't give jobs to Liberians. My man, they even bring their own *prostitutes*!"

The widened road continued for a long time, and we passed dozens more OTC trucks. I felt a surge of relief when we reached Krahn-Bassa National Forest; OTC had not made it that far.

The rest of the way to the village outside of Greenville was a cinch. Palm Butter Hill, Face-to-Face, and the area around Theresaville where we had been waylaid for the night on the previous trip a few months back were now dry, and we sped through to Vanjahtown.

"Hey, man!" muttered a long-faced Momo. "Where the people-o?" We had arrived in Vanjahtown, but neither the town chief, Dickson, nor any of the villagers were there to meet us.

I climbed out of the Jeep and spotted a group of men

under the village palava hut. Walking toward them, I felt mildly depressed. What was I doing here? I leapt over a ditch, silently cursing Dickson for not having informed the villagers we were coming. When I reached the palava hut, one of the older men stood up. He was reminiscent of the Yoda character from the *Star Wars* series and couldn't have been more than five feet tall. His stained and tattered T-shirt read: NOT A BALD SPOT. IT'S THE SOLAR-POWERED PANEL FOR A SEX MACHINE. There was a moment of silence, in which I suppressed a chuckle over his shirt, and then he asked me in a serious voice, "Are you Mr. Power?"

"Yes, I am."

"I'm Chief Wah. *Welcome!!!*" The half-dozen men swept me along to the main road. I spotted Dickson strutting down the road along with a group of a few dozen women and children singing, dancing, and beating drums. The women's faces were painted white. They formed a dancing circle around me and chanted in Sapo.

Chief Wah translated the chant: "The women are singing, 'We give praise because the white bossman has come!'"

Still enclosing me in a circle, they walked me back up the street to the other side of the village, singing in Sapo. An old woman with a painted white face smiled vigorously as she shimmied inches from my body, bending down to brush my stomach with her gray mop of hair. I shuffled and clapped along with them, all the way up the street, feeling joyful over this enthusiastic welcome.

After some formal introductions in the palava hut, I suggested we drive to their community forest. When I asked Chief Wah if he would join us, he replied, "Wherever Power go, I go!"

After a short drive, Dickson, me, Chief Wah, the school

principal, and half a dozen other men from the village tromped through the secondary rainforest, along a baseline boundary. The beauty of the forest overwhelmed me. We heard ibis calls and saw anteater and bush hog diggings. Our path was interesected by "animal roads" cut through the forest by pigmy hippos, bush hogs, and elephants. Chief Wah macheted a branch that secreted a red liquid that was used as iodine. Another plant cured snakebite. At one point, a small black snake crossed in the marshy ground right in front of me and someone cried, "Cobra!"

After a few hours of hiking the baseline, I was exhausted and had that familiar satisfied feeling you get after completing a hike. We drove the five kilometers back into the village, where Chief Wah offered me his own bedroom. The official program, a necessary part of every village visit, would begin at three o'clock. I lay down to read and then curled up for a nap on the straw bed. Sweat was pouring from me in the ill-ventilated mud room, but I was able to fall into a thin sleep.

A knock awoke me, and the chief announced that the program would be delayed until five or six. Not long after, an excruciating pain invaded my intestines. I gulped air as the pressure and pain attacked my stomach from all angles. I lay on the bed, but that worsened the agony. I desperately needed a drinking cup to take my antacid, and I tried to communicate this to the family in the neighboring hut. Speaking no English, they just smiled and ignored me. I stumbled outside to a place behind my hut, where I threw up, and then I returned to my neighbors and pointed to a cup that a small child was holding. They understood and went to find one for me.

While waiting for the cup, I clutched my gut in the rattan

chair in my room. Through a lens of pain, everything looked different, very foreign, even scary. Even the wasps nesting in my hut's earthen walls seemed to have it in for me. A group of chickens walked into the room, and I kicked dirt at them. A puppy flopped in as well and, instead of being cute, was menacing. A toddler walked by pulling a tin can car on a string, and the noise of the can grated on me. I was eight gut-wrenching hours from medical care in Monrovia. What if it was cerebral malaria or some other quick-acting disease? I stared at the dirt floor and tried not to think about it as flies landed on my legs. A mug finally arrived, and I took the antacid. Miraculously, within two hours the pain had subsided.

The program began at sunset. The school principal handed me a handwritten agenda, and I was initially relieved to see that there were only six items. Then I noticed that item six ("Other Speeches") had sixteen subitems ("a." through "p."). As one speech led to another, the day's light faded out of the thatched roofs, out of the children's faces, out of the palm trees. Candles were a great luxury, but two were lit for the occasion when it was completely dark. I made my speech, talking about the importance of the community forest that I had visited that day. I also responded to several requests for more free food from CRS. I noted that CRS now required community contributions in all activities and was no longer giving food-for-work for everything, only for selected activities such as school feeding. This, I said, would help ensure ownership of the projects so that they would last into the future. I said that instead of *giving* them golden eggs, CRS would now help them maintain the hen that *lays* the golden eggs. Clapping and exclamations rang out as my words were translated into Sapo.

One woman noted in her speech, "This is the first time in our history that a *white bossman* has slept in our village. We thank God that this *whiteman* has brought light to our village." A schoolteacher said that although the government was failing to pay them, they taught anyway as volunteers, "so that their children would not have to live in darkness." Chief Wah had the final words of the two-hour event: "You see that duck there that is now alive and breathing? That will be for Bill Power soup!" A dozen children leapt up and chased the duck, subdued it, and brought it over to the chief, who presented it to me as a gift.

After the speeches, the women and children danced in circles, chanted, and played drums. The celebration went on well into the night. As the sugarcane wine was passed around, I felt as if I were in a womb of community. It was a tiny, isolated town, yet the people were unified and full of life. There were many references to their joy over my visit and how they had danced and sung until late the previous night after they heard I was coming.

Over the wine, the men talked about the effects of the three-month rice gap, when people "wasted plenty," or starved. "But we are used to it," one said. They talked about the difficulties of farming with monkeys, chimps, and duikers constantly poaching from their agricultural fields.

The next day, I visited the new aspects of our program that I had recently introduced: the wood-saving ecostoves, the integration of environmental education into the school curriculum, and agroforestry plots, which reduced deforestation by intensifying production of fruit trees and ground crops in the same area. These projects used much less food-for-work and considerably more direct technical assistance. But while inspecting the nascent projects, I finally understood the immensity of the chasm that separated my world from the world of Chief Wah's Vanjahtown. The people of Vanjahtown still lacked even a basic notion of the project goals. For example, despite the dozens of community meetings we had held together to discuss the community forest (explaining that the purpose was to get legal title for the community forest so that it would belong *exclusively to Vanjahtown* for education and sustainable use), I was still asked by Chief Wah, "When will CRS begin logging in there?"

It also finally struck me that the idea of providing environmental education for Vanjahtown was a bit absurd. They were not only completely enmeshed with nature, but also consuming a tiny fraction of the resources of a Westerner like myself. This became especially apparent when I was leaving Vanjahtown and offered Chief Wah my shoes. I asked him if he wore a size eleven. The tiny man just grabbed them from me, thanking me profusely. I followed up, asking, "But are you sure they are your size?"

He replied simply, "I have no shoes."

CHAPTER 16

"HEY, BILL," THE Jacket says, "here's a riddle for you: What's the difference between 'ignorance' and 'apathy'?"

I'm back in Monrovia, having my morning coffee in my air-conditioned corner office at the CRS office on Randall Street, and the Jacket has just stepped in. I shrug.

"The answer: I don't know, and I don't care," he says, blue eyes flashing above a big grin.

This gets me thinking about what it takes to change; to slash through the thicket of our own conditioning and defenses, awaken to a deeper reality, and act. What forces transform ignorance and apathy into enlightened action?

Later that evening, I'm having a beer at the Anchor with Gabriel, and he says to me, "I know I can trust you now." He leans toward me and says barely above a whisper, "We've got an underground group forming to explore ways to undermine the Oriental Timber Company's illegal logging."

Some Save the Children staffers are giggling over mugs of beer, and stone-faced Liberian waitresses stand at the edge of the room. Gabriel's long, solid frame overpowers the small bench he's sitting on, and his eyes hold a determination. "It's hard to sit still while OTC works with military efficiency. If we don't act now, OTC will turn the country into a desert."

We are quiet for a moment, and then he says, "You're

invited to a meeting tomorrow evening. No one else can know about it."

A few weeks earlier, I might have declined Gabriel's invitation. Dangerous stuff, opposing Charles Taylor's main source of personal income, even if it was just a discussion group. However, some recent experiences in Greenville have impacted me deeply; I tell Gabriel to count me in.

The week before, in Greenville, Dickson, Momo, and I drove over to Atakai Timber in the Land Rover. Dickson had befriended Jihad Georges and Moukhayber, the owners of this Lebanese logging company. A servant showed us into a wood-paneled living room, where half a dozen Lebanese were drinking beer and watching an Arabic-language game show beamed to their Greenville home via satellite.

"Dickson!" Jihad Georges said, rising from his recliner and shaking Dickson's hand and then mine. "You want beers? Yes?" He then turned to the servant. "Bring two very cold beers!"

As we chatted, Jihad emerged as the brains behind the logging operation, whereas his brother Moukhayber was the bean counter. Moukhayber's wife and sister were also there, on a three-month visit from Lebanon. Jihad and Moukhayber's younger brother, Youssef, seemed mildly retarded. He sat two feet from the TV and flipped from one Arabic channel to the next.

"Youssef!" chided Jihad Georges. "Please don't play with that!" Youssef turned puppy-dog eyes to his brother.

A servant and cook loaded eggplant salad, baked fish, and kibbi stew onto the dining room table. My mouth watered even more when I spied our dessert on a side table: baklava, farina squares, and spiced rice pudding. I was just wondering when we would eat when Youssef tapped my shoulder from behind. "Do you want to see my pets?"

"Okay," I said. As we walked to the door, I heard Jihad quip that "we will feast on one of Youssef's pets tonight." In their backyard, a variety of animals wandered about, including a duiker, a Diana monkey, and a baby chimpanzee.

"Where did you get these?" I asked.

"From the bush," Youssef answered. "They are mostly babies from animals we kill for bushmeat."

"Why?"

"To feed the men in our logging camps . . . I love my animals. Do you love them?"

"They're beautiful, Youssef," I said.

"I have to watch over them carefully," he said, suspicion in his eyes. "My brothers are always trying to eat them."

The next day was Saturday. Dickson, Ciatta, a few others, and I piled into the Land Rover and headed to the Greenville port. Greenville was surrounded by gorgeous beaches, but swimming was safe only at the sheltered port because of the deadly riptides everywhere else.

I dropped off the others at the port beach and continued alone to the ATI port office. At dinner the night before, Jihad Georges had invited me over to visit them. I pulled into their work yard. Though it was Saturday, dozens of Liberians unloaded logs and used a wheezing sawmill to cut them into planks. A stone-faced Moukhayber approached my car and led me to Jihad Georges's air-conditioned office.

As we talked, Jihad showed me a full-color wall map of the timber concessions in the Greenville area. "Look at OTC's concession," he said with a scowl. "It goes right to the edge of Sapo National Park! Our concession touches the southern side of the park. We've been logging right up to the boundary for years and have never crossed the line. Did we ever cross that line, Moukhayber?"

Arms crossed, his brother shook his head vigorously.

"My friend," Jihad continued, "do you really think anyone is guarding the park? Ridiculous! There is no one out there! We seen sixty-thousand-dollar mahoganies right over the so-called boundary, but did we give in to temptation? *Did we give in to temptation, Moukhayber?!*"

Moukhayber shook his head again.

"No! We did not give in to temptation. Moukhayber knows. But let me tell you a secret," Jihad said, lowering his voice to just above a whisper. "Liberians say OTC stand for what? One Time Chopping. That simple English for this: OTC will cut everything down and then leave for somewhere else in the world. My patience is running low. If OTC cuts one tree in the park . . . *one tree* . . . I am going into the park, too."

None of my Liberian colleagues could swim. They were splashing in knee-deep water when I arrived from the logging office. Ciatta would barely go in above her ankles, but I coaxed her out to chest level. "See, it's not so bad," I said. "Just float at first. *Float.*"

Floating face-up, she breathed in gasps, whimpering when a foamy wave passed over her face. I held her up at first, but within an hour Ciatta floated on her own, with just the very tips of my fingers touching hers.

After the swimming lesson, we ran some giddy relay races on the beach, and then Dickson and I hiked off with our fishing rods. We circumvented a tangle of bush and eventually wound our way to an inlet.

"The fish here-o!" Dickson said. We cast and reeled in, cast and reeled. My bare feet nestled in a warm pool of water in the rock face, and a steady breeze massaged my whole body. The ocean water surged through the inlet. The tension that had been building within me eased away. Though the fish refused to bite, I didn't care. I looked over at Dickson, and he flashed a smile, which I returned.

Later on the beach, Ciatta and Dickson were teaching me how to break the ice with "country folk" during project site visits. Ciatta said, "Okay, pretend Dickson is cooking. I say, 'Hello, ma'!'"

Dickson smiled and answered, "Hello!"

"Y' all right?"

"I all right. How you day?"

"Trying. Wha' you cooking? Wha' kinda soup?"

"Potato greens."

"Good."

"How's Mo'rovia?"

"All right."

The exchange flowed soft and subtle, a singsong Liberian English. Ciatta told me it was my turn, and I exclaimed, "Hello, ma'!"

"Hello!" she answered. "How'da body?"

"Body fine-o," I said, grinning big. "What kinda soup you cookin'?"

That evening, as the sun set over the ocean, Dickson and I devoured bowls of palm butter on his Mississippi Street porch. Palo (who was three going on four) stopped by for his share of the food. Palo was one of the neighbor's children, but Dickson had essentially adopted him since his family lacked the money to feed all of their children. Dickson referred to Palo as his nephew, and Palo called him "Uncle Dickson."

"Where you were?" Palo asked me, eyes wide.

"Guess!" I said.

"To checka?" he said, referring to the place where Uncle Dickson plays checkers.

"No."

"To working place?"

I nodded my head.

"Walking?"

We had reached the limits of Palo's universe. He was out of ideas, so I told him we were swimming and fishing at the beach.

Dickson's houseboy handed Palo a tiny bowl of palm butter. After chewing for a while, Palo said, "God i'da breeze."

"What?" I asked, blinking a few times.

"The boy said, 'God . . . is the breeze,'" Dickson clarified with a smile.

God is the breeze. That animist sentiment arose naturally out of Palo's three-year-old consciousness. It was a lovely thought, and I let it sink into me as I stared out at a sun bleeding into the ocean. I had been charmed by the magic of unhurried Greenville and the ancient forests around it holding tiny communities like Chief Wah's Vanjahtown. I felt at home.

On the way back to Monrovia with Momo and a CRS monitoring officer, a fleet of yellow log trailers rolled past us. One of them hauled half of a double-wide home; others were loaded with Caterpillar skidders and backhoes. OTC was heading toward Greenville, toward the country's only national park.

As we passed all that expensive hardware, Momo said, "I always tell my people in Monrovia, 'At least OTC is not in Greenville.' What!? This is our last reserve forest."

"The Malaysian people so greedy," the monitoring officer said.

"My man, the Malaysians only come from their places because Ol'Pa Taylor lets them come! If Taylor says no, how they gonna go in there? The only thing is for *that man* to be removed." Momo was visibly angry. "I'm going to America; I'll drive a taxi there. This country run by criminals!"

We rolled past a pair of Asian businessmen in safari shirts. They were ringed by men I assumed to be forestry engineers, and together they pored over a blueprint. We rolled within five feet of them. Momo glanced in their direction, a deep frown etched in his forehead. An Asian man looked into my eyes, and I looked into his. Sunglasses hung from the breast pocket of his safari suit, and his hair was gelled back. He offered me a wave and then, ever so slightly, bowed to me. My insides locked up tight, and I stared past him into the rainforest he was about to destroy.

CHAPTER 17

"JOSEPH WONG KIIA Tai," a blond-haired man of medium build says as I slide into the dark corner of the room. The image of an Asian man with gelled-back hair flashes onto a screen via PowerPoint. "Usually known simply as Joseph Wong, he is the first of three links in the 'dirty triangle.' Wong, who is ethnic Chinese but travels on a Malaysian passport, is the director of the Oriental Timber Company. OTC is linked to the Hong Kong–based Global Star Holdings, which is part of the Djan Djajanti Group of Indonesia."

Another photo flashes onto the screen. "The Djan Djajanti Group's chairman is Gus van Kouwenhoven, a longtime friend of Charles Taylor and owner of Hotel Africa here in Monrovia. He is the second part of the dirty triangle. In the 1990s, Gus succeeded in acquiring five concessions in southeast Liberia—a good part of the country's forest bloc. While no maps of the concession area are publicly available, it may be as big as four million acres.

"The last corner of the triangle needs scant introduction." The screen flashes the official state photo of Charles Taylor seated in a throne in front of the Liberian flag. "Taylor makes it possible for timber barons like Wong and van Kouwenhoven to make millions on the fringes of the global economy. Taylor has declared OTC his personal 'pepperbush' that no one can touch.

"In short, what we are witnessing is a clearance sale of one of the world's twenty-five precious hot spots of biodiversity, Liberia's ancient forests, for the wealth of these three men. Additionally—" He stops suddenly. "Who's back there?"

Approaching the group, I say, "Sorry, I didn't want to interrupt."

"Gabriel, you said it would just be us!"

"Relax, Randall, he's one of us," Gabriel says with a smile as he extends his large frame and gives me a bear hug. I shake hands with Gabriel's Swedish girlfriend and co-worker, Liza, and then with Ross, a young Irishman volunteering with Gabriel. Randall offers the limpest of handshakes, still eyeing me suspiciously.

"Randall is gathering information for Global Witness, a British environmental and human rights group," Gabriel explains. "He is investigating OTC and is gearing up to launch a worldwide campaign to ban Liberian timber. We asked him to share information with us while he is in-country. Shall we continue?"

As we sit down, Randall clears his throat authoritatively. "Now where was I? Ah! The famous 'conflict diamonds': a term that refers to diamonds mined in places like Sierra Leone, Angola, and Liberia in order to fund war. Friends, the new buzzword is not 'conflict diamonds,' but rather 'conflict timber.'" The blond-haired man clicks to a photo of an immense area of stacked and numbered tropical timber at the Buchanan port. "Each of these logs sells for thousands of dollars and is then further converted into high-value items that grace the living rooms of Europe and North America. Big money. The logs go onto these OTC ships and are exported primarily to France, but also to other European countries, the United States, and China. The 'empty' ships come back with military hardware for Taylor, in breach of the UN arms embargo against Liberia. In addition to arms, Taylor receives lots of cash from timber. This is unrecorded, extrabudgetary income used to beef up his personal security forces, which are terrorizing his own people and destabilizing neighboring Sierra Leone."

He pauses to let this sink in and then says, "So we've seen how OTC is fueling the current conflict . . . but what about the environmental impact? Well, they say a picture is worth a thousand words." He flashes a photo of a clear-cut. A shirtless man holds his small son's hand as they both stare into the destruction. "This photo was taken in the OTC concession between Buchanan and Greenville. I like this photo because the father is literally scratching his head, as if asking himself, *What happened?* This is the Liberia his son will inherit.

"OTC's timber operations are expanding deeper into the rainforest every day. What is now a towering, untouched jungle habitat filled with rare pygmy hippos is turning into a honeycomb of quarter-mile-wide strips of deforested bush and road. OTC is operating at a remarkable speed! They've got two hundred Caterpillars, D7 size, plus seventy trucks that carry out forest clearance, log transport, and loading. OTC never closes. They work seven days a week, three hundred and sixty-five days a year."

"They work all weekend and even on holidays," Ross says. "I saw trucks unloading last Sunday night at the Buchanan port."

"Exactly. OTC likes to take a remarkable amount out of a country in a few years and then split. It's a gold rush mentality. They're scrambling to get what timber they can while

Taylor is protecting them because it's anyone's guess when he might fall." The British consultant switches off the computer. "That's really all I have by way of a formal presentation."

There is a long silence as our small group reflects on the images we've seen. Liza gets up and flips on a light.

Gabriel breaks the silence. "Randall . . . are you sure it's a good idea to launch a campaign against Liberian timber?"

"What do you mean?"

"You live in *Europe*," Gabriel says in a mock British accent. "We are here on the ground a mile from Taylor's presidential mansion. When you publicly attack OTC, who will Taylor come after . . . *you* or *us*?" The visiting consultant fumbles with his pen, and Gabriel continues, "We all know the answer to that. Taylor will accuse us of providing the information for the campaign and 'aiding and abetting enemies of the state.' This could mean prison, torture, disappearance . . ."

"They'll want to make an example out of innocent people here to send a message," I say.

"Hold on a minute!" Randall says, frustrated. "So we should remain silent? Just let this happen? The Liberian forests are *globally* significant pristine rainforests. Indonesians and Dutchmen are cutting them down to make furniture for Parisian families. This goes way beyond the borders of Liberia."

"I agree," Gabriel says slowly, "but it's delicate."

"And what if your international campaign brings UN sanctions against Liberia?" Liza says. "Sanctions will hurt ordinary Liberians."

Randall's face reddens. "Yes, but we need to think in terms of the bigger picture. Okay, so there are a few short-term casualties!"

"So starving babies are acceptable casualties?" Liza says.

The debate continues. It becomes apparent that we can do little to battle OTC within the borders of a dictatorship allied with that very company. And our group is divided on how to run a global campaign. I find myself, strangely, tuning out of the discussion as my mind wanders south, and east, back into the mysterious jungles near Greenville.

CHAPTER 18

LEAVE GREENVILLE AT dawn with Dickson, Ciatta, and Momo. We cross into the overgrown rubber farms outside the town, finally reaching the checkpoint where the wider road forks left back to Monrovia and the other forks right toward Sapo National Park. We take the road less traveled, the road to the interior.

"Hey, man!" Ciatta says. "I still don't see what we are gonna do back there in the bush."

"It's a small detour to see Sapo National Park."

"You crazy? There are no *national parks* in Liberia!"

"It's on my map," I say. Repeating my phrase, Ciatta and Dickson laugh hysterically as we roll forward along a worsening dirt road and enter solid forest. Momo keeps a straight face and seems to be lost in thought.

Dickson takes a break from laughing and says, "People used to live here before the war. They all left because of the rebels."

We drive along. The solid bush continues. When we have arrived at what I am sure is the very center of nowhere, a military checkpoint appears. A lanky soldier approaches Momo's window, staring at him through pink-veined eyes and emitting one of the most menacing *weekend* requests I've heard.

"Bossman," Momo rasps, "we just going to the park-o."

A tense moment ensues as the apparently drugged soldier

continues to stare down Momo, running his finger back and forth on the trigger of his gun. He has obviously never heard of our destination.

"There's a national park back there! I not lying!"

We wait a full five minutes. The soldier keeps his gun trained on Momo's head. Momo stares forward. I am feeling selfishly relieved that the soldier at least hasn't noticed me, until he suddenly steps back from Momo's window and opens the car door next to me. "Get down," he says.

I sit firm. Momo says, "Why you gotta bother the boss-man-o! He not getting out of this car! This official NGO vehicle." The man is so close that I can smell his dank odor. The smell of being in the jungle for weeks, maybe months, without soap. Momo continues to talk. "None of us are getting out of this official vehicle! Leave the bossman be!" But this guy pays no mind. He is what Liberians call a "don't-care bitch": Nothing can faze him because life has ceased to matter to him.

I recently saw two faces like that. A CRS colleague invited me to Monrovia's only health club. He failed to warn me ahead of time that the place was a collection of mining and vehicle parts strewn about a windowless warehouse. A dozen men performed quasi exercises with these odds and ends, while others did situps on the cement floor. Two young men, perhaps in their late teens, kept trading off what looked like a large drill bit, heaving it skyward while lying on the floor. Tupac Shakur's *Resurrection* emerged from their radio. Their ragged clothes and a vacant look in their eyes told me they were ex-combatants, maybe from the Small Boys Unit.

Like those boys in the gym, this soldier seems ambivalent about whether he lives or dies and is thus without a trace of fear. The moment feels endless, with the soldier insisting I step out of the vehicle and Momo trying to smooth-talk him out of it. Finally, Momo tries a different tack, reaching into his pocket and holding out a generous wad of bills, saying, "Here's something for a sof' drink, all right, boss?"

The soldier's hand comes forward to accept the money, and then he ever so slowly ambles over to the thin wire and drops it down.

"Close your door," Momo whispers, and I obey. We roll forward through the checkpoint, and I look at the soldier, who stares into the thick forest beyond.

"That checkpoint is deadly!" Dickson exclaims, looking over his shoulder at the soldier and flashing his trademark smile. "Or at least it was during the war-o. One time I came this way to go to Zwedru and two small-boy rebels right there told me to get down from the car because they were gon' kill me. I asked them why, and they said I was *fat,* so I must be with the government. So what did I do? I *smiled*!! I smiled and said, 'You're not going to kill me-o!' My man, this confused those boys. *What?!* They were used to fear and crying, not a smile like that. One of them said, 'You gonna shoot dat smiling man?' The other said, 'He's with the government, and I will shoot this man.' They had a whole lot of palava, and then one asked me: 'What your team?'"

Dickson pauses. He has our rapt attention. "I had two choices: Millennium Stars and Mighty Barolle. One meant life and the other death. My heart was beating-o and the sweat poured out of my smiling face. Stars or Mighty Barolle, Stars or Mighty Barolle. I couldn't get either word out of my mouth. I finally said, 'Millennium Stars!' and one of them said, 'You can't kill a Stars man!' and they let me go! My face pained me because I'd been smiling so hard. My man, that's why I'm still smiling today."

As Dickson finishes talking, we come to a decaying sign: SAPO NATIONAL PARK, 3 MI. SPONSORED BY THE EUROPEAN UNION. We wind our way through increasingly higher forest to Jalaystown, on the park's border. We park in front of a shack that a sign identifies as Sapo National Park's headquarters. It looks to be abandoned, but after a moment a pudgy man yawns at the entrance.

He walks over to the car, and midway he stops and cries out, "Bossman!" My first thought is that he is speaking to me, but then it occurs to me that he can't know me. Then I assume he is talking about Dickson, who directs the CRS Greenville office. Wrong again. He's talking to my driver, Momo.

Momo steps out of the car and hugs this man, who continues, "Boss! We thought we lost you for sure!" We join the two of them beside the car, and the story unfolds. Momo had been a lead park guard in Sapo before and during the early years of the war! The pudgy man (who introduces himself as Lincoln) is one of the junior park rangers who had worked with Momo. The park is nothing but a paper park now, but Lincoln and a few other guards continue to work for a tiny monthly stipend. Momo tells Lincoln that he took the job with CRS as a driver to feed his family. I ask Momo why he never told me about all of this.

"I don't like to talk a whole lot about the past," he says.

As Momo and Lincoln catch up, we drive the final ten minutes and park at the "Safari Camp" near the Sinoe River, which forms the park's western boundary. An American businessman put up a luxury safari tent and makeshift gift shop the year before. He flies in wealthy Texans who want some of the rare trophies only Liberia can offer, such as certain endangered varieties of duiker. Lincoln tells us that it is not only endangered species that are going out in the Safari Camp's single-engine Cessna. He suspects diamond smuggling as well.

We walk down to the Sinoe River, and Ciatta insists that she is not "going anywhere near that canoe." Dickson, too, is frightened by the canoe and decides to stay back with Ciatta. So Momo, Lincoln, and I paddle upstream in a single canoe. Lush greenery towers on both sides of us and pushes its way toward the sunlight, where the wide river splits the forest. Humidity blankets us. Flies swarm around our legs, biting frequently. Lincoln slaps at them with a rattan vine. Colobus and Diana monkeys crash through the canopy above, alerting one another to the presence of humans. I notice a number of smooth, muddy indentations that slope down into the river. Lincoln explains that they are "hippo slides," where these tetrapods have tobogganed into the water.

After paddling through a long reach, we ford a shoal and reach the trailhead. Lincoln tells us that it is the only trail in the five-hundred-square-mile park. He and a crew of villagers cut it a few weeks back. Vines have already invaded the path, and Lincoln hacks our way through the tangle with his cutlass. While little sunlight penetrates the two-hundred-foot canopy, the moist heat causes my T-shirt to be soaked with sweat. We come upon the skull, spine, and rib cage of a duiker, which Momo identifies as "leopard kill." I look at the unarmed Lincoln and think, *What would stop us from being the next leopard kill?*

Walking on, we reach a place on the trail where

chimpanzees used stones as tools to crack open betel nuts, the remains of which are scattered on and around the trail. Lincoln says, "The chimps were just recently here, so keep your ears open."

The trail suddenly widens. "This is the elephant road! We found this while cutting this trail, and joined with it to save work." Forest elephants had trampled down the ground cover, sliced through large vines, and ripped down many smaller trees. While there is no official count, hundreds of elephants roam the park. "The elephants were almost extinct before the war, but then flourished during the fighting because *nooobody* could waste their precious bullets on animals!"

Not only were the elephants safer in the park during the war, the people were, too. Small bands of humans roamed and scavenged for many months at a time within Sapo Park, including Lincoln and Momo. "I was here for four months one time! The LPC rebels killing everyone they could over there," Momo says, gesturing toward the far side of the Sinoe River, which lies outside the park. "There was no more ammunition, so they were using cutlasses. Hey, man! It takes a lot to hack a leg off with a blunt cutlass."

"How did you survive?" I ask Momo.

"We trapped fish at night to eat and trade. Other people would sneak across the river to gather cassava from over-grown farms. That was more dangerous. We would wander in the forest and find other people. You could trade a fish this size for this much cassava." He gestures these measurements with his hands. "We watched what the monkeys and chimpanzees ate, and ate the same. But I *never* hunted the animals in the park, not even when it was really bad. I would catch more fish for them or find more berries.

When I saw someone who had killed a zebra duiker or hippo, I would admonish them: 'Those are protected species, my man! You can't go butchering them! I could arrest you!'"

We walk for an hour on the elephant road and then on a smaller trail again. We are mostly silent, taking in the symphony of tropical life that surrounds us. We are nearly back to where we'd left the canoe when Lincoln abruptly comes to a halt. Momo and I stop, too.

Not ten yards away are two large chimpanzees, one black and the other nearly ginger. I blink and stare into the ginger-colored primate's eyes. After a moment in which time completely stops for me, the chimps turn, as if in slow motion, and then bolt away from us, their cries echoing through the forest. Hoots ring back from beyond my sight in the jungle, perhaps from other members of their family group.

Later, while paddling back in the canoe, Lincoln tells me about a "conservation-friendly taboo" held by Sapo tribesmen such as Chief Wah who live around this side of the park. "The people say that long ago, in the time of the tribal wars, the Sapo were losing badly in battle. Pushed back to this wide river and unable to swim, they were cornered and about to meet a certain death. Just then a clan of chimpanzees appeared. What did these chimpanzees do? The people say they carried them across over their heads, swimming with powerful legs and hoisting the people above their hairy bodies. Because of this, the chimpanzee is revered as a brother, and nobody eats him."

Rolling toward Buchanan, Ciatta complains about how bored she was sitting in the Safari Camp with Dickson all day. As Momo tells the others about our rare chimpanzee sighting in the park, we drive past the familiar site of a shirtless child hoisting the bloody side of a duiker over his head. Dickson instructs Momo to pull over. "How much you want for that meat?"

"Two hundred dollar!" the child answers.

"What?!" Dickson screeches. "I give one fifty. Meat small!"

Seeing the potential customer, the boy's father runs down to our truck. Dickson is counting five liberty bills off his wad when Momo says, "Wait!" He examines the markings on the side. The stripes indicate that it is a zebra duiker. "Bossman," Momo says to Dickson, "this animal is endangered. It's on the FDA list . . . It's illegal to buy this."

Ciatta jumps in to defend Dickson. "I say, are you crazy, Momo? There's no cow meat or goat meat in Greenville! Bushmeat's all! Besides, this family only survive by selling that meat."

I look into the little boy's hopeful eyes, framed by a dirty face. His father, also shirtless, is just muscle and bone. I can tell he is hungry for the sale.

"Yeah, Momo," Dickson says, counting his money. "One less zebra duiker won't make a damn difference."

The man's wife stands by the door of their tiny mud hut on an embankment above. She holds a baby. I look back at the cut of meat and feel trapped in a paradox. My mandate to "fight poverty while conserving the rainforest" guides me little in this moment, a moment in which I must make a choice. As the highest authority in the Jeep, I have the final word on whether or not Dickson buys the duiker. As he continues to count out the liberty bills, my thoughts turn to the chimpanzee family that I witnessed today: those old eyes and their echoing cries in the forest. Those cries of the chimpanzees telling me that the extinction of a species is not the right road out of this family's poverty.

"Let's go, Momo," I say. "We can't buy zebra duiker." I take one last look, blood on stripes, as we begin to roll toward Monrovia.

CHAPTER 19

I'M TRYING TO call Jennifer from my kayak using a CRS satellite phone, since I wasn't able to get a signal from Carolina Farm. I dial her number, and it goes through. I don't know what I'm going to say if she answers. I ache for the intimacy we once had during our shared life in Washington and desperately want the call to connect. Looking out over the bay and into the ocean beyond, I feel tears coming on.

Someone picks up the phone on the other end.

My colleague Susan and I were driving together from Carolina Farm to work one morning. We often carpooled since we lived in the same compound. I steered through the Carolina Farm gates into the moonscape half mile to the main road, and as we lurched along I noticed a slim man thirty feet ahead, waving us down. When we reached him he sidestepped in front of the car, and I slammed on the brakes. "Bossman!" I said out the window. "What the matter-o?"

"Sorry, boss," he said. "I got to show you something."

He stuck two filthy fingers into his mouth and probed around until he found what he was looking for: a diamond. He wiped it off with a handkerchief and tried to hand it to me. "It's from Sierra Leone," he said.

Susan leaned in to get a closer look.

"I think bosslady missy like my diamond. I sell it cheap-o!"

Susan shook her head. I began to pull away, saying, "Thanks, but we're really not interested."

That same evening, I was enjoying a sundowner in my hammock after a day in the office. The sky's orange bled into rust red over the surf. I began to bite into an ice cube but stopped when I noticed a flash of white against the lawn. As I slowly chewed the ice cube, the white spot began to take the form of a man in a wheelchair heading my way.

Before long he had pulled up right below my deck. "Y'all right?" he asked, gulping air.

"I'm tryin' small," I answered, wondering how he got past the guards.

"I want to be your friend," he said. "Yeah, boss . . . I want to get to know you."

I let this hang in the air as I chewed on another ice cube.

"Could you help me get to America? You could help me with the embassy. I want to go to America to work."

"I don't even know you."

"Yes, this is very true. But since you are my friend you can help me. I had a job as a security guard. Liberians are a jealous people. You get a little successful and they want to push you down."

He had a worn, knotted black face and pink-veined, paranoid eyes. His wheelchair seemed about to collapse, and his shorts concealed only the tops of two broomstick legs. Tiny poles, not really legs.

"I'm from Freetown." His face was a clenched knot.

He stared out over the bay and then back at me. "I wasn't always like this. I used to walk around on two legs just like you." He gestured toward his broomstick legs as if they were an exhibit at a courtroom trial. "The rebels up there . . . ," he said, nodding his head up the coast toward Sierra Leone, his knotted face looking like a flexed biceps. Tears squeezed out.

A long pause hung between us as the waves crashed under the fading sky. I drained my sundowner.

"You know, I sure could use some soap," he said. I reached into my pocket and stuffed a wad of liberty into his hands, and he pivoted his rickety chair and rolled across the lawn to the next villa.

"Hello?" comes a voice over the phone. It's Jennifer.

"I miss you," I say.

"I miss you and I love you," she replies, her voice taking that wavy, dreamy quality of satellite communication.

"I can't believe I've been here a full year."

"*I* can."

"Jennifer, it's all just so *brutal* . . ." I don't know if I'll be able to hold back the tears.

"It's all right, baby, you'll be home soon. And I'm here for you."

John stuck his head into my office. "Meeting! My office. Regional crisis!" he said, punctuating his staccato command with a wink and vanishing.

I was waiting for a call from Jennifer and didn't want to miss it. On the other hand, some CRS big shots from other countries were in town, and I couldn't easily get out of the meeting. I asked my secretary to interrupt if an international call came for me.

A gray-bearded CRS Sierra Leone adviser, Brian Cootner, nodded gravely to me as I came into John's office. I sat on the couch next to another man, CRS global technical adviser

Jay Frayne, a tall man with an English professor's tousled mop and a walrus mustache. Jay nodded solemnly to me as I settled into the couch.

Brian was in the middle of a story. "Colonel Bloodshed, that's what I think they called the fucker," he said, taking a drag on his pipe. "He can't have been more than fifteen years old. It happened right in Freetown, after the mobs of child soldiers sacked the capital in January. The BBC reported the whole thing, had an eyewitness. Colonel Bloodshed's teenage cronies wore Tupac Shakur T-shirts and American flag bandannas tied around their heads. They had dragged a baby-faced kid, a real middle-class pretty-boy, into this . . . shell of a building, kind of like that one." He pointed with his pipe out the window toward one of the bombed-out buildings outside of our office.

"The pretty-boy was begging to go with them, back into the bush, to be indoctrinated as one of the rebels. Anything to escape his fate. 'No!' Bloodshed told him. Some of the rebels threatened to shoot him, while others wanted to hack off a few of his limbs to send to the Sierra Leonean president. The boy, who had been whimpering all along, positively bawled when he saw the object in Colonel Bloodshed's hand: an ax."

I winced.

"Drug strips covered Bloodshed's face—adhesive bandages that masked incisions where he had ingested cocaine or amphetamines. These were the drugs that wired his head for battle. As the pretty-boy wailed for his mother, the other rebels stretched him out on his stomach on the concrete floor and extended his arm. Bloodshed held the ax high over his head for a long moment, reveling in the power, soaking up all the screaming."

Brian turned to face us and continued, "*Slam, slam slam!* came the sound of metal on concrete as he hacked at the hand until it practically jumped away from the screaming boy."

Chopping off limbs is the signature strategy of the Revolutionary United Front. They are Sierra Leone's major rebel force and control half the country. RUF leaders like Colonel Bloodshed are fond of repeating their group's motto: "Everyone must *lend a hand* to the revolution." This practice terrorizes rural populations into fleeing an area before the RUF advances, allowing them to easily capture diamond fields.

In surprise attacks where people cannot flee in time, the RUF sacks a village and abducts the surviving children. These kids, who have often seen their parents slaughtered, undergo a brutal initiation in RUF jungle camps. The leaders inject drugs into the initiates, which removes them further from reality and begins the process of addiction. Light weapons such as the AK-47 mean that boys as young as eight can be easily armed. These children are fearless and unpredictable in war, particularly the smaller ones, who are placed closest to the enemy. Once they've committed heinous acts, they are often rejected by their own villages and find their only sense of belonging in the military unit. They imprint on their commanders as father figures and are fiercely loyal to them.

Jay, CRS's technical adviser, had been silent since I'd come into the room. Still apparently lost in thought, he muttered, "Diamonds."

"I sense a thought forming," Brian tried to joke.

"Diamonds and timber are the lifeblood of dictators like Taylor. His cash comes mostly from timber and Foday Sankor's from diamonds. They use repression and terror to maintain their control over these resources. Without the timber and diamonds, these men don't exist."

"It's not about ideology in Africa, is it?" Brian said, taking a drag on his pipe. "You never hear of left or right, conservative or liberal. This war, like all African wars, is a war of the belly. It's purely about money. I mean, look at the history of it . . . First the colonialists extracted the resources, then neocolonial African governments propped up by cold war interests, and now—strategic interest in Africa having lessened after the fall of the Soviet Union—rebels like Sankor and Taylor control the resources."

"Hard to get much done in this context," I said.

"Aren't we supposed to think about how the CRS programs in Sierra Leone and Liberia can act together to tackle this issue?" John suggested.

"Let's not inflate our sense of self-importance, for Chrissakes!" Brian said. "Look at the bigger picture. Foday Sankor and Charles Taylor are in bed together and have been since they teamed up to start the wars in both countries! Both are kept in power through ongoing conflict. As long as the situation is anarchic, the diamond industry can't be regulated. Do you know that Liberia exported one hundred times its national capacity in diamonds last year? Those are Colonel Bloodshed's diamonds."

This got us going on the demand side of the conflict diamond dilemma: A diamond is basically required for engagements in the States as a pricey symbol of one's love. Its supposed rarity gives it its value.

"It's a damn lie," Brian muttered in response to this, his back turned to us as he peered into the wreckage of Monrovia out the window. "De Beers controls two-thirds of the world's rough-cut diamonds. The company carefully manipulates scarcity through hoarding diamonds in London and letting them trickle onto the market at the time and price they choose. It is the myth of diamonds being rare. And as for 'a girl's best friend' . . . do they mean a Sierra Leonean girl's best friend? And where would she put the ring, with her hands chopped off?"

John got up and poured himself a cup of coffee, offering me one as well. Brian continued, "The idea of romance surrounding the diamond is an invention of De Beers! They hired an advertising agency back in the 1930s to instill that myth. In the sixties De Beers waged a similar campaign in Japan, creating the diamond ring 'tradition' there as well."

"But the conflict diamonds awareness campaign will cut down on demand," John said. "Consumers will stop buying diamonds once they know the gems are directly supporting people like Taylor."

"Consumers of which planet, John?" said Brian. "Not this one. The exact opposite is happening. Diamond sales are booming, despite the international awareness campaign. De Beers had record sales last year—five billion!"

My secretary poked her head into the office and said, "International call from one Miss Jennifer."

I almost knocked over my coffee cup as I excused myself and rushed to the phone in my office.

"Hello?" I said, out of breath. Silence. The phone line had gone dead.

I meet Gabriel and Liza after work in front of CRS and we drive a few blocks up Randall Street to Stop-N-Shop, the Lebanese grocery store. Liza goes in to get the last few ingredients for the meal we're to prepare at my house. It is to be a working dinner, where we plan to strategize about further ways of combating OTC's illegal logging. Gabriel and I get out of my Land Rover and are immediately surrounded by a dozen war-affected youths.

My usual reaction is to look away. They are always there outside of Stop-N-Shop, begging as I go in and come out, in their rickety wheelchairs, missing an arm here, a leg there; one boy is missing both arms and has a cup tied around his neck for donations. The Liberian government officials and expatriates who go in walk briskly through this small herd, sometimes stuffing dirty liberty bills into a few palms before slamming their car doors shut. Whenever I get out of my car, my chest tightens and I try to suppress the desire to help, to do something, to reach out, mostly because I think I can't handle it. They are a riptide that would suck me in and drown me, so the safest course is to head straight to the air-conditioned aisles of Stop-N-Shop.

Gabriel's reaction is different: He reaches out to them. What's your name? Where are you from? Nimba! Ah, where? I've been there. What football club do you like? Really, I prefer Lone Star. And: What are your dreams? You ... what's your name? Robert, what's your big dream? How do you plan to make it happen?

I watch the young people's confrontational begging posture melt away. The furrowed brow, the rush to edge a wheel-chair or crutch in front of the shopper, all of this is trans-formed into a relaxed attentiveness. They feel listened to, noticed, cared for, because Gabriel touches them, touches their stumps and faces, engages them in conversations. He sees them, they see him, and a barrier is broken.

On the ride to Carolina Farm, I tell Gabriel that I feel like Sisyphus pushing the rock up the hill, that the task we are taking on is hopeless to the point of absurdity. Gabriel replies by quoting Mother Teresa: "'There is no such thing as doing great things in this world. We can only do small things with great love.' It's like with those kids. You can't give them their arms and legs back, but you can show them love in front of a supermarket. And we can't stop all rainforest destruction, but we can take our small stand against OTC."

At Carolina Farm, Gabriel and Liza start cooking in the kitchen, and I excuse myself to call Jennifer. The landlines have crashed, and there will be no regular phone service in the country, possibly for weeks. Luckily I have a CRS-issued satellite phone. It works best out on the water, so I cover it with plastic and again row out in my yellow kayak, until I am in the center of the St. Paul's mouth and drifting toward the Atlantic. I aim the panel up at the heavens and dial Jennifer's number.

"Only a few days and you're back for vacation," she says.

"I've got so much to tell you . . . *Liberia* . . ." I look out over the water, over the curl of waves, into the blue sky, the clarity of the late dries.

CHAPTER 20

AT THE TOP of the Woodley Park Metro Station escalator in Washington, D.C., Jennifer quickens to embrace me. Her tall, thin body folds into mine as I run my hands over her hips and stare into her blue eyes. Long blond hair blows around her face.

"Deb's probably waiting," I say. We cross Connecticut Avenue together, holding hands. I am back in the States on mandatory absence for the relief of stress, or MARS, a week-long vacation required for many aid workers in danger posts.

"Hey!" Deb exclaims as we enter the coffee shop. We all hug and then carry our lattes across the street to a pocket park. Jennifer coos over Deb's ring.

"Yeah," Deb says, blushing. "Dave finally popped the question!" She moves her extended hand from side to side, and the stone catches the sunlight, reflecting brilliantly.

"That's a big rock," I point out.

"I know! Dave's aunt in New York showed him around the diamond district, helped him get a good deal . . . Of course, he still spent a bundle."

"It did the trick," I say.

"Huh?"

"It produced 'another tearful acceptance speech.'" Blank looks from the women. "You know, the De Beers ad?"

* * *

After our coffee with Deb, Jennifer and I head toward her apartment. She's invited some guests over for dinner. Her apartment is bathed in color and light. Modern art and textiles from around the developing world clothe her walls, and a burgundy rug I once purchased in New Delhi covers part of the hardwood floor in her bedroom. Mayan *huipils* and Tibetan prayer flags are interspersed with framed photos. One shows the two of us soaked in sweat at the end of the Lost Coast trail in California; another is from Halloween two years ago, in which she is ironically dressed as a devil and I as our Indian friend Rohit.

Jennifer flows gracefully around her kitchen and dining room, cooking and setting the table as if on ice skates. The guests arrive—Rohit and two of Jennifer's Japanese friends. They are all in their late twenties and full of upwardly mobile energy. As we dig into tortellini, Rohit launches into a story about his life as a fledgling investment banker.

He says, "The freakin' dinner bill was eighteen thousand dollars for the dozen of us."

"Come on!"

"No, really, it was sick. There were a couple of associates and ten of us new guys. We'd been working seventeen-, eighteen-hour days as always, including weekends. Everyone was freakin' stressed. So the guys ordered the most expensive wines and brandies, and there were dozens of plates of food at fifty bucks a plate. People got drunker and drunker, and ordered more drinks, taking a sip or two and leaving them to order another, and the plates were barely touched. It was some kind of orgy. But no one cared because it was all going on the expense account."

When Rohit finishes his story, one of the young women turns to me and asks, "So how's Libya?"

"Liberia," Jennifer corrects her gently.

"*Oops*, Liberia. Sorry. God, I can't even imagine what it's like there."

I open my mouth and then close it. My heart quickens. A thousand images and feelings fill me. Silverware clicks against china, and I hear the muted honking of cars on Connecticut Avenue below as the others eat, waiting for my response. I can't think of where to start.

Jennifer tries to break the tension. "More wine, anyone?"

One of the girls stretches her glass across to Jennifer and seems to think of something. "Mmm!" she says, swallowing a bite. "I've got a concierge now!" She describes her new Old Town, Virginia, apartment. Swimming pool, complementary breakfast in the lobby each morning, concierges in top hats. "And it's furnished!" she says. "It's got a mahogany dining room set. Can you believe it? *Mahogany!*"

The next morning, Jennifer and I are hiking the Great Falls trail on the Virginia side of the Potomac outside D.C.

"The sticky buds," Jennifer says, stopping trailside to touch a flower just about to open up. As I stroke the bud as well, our fingers meet, and we kiss. She's referring to her favorite book, *The Brothers Karamazov*. To Dostoevsky, and to Jennifer, the sticky buds represent hope. Jennifer is deeply religious, though she doesn't wear it on her sleeve, just exudes joy and selflessness. She adores infants, whom she believes come out of the womb fully divine. No matter how far a person might stray as an adult, she said to me once, that person still contained his or her inborn potential for goodness.

"The sticky buds," I repeat. "Hey, you never e-mailed back about my question." I take her hand and we continue our walk along the box canyon ridge.

"What question?"

"Whether you relate to Dmitri, Ivan, or Alyosha."

"Oh . . . well, personally, I really have a hard time relating to Dmitri, or even Ivan."

I need Jennifer to show sympathy for Dmitri. His binges and passion, doubting love, doubting God. Where is Jennifer's dark side? I still want to believe in a loving, involved Creator, want to forget all about the glimpses of evil I have seen in Liberia. Jennifer and I know each other well, and she can tell that I want her to relate to Dmitri or Ivan, so she tries to show traces of empathy for them. But she convinces neither me nor herself. So I change the subject to our future kids.

We dance around the topic. I ask, "How do you feel . . . about living abroad with children?" She says it could be fine, under some circumstances. I ask which circumstances. She replies that she wants to "of course" have her babies in the United States and that they would spend their first years here, where there is superior medical care.

"But we are all in this together," I protest. "All six billion of us who share the planet. Why should our babies have such better medical care?"

"Because they can! It's a no-brainer. Liberian parents would give birth in an American hospital if they could. What, you would *choose* to put your own children at risk?"

"Jennifer, in any developing country there are very good hospitals for those who have the money."

"Bill, you just don't get it." Her blue eyes begin to well with tears, and we stop on the path, the river now entering a rapid below us.

"What don't I get? Don't you want to embrace the *adventure* of life together?"

"I don't want to live in Liberia," Jennifer says, wiping

away a tear. "I don't want to live in Sierra Leone. Or Cambodia or Burma, or Haiti or Afghanistan. And I certainly don't want my children living there. Maybe I'm a third world person but not a fourth world person. Buenos Aires or Capetown, Kenya or Chile, those places are fine. But I'm not cut out for danger posts. It's not that I'm scared, I just have nothing to offer in those places."

"I understand. But will you just consider for a moment that maybe you *are* scared?" She stands silently, looking at me. "I really feel a person needs to take risks in life."

"There are sensible risks, and then there are dumb risks."

"I want children who are involved in the world."

"Involved in which world?"

"The real one."

"What? So only carnage and death are real? Only political repression and environmental destruction?"

The Bethesda Mall straddles the city of Washington, D.C., and its suburbs. Jennifer and I browse one of the mall's jewelry boutiques, trying to solidify our unraveling engagement with something solid.

"How about a pearl necklace?" I ask.

A huge, weighty pause.

"Well! Do we have to do what everyone else does?"

"No one will know that a pearl necklace marks our engagement. Do you know, every day I'm sitting around conference tables full of twenty- and thirty-somethings, and the first thing all the single men do is look at our hands for rings? I am constantly being hit on. Is that what you want?"

"Okay, fine, a ring. But how about inset with something besides a diamond?" We spend the next hour looking at amethyst and agate, onyx and opal. Nothing is quite right.

"Honey," Jennifer says, "I agree with you about conflict diamonds. I know it is very important to you . . . as it is to me, of course! But none of these other stones say what a diamond does."

"I'll mention that to Colonel Bloodshed next time I bump into him. He'll be pleased you feel that way."

"Colonel who?"

"He's a guy with a diamond fetish. Likes axes, too . . . Never mind. So, the bottom line is that you want a girl's best friend."

"No, I don't know. Not if it can't be traced to its origin. But what else can say what a diamond does? Let's keep looking."

We left without a ring.

It becomes a mantra: *I can't believe I'm losing her.* I worship this woman's clear white light, her boundless hope, and a large part of me wants to wrap myself up in this love. She is a path to my children, my family, to the kind of adulthood I've always imagined. *I can't believe I'm losing her.* There are several tearful conversations. At one point we lie sweating in her bed together, a helicopter swooping over, its floodlights periodically illuminating the room.

"I love you," she says.

"I love you," I answer.

I can't believe I'm losing her. Would I ever find another Jennifer? We lie together in the sticky D.C. night, and the *thwack-thwack* of the helicopter continues overhead. I get up and go into the living room, which is draped in *huipils* and prayer flags, a conglomerate third world. I imagine that I can stay in D.C., that I can cash in my return ticket on Air Afrique, sign my letter of resignation from CRS, and hang

Liberian masks and weavings on the walls. Jennifer and I will send our kids to cello lessons in Bethesda and collect pensions. There can still be a happy ending.

Looking out through Jennifer's living room window, I see a thin blue light permeating the oak and birch trees, giving edges to the freshly painted brownstones; it's the *heure bleue,* the hour before morning breaks when it's still solidly night but with an illusion of daybreak. The streets are mostly silent. A taxi stops in front of Jennifer's building, its headlights still on, and a man loads his baggage into the trunk, probably headed to the airport. At crossroads in life, we often choose not between right and wrong, but between two rights, between two loves. I feel a tug in my gut, a gnawing, frightening sense of destiny. In that silence, looking down over Connecticut Avenue, I know that I've lost Jennifer. I am meant for something else.

PART III
Burning Season

Kind of Blue

True morality consists not in following the beaten track, but in finding out the true path and fearlessly following it.

—Gandhi

CHAPTER 21

WHEN I SEE the syringe, I stop in my tracks. I'm walking on Poo Poo Beach, Monrovia, and did not even consider the fact that I was barefoot until the needle appears, interspersed with trash and piles of poo. I slip on my sandals and keep walking.

Back in Liberia for a week, I've reached rock bottom. Jennifer had always been there for me throughout the first year, not physically, but as a bridge across the ocean to my old life. She was a touchstone, something solid that I could grasp on to for strength. Like the holy guinea pigs of my Long Island childhood, she was proof of a loving world. I walked away from her, and that life, and toward a crumbling Liberia. The UN Security Council voted to impose sanctions against the country while I was in the States, and they are to take effect in two months if Charles Taylor does not stop trafficking Sierra Leonean diamonds. Liberians fear the coming sanctions, fear the effect on their families. Meanwhile, the border war is picking up steam as anti-Taylor Liberians operating out of bush camps in Guinea take one town in Lofa County after the next. New rumors surface each day: The rebels are in Buchanan. The rebels will sack Monrovia.

Walking on, I pass a thatched adobe school right on the beach. Some of Monrovia's poorest people live in oceanfront homes. (I tack this up to security, that the shore is more open to attack and therefore home to the marginalized.) Fifty students line up in front of the school, place their hands on their hearts, and sing out, "All hail, Liberia, hail!" It's the first line of the Liberian national anthem. Lacking a flag-pole, their principal thrusts a Liberian flag over his head, and it flaps in the wind, red, white, and blue, but with only a single star. The children belt out:

> All hail, Liberia, hail!
> This glorious land of liberty
> Shall long be ours . . .
> And mighty be her powers.
> In joy and gladness
> With our hearts united,
> We'll shout the freedom
> Of a land benighted.
> Long live Liberia, happy land!
> A home of glorious liberty,
> By God's command!

I've heard this anthem sung many times, but never with such sadness. On another occasion, wondering why the anthem praised Liberia as "a land benighted," I thumbed through my thesaurus for the reference: "Benighted: blind, visionless, unseeing, undiscerning, unperceiving, stone blind, blind as a mole, hemeralopic, nyctalopic, mind-blind, soul-blind, spiritually blind, dark, 'dark, dark amid the blaze of noon' (Milton)."

Poo Poo Beach: rock bottom, the world's armpit, *dark, dark amid the blaze of noon*. What strange force has drawn me here? I've been back only a week and have already been sent on an all-Liberia tour to fire a good number of my employees.

* * *

"Hi, bossman . . . Can I bother you small?" It was Mohammed, one of CRS's driver-mechanics. I'd returned the day before and was busy catching up on missed work.

"Sure, please have a seat."

"Whew, cool in here!" Mohammed said, sitting in my rattan chair. He then cleared his throat. "Bossman, I want to lecture you about a small-small problem." He shifted in his seat. "Spare parts. Thousands of U.S. dollars of vehicle parts missing-o."

"Go on."

He wiped the sweat off his profusely sweating brow; his shifty eyes were those of whistle-blowers from the movies. "Everyone involved, from the managers upstairs down to the drivers and mechanics in the lot."

"Except you?"

"Yeah." He looked away. "I didn't know what was happening until soon."

The generator droned outside. I massaged my temples to try to stave off a headache. A first round of CRS layoffs was imminent. With UN sanctions scheduled in eight weeks, the American government notched up the pressure by enforcing the Brooke Amendment, which halted U.S. aid to countries not current on their external debt payments. The Brooke Amendment was disastrous for CRS; USAID slashed our primary budget, forcing us to cut staff and programs.

"Why didn't the security guards catch this?" I finally asked.

"Parts going out right under the hood, bossman! Or under a seat, anywhere. Who notice? Those Toyota parts cost four, five hundred dollar U.S. Forms are filled out to replace good parts, and Johnboy signs off. Everyone eats some."

The generator drone seemed to be increasing. "Mohammed . . . do you have any proof?"

"I have someone else who will back up what I telling you."

I thanked the driver and got up to go to an executive management meeting. As I walked to the conference room, I had no doubt that Mohammed was telling the truth, but I knew he had also "eaten small" like the others and was coming forward now only to try to escape the ax.

"Downsizing is healthy," John was saying to the other four expatriates when I entered. He leaned his small frame forward, having to sit on the edge of the chair for his feet to touch the floor. "Okay, I won't deny it hurts a bit at first, but we will be a leaner machine for it. The first step: Outsource everything possible to cut costs!" As John issued his Napoleonic decrees, I noticed the Jacket right next to him; he rarely left John's side these days.

"Here are the severance letters," John stated, pushing piles to the various managers. Mine was the thickest, and I noticed the Jacket's was barely a centimeter high. I flipped through, and my heart sank as I saw Ciatta's name among the casualties in my pile. "Okay, team. You've got your marching orders, now let's go out there and downsize!"

Probably too loudly, I said, "Why wasn't I included in this decision?" Susan nodded in agreement, equally upset about being sidelined.

"There are some decisions made by consensus, and others of which you are *informed*," John stated dryly. "This decision was the latter variety."

"Shouldn't the whole executive management team have input into such a big decision?"

"You were out on MARS. And besides, this was a decision of the U.S. government, per the Brooke Amendment. In consultation with the Jacket, I made the staff cuts based on a U.S. government mandate."

"But you cut the heart out of our field offices, which are the ones implementing our programs. Meanwhile, Jacket's pile of severance letters looks rather thin. So we'll have no one left to carry out our programs in Greenville and Gbarnga, but will have plenty of corrupt staff sitting around in Monrovia." I knew I was crossing the line, but my temper had overtaken me.

"There is no corruption in my team!" the Jacket shouted.

"Vehicle parts are slipping out under your nose, with everyone in on it. One of the drivers just blew the whistle in my office. And he has an alibi."

A silence fell over the conference room. John and the Jacket looked at each other, and John said, "I don't think our staff is capable of that. But I will ask the Jacket to investigate."

"But they are from his team. Shouldn't someone else investigate?"

John looked me squarely in the eyes. "Sanctions nip at our heels, and the U.S. government has slashed our funds. In this context, no one is indispensable." He looked around at the other white faces and than back at me. *"No one."*

CHAPTER 22

"I WALKED INTO THAT office with a dozen different opening lines in my head," I told Susan. "When I came in a hush fell over the room, and I was looking out into the nervous eyes of my friends. All I could do was stand there . . . People cried when I handed out those severance letters."

"It's not your fault."

"That sounds like a line from a movie. Anyway, it feels like it is."

I stared out the window. OTC had penetrated even farther into the Krahn-Bassa National Forest, supposedly a protected rainforest. Two OTC trucks tailgated us, flashing their lights to pass. Momo let them by, and a cloud of dust covered our Land Rover. We rolled up the windows, coughing. The drivers were Asian. We rolled on for a long while, no one speaking. Finally I said, "Do you know one CRS paycheck here feeds *fifty* people?"

Momo jumped in when he heard this. "Yeah! *Everybody* want to eat some. Next minute—*what?!*—money small!"

"Then why do you give to everyone?" Susan asked him.

"People talk. They say you mean, you greedy. Your relatives gossip. Anyway, they gotta eat, too. How I going to let them hunger when I got something in my pocket?"

"It's the original insurance policy—a traditional social safety net," Susan said.

"Also a race for the bottom," I said. "What is the incentive to get ahead personally if everything gets shared equally in the end?"

"Ah, but when you give, you get to be the bossman!" Susan said.

"Hi, Ciatta . . . Have a seat, please."

Susan and I arrived in Greenville an hour before and would be leaving for Monrovia the next morning at daybreak. The executioner's job was quick. Three of us sat behind a table in front of Ciatta: I was at the center, with Susan to my left and Dickson to my right.

"Ciatta," I began, "in your three years with the agency, you've served Liberia's poorest in remote areas."

I paused and took in the sounds from the street below: women crying out, "Mango three-fa-five, three-fa-five!"; hands slapping and snapping; a truck racing to the port. The backdrop was too perky for what I was about to do.

I wiped my forehead with my sleeve, but sweat had already made it into my now itching eyes. "Ciatta . . ." I couldn't say it. She sat there in the middle of the room like an accused person under interrogation. But she was innocent. Her blue braids fell from a maroon head wrap onto her shoulders and over a batik dress. Each of her braids was exquisitely tied.

Susan tried to help me out. "Ciatta, the Brooke Amendment—"

"Yeah, I know. You're firing me. Just get to the point."

I looked over at Dickson. He was slumped in his chair. The ultimate defeat was letting your own staff go.

"How I gonna manage?" Ciatta went on. "I got a daughter. You know Yeanue. She only four! Who gonna pay her school fees? My mother, father, and stepfather, most of my aunts, they working? No! I the one feeding them. And my brother, Jackolie, and his daughter . . ."

Susan took the letter from my hand, walked across the room, and placed it on Ciatta's lap. "Thank you for aiding Liberia's poorest."

"Maybe we should just forget about the environment for now," I suggested to Gabriel, who was in Greenville installing ecostoves. We had met up at Mississippi Street Blues for a beer just a few hours after I had fired Ciatta.

"How so?" Gabriel asked.

"I mean, let's focus *all* of our efforts on reducing poverty. Basic nutrition, literacy, food production, education. Once we have the economy at least sputtering along, we can start talking about a luxury like the environment."

"So it's 'either-or'?"

"Hmm?"

"Your paradigm is *either* we have economic growth *or* a healthy environment?"

"Maybe. And anyway, what kind of crazy Ghanaian uses words like 'paradigm'?"

"Crazy ones like me," Gabriel said, laughing. "But my own paradigm—sorry, *ma-way-ah-do-see-da-world-o*—is sustainable development, not 'either-or.' Conservation can actually help the economy and improve people's lives. Our ecostoves reduce the labor needed to collect wood while maintaining the forests for future use."

I sipped my Club beer as Gabriel talked about what he called "production through conservation." His reforestation projects deliver wood for poor households; agroforestry intensifies production and thereby reduces slash and burn while increasing nutrition. I told him that these are the types of improvements I had begun introducing into my own projects, but that the layoffs had gotten me feeling skeptical.

"Keep your eye on the side of the road on the way back to Monrovia tomorrow," he said. "I think you'll see why we need to integrate conservation into small-farmer practices."

Our friend Jim, who worked with the British NGO Tearfund, sat down with us, looking bedraggled.

"How's it going, Jim?" I asked.

"Terrible. We're firing everyone. Closing shop in Greenville." He raised his hand to flag down a waitress. "I've got a brigade of security guards in the compound. Tomorrow we try to ship the stuff back to Monrovia. Bloody hell, I need a cold one!"

My head pulsed with a hangover as we drove through the Krahn-Bassa National Forest the next morning along what everyone now simply called the OTC Road. A pair of hornbills sailed above the verdant canopy, but my usual joy over such a sight was absent. I had accepted the sad task of transporting the unemployed Ciatta and her belongings back to Monrovia. She sat next to me in the back, not having uttered a word since we'd left Greenville hours before. Susan sat shotgun next to Momo.

A few hours earlier, we had passed the Tearfund office. The scene was one of total mayhem. Half a dozen trucks ringed the office, and hired hands tried in vain to load them with furniture, office equipment, and generators. As soon as they placed something in the truck, a group of ex-employees would jump in to try to snatch it. Other former employees, some of whom I recognized, ran in this direction or that, their arms loaded with booty. Jim, the Brit we'd seen the night before, was trying to rally an unenthusiastic squad of security guards. One guard chased down a young woman who was escaping with a metal bucket. They struggled for it. The last image I saw as we drove away was the security guard successfully yanking the dented pail from her.

A few hours later, the image of the struggle for that bucket was stuck in my throbbing head. I was considering trying to sleep when the amazing sight that Gabriel had hinted at the day before jolted me: a family in the middle of the Krahn-Bassa forest.

It was a young family, father, mother, and a few children. They had cut down a couple of acres and had constructed a crude wooden home, held together by tied vines. Smoke and pockets of flame rose all around their house.

"Colonists," I said aloud.

"You mean *settlers*," Susan said. She was trying to be politically correct, but I preferred the word *colonists* with its more intrusive undertones. This was the exact same pattern from throughout the developing world: Logging companies like OTC are the shock troops, cutting roads into primary rainforests, while poor farmers like this family are the regular infantry, finishing off the forests with slash-and-burn agriculture.

Through smoke I saw them staring at us as we slowly drove by. The young pioneer and his wife looked to be in their twenties. They had two small children, and another was strapped to the woman's back. While their skin was deep brown, I would later picture their faces as a fresh pink. Pink faces glazed over with the sweat of work in a humid place, sweating also from the heat of the burning land. Environmental regulation had collapsed, and the land was theirs. It was indeed a colony, and they looked alien. Pink, cuddly, and sweet, but aliens nonetheless.

More would follow. They too would slash and burn. Each family that came would deforest several acres each year, bringing a far greater devastation than even OTC's logging. My heart went out to this young family, unaware, but it went out further to the integrity of our planet. What already happened in the Amazon, Indonesia, and throughout the developing world was beginning to happen here. As the world's last wild pigmy hippos, dwarf elephants, and red colobus monkeys fled the flames, who would take a stand for them?

Back in Monrovia, I dreamed of wilderness and fire. Chief Wah and the rest of Vanjahtown were burning their CRS-sponsored community forest. Some hacked away at iron-wood trees with machetes, while others stood watching. I pleaded with Chief Wah not to do it, but he shrugged dramatically and said, "Rice small! It hungry season-o!" The fire began to spread beyond the community forest. In no time, the Sapo National Park buffer zone was ablaze and the flames raced across the canopy toward Sinoe River, the park's border.

I ran.

Running, the heat burned but didn't scald. When I reached the river, I saw Ciatta and the other Greenville, Gbarnga, and Buchanan staff I had fired that week. Their families were with them, and they all hacked at the trees. Dozens of babies lined the river, and the adults shoved leaves and wood chips into their mouths to quiet them. The babies chewed and swallowed the chips and leaves and then cried for more. Amid the chaos, one clear thought formed: *I must find Gabriel.*

Momo suddenly appeared in a motorized canoe. I climbed in and we raced downriver, under a bridge of fire as the flames jumped the river from one side of the canopy to the other, into the park where Ciatta and all of my CRS friends frantically chopped down trees and stuffed their babies with wood chips. The babies began to cough and whine as the smoke started to enter their lungs. I yelled against the drone of the motor to Momo that he must go faster! We must find Gabriel!

Momo banked the canoe near the top of a waterfall. Leaping out onto the shore, I saw Gabriel below in the center of an enormous refugee camp, building ecostoves and planting trees. He gently coached the refugees as they constructed the energy-efficient stoves. Gabriel glowed with optimism, oblivious to the mayhem all around. I cried out, but my voice was drowned out by the waterfall that separated us.

"Gabriel!" I screamed into the crashing falls. "*Don't you see the fire?* My God, Gabriel, there's a fire."

CHAPTER 23

"I WAS NOMINATED TO be Ms. Liberia. I would have sung at the pageant," Ciatta says. "But I didn't participate because Charles Taylor makes sure it goes to his favorite girlfriend each year. It's rigged!" She puts her empty beer bottle on the table and says, "Why don't we walk-small?"

I've brought her to Miami Beach, my secret hideaway, the place where my nightmares of burning forests vanish. It's less than fifteen minutes from Carolina Farm in my Land Rover. Ciatta and I crossed the bridge into Virginia and followed the sand roads behind Hotel Africa to a wooden sign: MIAMI BEACH. A waiter came up to my jeep, exclaiming, "Mr. Powers!" and escorted us to one of the beach restaurant's dozen white plastic tables, inevitably unoccupied during the week.

I follow Ciatta along the beach. Grasses dance to our right, and I scan the ocean for dolphins. We pass through a Fanti fishing village. The Fanti are an ethnic group that migrated to the Liberian coast from Ghana. As we pass, this particular Fanti community is struggling to work a net to shore, and Ciatta and I stop to watch. Dozens of men, women, and children pull at each end of the enormous net as if locked in a tug-of-war with the sea. Two muscular men splash in the center, trying to scare the fish into the net.

The sun has begun its dip below the horizon when they finally pull the last of the net to shore. Ciatta and I walk down to the water's edge to examine the fruits of this long effort: three scrawny grouper, no bigger than the snapper blue-fish that I tossed back into the Long Island Sound as a child.

We turn back toward Miami Beach, and a project idea comes to mind: Fanti Food Security Through Improved Fishing Techniques. I mention it to Ciatta.

"You think you know more about fishing than the Fanti?"

We laugh, and the background noise of my handheld radio continues: "Charlie Foxtrot, Alpha One. Go ahead, Alpha One."

"Hey, man, why don't you turn that thing off?"

"For security reasons."

"*Security?!* If fighting starts now, we'll just run up the coast to Sierra Leone."

"That's reassuring," I say, switching off the radio. "You're right, though. I wake up at all hours of the night with this thing. You know, the Intercon guards' radio checks. And when you combine that background noise with Monrovia's generators . . . Was that Camus' or Sartre's metaphor for hell?"

Ciatta raises an eyebrow at me, and we keep walking. After a moment she says, "I remember this beach." The last bit of the sun has sunk below the horizon, and the sky is aglow in burnt orange. "When the war came to Monrovia, I fled right along here with my twin brother, Jackolie. We walked for three days straight. Bodies . . . floated and washed around like some kind of logs. I thought for sure I'd end up floating there with them." We walk along in the firm wet sand, the waves lapping up against our shins. "If I hear anything, Bill, I will come for you. This country not correct. Sometimes I hear things that you might not."

Not knowing how to respond, I mumble a thank-you.

Abruptly changing gears, she yells out, "I'll race you!" She sprints up the beach, and I run after her. Ciatta is quick, but my longer legs ultimately give me the advantage. As I pass her, she dives at my legs, tackling me.

"*Errrr,*" she growls, assuming a wrestler pose on her knees. I do the same, and we roll and wrestle, our clothes and hair covered with sand. She rips at my shirt, popping off a few buttons, and scratches me hard. I try to pin her down, but she wriggles loose and then lunges at me, bringing me down under her. I finally secure her wrists and pin her down, the larger bulk of my chest and torso on top of hers.

"You win," she concedes, gasping for breath.

"Where did that come from?" I ask, rolling into the sand beside her and panting. She flashes a smile at me. "I'm going for a swim," I say. "You coming?"

"With my swimming teacher? Of course!"

We strip to our underwear, stash our clothes among the grasses, and run down to the water, splashing our way in. I can never believe that these warm tropical waters form part of the same Atlantic Ocean that wash up ice cold against Long Island.

"Careful, it's getting dark!" she yells as I swim out into deeper waters.

I do a slow backstroke toward the shore. And then I begin to float. The water is calm. A jagged barrier of rocks a hundred feet out shields us from the rough surf. I roll from my back to my belly and see Ciatta five feet from me, also floating.

I propel myself toward her, and eventually my hand and wrist find her body. She takes my hand loosely in hers, and then our hands separate.

We float close together, she on her back and I with my head underwater, an entombing silence, like pressing the mute button on the world. Just the sound of sands rubbing below me. I periodically lift my head slightly to take in air and then dip back into the silence. A gentle wave brings us together again, and we bob against each other. Then the waves separate us. I eventually take a gulp of air and launch myself back in her direction with my foot. My arm slides into the dip of her lower back, and she laces her fingers into mine. I roll to my back and open my eyes to the first shimmering stars. Only the faintest traces of the day linger.

"Ready for a real Swedish massage?" Gabriel asks with a laugh. I follow him and his Dutch girlfriend through their Monrovia apartment into a bedroom.

"Strip!" Liza says, turning around to light an incense stick. Meanwhile, Gabriel slips an Enya CD into the stereo; the soothing melodies accompany the sound of the whiny generator outside. I slide under a sheet on the massage table.

Gabriel asks if I've been in Greenville recently. I tell him I have and that new settler families had entered Krahn-Bassa. I tell him about how I still picture the first family I saw there as cuddly and pink against the smoky wasteland, adding, "All of this has led me to a new theory . . . Picture a diagram of a vicious cycle: *Poverty* causes *environmental destruction,* which causes further *poverty.*"

"An elegant theory," Gabriel says, "but incomplete."

"It was poverty that drove that family into the Krahn-Bassa Forest so that they could eat, right? And they do eat for today! But the longer-term impact is a loss of soil quality, species to hunt, and watersheds—"

"Which leads to greater poverty, forcing further environmental degradation," Gabriel jumps in. "Your logic is correct. But you're forgetting the most important part of the equation."

I am getting annoyed. Liza returns with hot oil and rubs it between her hands. "Turn over," she says. "We start with the front."

I flip over and turn my head to Gabriel, who sits in a full lotus position on the floor. "I'll stand by my theory until you tell me what you think is missing."

"You mention poverty," Gabriel says, breathing deeply. "But what about *wealth*?"

"I didn't spot any rich farmers cutting down the forest."

"No? How did those 'cuddly pink aliens' get there?"

"The OTC Road," I say, finally getting what Gabriel is driving at. As Liza works the hot oil into my shoulders, I flash back to Washington, D.C., and Jennifer's friends' mahogany furniture.

"Here's a fact I like," Gabriel says, getting up to retrieve a book from his bed table. "'Recent scientific estimates indicate that at least four additional planets would be needed if each of the planet's six billion inhabitants consumed at the level of the average American.'"

I let these words sink in, as the hot oil does, my body relaxing even as my mind struggles to absorb this statistic.

"It's similar for Europeans or Japanese," he continues. "So what's the real source of rainforest destruction? Is it just those desperately poor farmers you see in Krahn-Bassa? I like the bubble metaphor."

"Let me know if this is too hard," Liza says. I mumble something in reply.

"Each of us six billion people is more than just our body. We're dragging behind us a bubble that represents our real impact on the environment, our true size. The bubble represents our consumption: the oil we burn, the trash we throw out, and so on. All of it has its root in a forest somewhere."

My New York investment banker friend's bubble is a Goodyear blimp, whereas most Liberians have soap bubbles. What of my own bubble? "Okay, you've got me feeling sufficiently guilty."

"Sometimes a bit of guilt is healthy."

"Gabriel," I say, my body relaxed but my conscience ill at ease, "you can't be as perfect as you seem."

"Far from it! I used to be unbelievably materialistic! You name it, I owned it . . . or wanted to."

I glance down at Gabriel, who continues his yoga stretching as Liza works my feet. "What happened?"

"I went to India!" he says, laughing. "I spent a couple of years wandering, meditating, learning the wisdom of the East. I still practice yoga and meditation every day. That experience in India changed me fundamentally. I was completely self-centered before, like a greedy, grubby worm, never satisfied with what I had, always hungering for more. India opened me up." He pauses and then adds, "And then there was something that Gandhi said that really influenced me: 'True morality consists not in following the beaten track, but in finding out the true path and fearlessly following it.'"

After the massage, Gabriel and I walk over to what everyone calls Star Radio, a simple outdoor chop shop next to the former radio station of that name that Charles Taylor had shut down a few weeks earlier. We order two Clubs.

"Sorry, Gabriel, but I don't believe you," I say, returning to our conversation inside. "I'm not Gandhi, and never could be. And neither could almost anyone else. He was a rare aberration, like Christ or Buddha."

"Do you believe in people's capacity to change?" I nod. "Does that capacity have limits?" I think about this for a moment, and Gabriel continues, "Through love there's no limit to how much we can change!"

"Gabriel," I say, shaking my head. "You don't realize what a legend you are here. Everyone knows about you. You're a myth. But it's because you're different, you're the only self-less person here." I unwrap the toilet paper from my beer bottle. The stark shells of buildings rise up around us in the dark, the occasional taxi honking its way by Star Radio. I still feel Liza's strong hands on my back.

"*Enough*," Gabriel says.

"Enough?"

"It's a beautiful word. Someplace between poverty and wealth there is an elusive point: *enough*. Do you know who some of my greatest teachers have been?"

I shake my head.

"Some of the average people here in Liberia! Many of the farmers in the so-called *bush* have a simple joy that they just exude. It's as if they are connected to nature in the same way we have been as a species for fifty thousand years. Material simplicity can be joy evoking. Haven't you noticed that in Greenville? The feeling you get from people."

I have, and that is part of what attracts me to Greenville and the communities around the park. But then Chief Wah pops to mind: how he hungrily snatched up the old sneakers I offered him, a treasure to him.

"There isn't enough here! Especially not enough peace of mind. Everyone is focused on survival," I say.

"The average Liberian who maintains her sense of dignity and joy even amid repression is resisting tyranny."

CHAPTER 24

"'I AM *NOT GOING* to uncross my arms!'" Ciatta is saying, acting out her encounter with one of Taylor's soldiers earlier that day. It's evening now, and we're relaxing at my house.

"I mean, that ATU soldier had a lot of nerve, asking me to uncross my arms for no reason. Just crossed like this." She demonstrates the posture. "That boy got angry when he heard this! He charged at me, the cold metal of his rifle against my arms, demanding, 'Uncross them, *now*!'

"I blinked at him, not showing a trace of fear. I said, 'Excuse me, but maybe *Your Excellency* did not grasp my meaning when I informed him that I will *not* uncross my arms.' I say! When that boy heard this, he got mad. A woman like me embarrassing him in front of plenty people. The Taylor convoy was coming and there were hordes of us stopped on the roadside. Sweat dripped into his eyes, and some snot gushed out of his nose like this. He was panting heavily . . ."

Ciatta pauses and switches gears: "Hey, you got some juice or something? I'm thirsty."

"Wait a minute! What happened?"

"Okay, okay . . . ," she says, enjoying my rapt attention. "He kept panting and staring at me, and *everyone* was watching. I crossed my arms across my chest harder than ever. His gun pressed harder against me. Finally he said, 'Fine girl think she got a friend in the government!' And, do you know, that boy walked away!"

I get up to get her juice from the kitchen, saying, "Ciatta, why risk your life over something like that?"

"I know how to handle military men. If you act like you are well connected, they respect you," she says, following me into the kitchen. She grins at me as she leans against my kitchen counter. I hand her a glass of juice and kiss her on her neck.

"Like the time when I was thirteen. I was a refugee with my family. We hid up in the bush, near Sierra Leone where you go surfing. We were hungry. My auntie sent me to a village to get bread, and I was stopped by some rebel boys. One of them said that I was a Mandingo girl! That I was a Krahn girl! As if I were both. Boy was stupid-o."

"So what happened?"

"He told me I was an enemy Mandingo girl. That I had eyes like a Mandingo. That he would rape me and then kill me. 'Take off your pants!' he yelled." Ciatta takes a sip of her juice. "I told them I would *not* take off my pants, and they insisted. I refused again. So that boy said he would kill me first, so I should give him six feet."

I flash a puzzled look.

"'Gimme six feet.' That's what he said to me. If you don't give six feet, the blood might splash back all over the person shooting. Something like that. Anyway, I told him I wasn't going to give him no damn six feet. He got all puffed up— just like that ATU boy with the gun today!—and I thought I was dead. But just then one of the other boy soldiers who had been quiet until then asked me if I was a Mandingo girl. I told him I was a Bassa girl. 'Speak Bassa!' he demanded, and I told him I'm not going to speak no Bassa. He asked me what village I was from, and I told him. I say! That boy was Bassa, too. We were brother and sister! From the same tribe. He told the other boy that they could not harm his sister, which caused a huge fight, yelling and screaming at each other, a gun went off, and I went down to the ground. The Bassa boy told me to run as he wrestled the other boy down, and I did. I jumped into a ditch and ran."

LIBERIA IS A COUNTRY OF LAWS, NOT MEN. LET'S KEEP IT THAT WAY.

I pass a billboard with this message each day on the way to work. Under these words is a regal-looking portrait of Charles Taylor above the inscription "His Excellency Dahkpannah Dr. Charles Ghankay Taylor."

The irony is so blatant that I imagine Taylor giggling hysterically when he commissioned the billboard. I can't help but laugh. Ciatta can't, either, and neither can Monrovia's taxi drivers. These very poor men drive Nissans, Hondas, and Toyotas that no longer pass emissions requirements in their first world country of origin and are sold off cheap in places like Liberia. These taxis are inevitably on the brink of total collapse but usually carry a hopeful message scrawled by the driver in white paint on the back bumper.

Things like HARD TIMES, HIGH HOPES or GOOD NEVER LOST. Others say PERSEVERANCE or THINK BIG.

I make a game out of spotting new ones on the way to work: NOTHING SPOIL; MOTHER'S BLESSING; MORE LUCK AHEAD. DETERMINATION, reads one. TAKE ADVERSITY WITH CONFIDENCE, proclaims another.

The Jacket quips to me on one occasion that the more beat up the taxi, the more religious the message on the back: OUR GOD IS ABLE; MY SOUL GLORIFY JEHOVAH; JAH IS MERCIFUL.

While I'm not certain his theory holds, many of the scrawled messages are religious: JUST BE GOOD, GOD WILL HELP YOU; GOD TIME THE BEST; GOD'S PLAN MUST BE FRUITFUL: FATHER TAKE CONTROL.

Other drivers passing beneath Charles Taylor's billboard celebrate themselves. LOVER ON DUTY, proclaims one. Then there's WATCH MY BACK, ALL EYES ON ME, and even ROYAL AMBASSADOR. Another simply reminds us, TAKE IT COOL.

A second Taylor billboard, right across from the Geneva Convention's fiftieth-anniversary monument (EVEN WARS HAVE LIMITS) on Providence Island features the president smiling down with an ambitious promise: ELECTRICITY BY THE NEW MILLENNIUM. Just before the year 2000, the lights did go on in a few square blocks downtown, but only for a few weeks—long enough for all four Communist-era generators purchased from Slovakia to crash.

Underneath the billboard, the taxis pass. One bumper asks simply, HOW COME? while another seems to answer with, IF I KNEW . . . while one laments, TO LIVE LIKE THE POOR MAN IS NOT EASY, another assures us, THE RICH ALSO CRY.

ONE NATION, ONE PEOPLE. TOGETHERNESS.

LIBERTY.

"I got dreams, you know."

Ciatta's dark and light blue braids fall over her naked back and shoulders. After she had told me about her encounters with rebel soldiers, we'd watched a Nigerian soap opera for a while (the TV competing with the air conditioner's hum and the roar of the distant generator) before crawling under the mosquito net into my bed.

"I'm going to Canada," she says. "The UN got this refugee resettlement program."

I pull her shoulder toward me so I can look at her face. "Be serious."

"I am. They'll send me and Yeanue to Canada. They'll pay for me to go to university, and give me housing for the first years I am there. I need to go. What I doing here? Nothing! Most of my friends from high school, they made it over to that side. They're advancing . . . I want to make something of myself, too."

I push her braids back and say, "You're not exactly a refugee."

"I been a refugee half my life. The only thing I need is *five hundred dollars* to get a space on the list."

"Ca'gaa'boiest!" Ciatta's four-year-old daughter, Yeanue, says from the backseat of my Jeep.

It's Saturday, and Ciatta and I have picked up Yeanue from her grandmother's and are headed to the beach. I have no idea what Yeanue just said, since her Liberian accent is so strong.

Ciatta turns to her daughter. "What you say?"

"Ca'gaa'*boiest*!"

"She says, 'The car is going to burst.'"

Just then we hit yet another deep pothole, which rattles the vehicle. We eventually shoulder and ease the Jeep onto a dirt road heading toward the coast. We bounce along until we arrive at a gate, pay our admission, and park in a lot packed with NGO, government, and private sector SUVs.

Stepping onto the hot sand is like entering a Club Med advertisement: the crash and roar of surf, a cobalt blue sky, and a limitless stretch of white sand punctuated by colorful beach umbrellas. A waiter in a white button-down shirt jogs across the sand to us. "Ooombrela?" he asks.

"Sure, boss," I say. "Please bring it to that table there. And please also bring us three sof' drink."

"Wa' flavor?"

We tell him and cross the sand toward the only empty table. A dozen European colleagues from other NGOs, including CONCERN, Action Contre la Faim (ACF), and Save the Children, sit around a long table. I wave to them, but only a few nod back. The rest just stare, wondering whom I will sit with, who my "friend" is, and oh-my-God, she has a kid. In expat circles there are specific spaces for including one's local girlfriend—nightclubs, your own home with the curtains drawn, certain beaches—but Thinker's Beach on a Saturday was not among them. This was an undeclared time to be among one's own. We are able to skirt the European table, but, no way around it, we have to walk right by the Surf Buddhas.

"Hey."

"Wa sup?" three Buddhas chime in. Most of them, including the Jacket, are out catching waves.

"I speared this one out by the rocks," one Buddha says, pointing to a grouper he is grilling. "You will eat fine today!"

"Okay, I'll stop back. We're sitting over there."

"Why don't you join us here?"

I look over at Ciatta and down at Yeanue. "Later. We'll come back."

The waiter is hoisting a red umbrella above our table when we get there. I scan the break line and spy the Jacket and a South African friend paddling to catch a wave. Popular African disco pulses from the restaurant area above. A slim girl in a bikini jogs toward our table: Ciatta's cousin.

"Hi! How are you, baby?" she says to Ciatta, kissing her. "Yeanue's so cute in her little beach clothes!" Ciatta and her cousin walk arm in arm down to the water with Yeanue in tow.

The waiter returns with our soft drinks. As I take a sip, I spot another Buddha I know emerging from the surf. He's from California, but I can't remember his name. He jams his board into the sand near the Surf Buddha table, opens a can of beer, and heads over to me.

"*Duuude!*"

"Hey." We shake hands and perform a quick Buddha hug. "Good waves?"

"Fucking excellent, man. Almost as good as R-port. *Almost.* Speaking of Robertsport, what do you say to next weekend?"

"Love to, but I'm busy."

"Busy?" he says, grinning. He notices me staring toward the water's edge where Ciatta stands chatting with her cousin. He continues, "That shit's good for a while, but you gotta go for some European pussy in the long term. Think of it this way: per capita investment. Look at the one I've got. That Norwegian over there." I see her at the Buddha table, her hair so blond that it looks white against her bronzed skin. "Hundreds of thousands, perhaps a few million dollars of investment created that twenty-six-year-old. Private schools, excellent medical care, not to mention all the bene-fits of Norwegian infrastructure . . . Fucking hell, the goddamn *dental work* she's had alone is worth ten times everything that's been invested in your Liberian chick her whole life!"

I glance out over the waves. The Jacket is coming out of the surf and heading our way.

"No, but seriously. Picture her in ten years. Picture the dinner conversation! Take it from me. Have fun for a little while, okay? And then get yourself a first world woman when it comes to settling down. Don't get lured in, my friend. She's only after you for the green card. No offense."

"Offense taken."

He blinks a few times and then bursts out laughing. "No, really," I say. "Offense taken." He stops laughing and bristles.

The Jacket comes over, and the other Surf Buddha says to him, "This dude is way too unmellow," as he shakes his head and walks back toward his table.

"What's up with that?" the Jacket asks me.

"The guy doesn't like Ciatta . . . You've got a Liberian girlfriend, Jacket, how can you hang out with someone like that?"

"Consult rule number one of being a Surf Buddha: You *riiide*. Who cares what that guy thinks? Opinions are like the froth after the wave has crashed, full of air. Ride, man, ride." He takes a surfing posture and grins. "Oh, and one correction: Mine's not a girlfriend. She's my wife. I paid her father the dowry and everything. I've gone native, my friend. I've got three others as well, deputy wives, as they say, who I'm happy to say now sleep on mattresses.

"But listen," he continues in a more serious tone. "Rule number two of being a Buddha is the same as rule one: You *riiide*. You don't create tension on the beach."

I pick up my board from the sand and thrust it toward the Jacket. "This is for you."

The Jacket looks at me for a moment and says, "What the hell are you doing?"

Sometimes your body just acts. I know in every inch of my flesh that I am no longer a Surf Buddha and that I never really was. I don't know exactly where I'm headed, but I do know I will not need that board to get there. The sun beats down hard on my face, and I can hear the Buddhas laugh at the next table. The Jacket stands there, hands at his side, not taking the board from me, so I let it fall toward him and he catches it. "It's a gift."

The Jacket examines the board in his hands. "You're making a big mistake. Don't care so damn much. It's not only useless, but neurotic to care. Because this is all beyond your control."

Ciatta asks her cousin to watch Yeanue, and we walk together down the beach. I tie a T-shirt into a makeshift turban as protection against the sun. To our right, the waters roll out blue and end in a dull haze; to our left, the wind howls through the skeletons of former mansions and hotels. I'm keeping a step ahead of Ciatta, and we're not talking. The surfer has unfortunately managed to plant a seed of doubt in my head: *She's only after you for the green card.* I'm suddenly seeing Ciatta differently, and this has caused something to click in my mind. I finally say to her, "The *refugee* program you told me about." She looks away, toward the sea. "I was talking with a UN friend last week and he told me about a refugee resettlement program for Sierra Leoneans. But not for Liberians."

After a long pause she says, "Maybe. So what?"

"You lied to me."

Ciatta stops short. "I have never, and will never, lie to you."

"You didn't mention the program was for Sierra Leoneans."

"You never asked!"

"So you just give me the portion of the truth that is convenient for you? Anyway, it's not a five-hundred-dollar *fee;* it's a bribe."

We walk for a long while in silence. "Look," I finally say, "I think you know that I'm not going to bribe a UN official. So if you can't think of any other way to get the cash, I suggest you choose another of your dreams—finishing your university degree here. Sure, it would be great to get to the States or Canada, but just a few weeks ago you were all excited about enrolling in classes so that you're not wasting your time here. Right?"

"Yeah, and? I don't have the money for that, either."

"I'll help you out with that. Why don't you enroll in the Methodist university. It's more expensive than the University of Liberia, but much better."

We walk a while more. Her fingers eventually touch mine, and we hold hands as she says, "I think I'll enroll."

CHAPTER 25

T HE SUN STREAKS into the living room and melts into the upbeat Malian jazz coming from the stereo. A breeze blows in, too, and twirls the tobacco smoke from a friend's cigarette. He's tapping his foot to the rhythm, and his whole body is pleased with the music.

It's Ciatta's birthday, and we are celebrating at her friend Maria's apartment on a Saturday afternoon. Her place is tidy and neatly painted, but raggedness pulls at its edges: Photos of her family hang a bit crookedly on the walls; the sofa's armrests are split, showing the foam inside; the bathroom doorknob is gone. A poster of the Virgin Mary hangs above the color TV in a corner. Maria sits across from Ciatta and me. She is very dark skinned, with deep black eyes. Her hair is dyed slightly red and suspended in an offhand way around her head. She wears a fishnet shirt that shows her black bra underneath, and a colorful wraparound skirt.

Ciatta says, "Hey, man, this is some *nice* music!" She slouches back in her chair next to me and closes her eyes, taking my hand in hers and holding it lightly against her stomach. The tune is Habib Koite's "Sarayama." Everyone is grooving to it now. Maria's head moves ever so slightly. The two other men with us, Liberians in their early thirties dressed in flowing, tie-dyed African shirts and blue jeans, smoke as they smile and nod. The music blends African drumming with a heavy baseline overlaid with vocals in a Malian language.

The tune ends and the news comes on. "DC-101 is proud to bring you the news in French, English, and simple English this evening," the announcer says. "We begin with the news in simple English."

The announcer clears his throat and says, "Let us begin with the economy. The bossman of Liberia's money business anounced that the Liberian dollar is struggling against the mighty U.S. dollar as it fell to . . ."

"'Bossman of Liberia's money business'?" Maria shouts. "Hey, man, why can't they just say 'finance minister'?"

One story involves an interview with several fishermen who witnessed two fish talking to each other. The debate is lively and deals not with whether or not the two fish had spoken (they all take this as self-evident), but rather with what exactly the fish said. The next story is about African forest buffalo attacking towns near Buchanan. Local residents describe the bush cows as being organized into battalions and regiments; the residents are preparing for an attack. Another is about a woman's vagina that informs her husband that she is cheating on him. This is not *National Enquirer*–style entertainment, but actual news stories that most average Liberians accept as truth. The idea of animals communicating and organizing armies—and even of human body parts speaking—is entwined with juju, or African sign. Witch doctor *zoes* cast spells that cause these events.

A story about the festering border war begins with Charles Taylor's voice: "Enemies of our great independent nation continue to threaten our vital national security." His English has the lilting cadence of the American South, but with crisper edges, warm, confident, intelligent, and commanding. "These rebel elements invading from Guinea are forcing us to stop road construction, health care, and education and switch those funds to national defense."

"That man is the chief of rebels!" Ciatta bursts out as she jumps up and switches off the radio. "I say let's eat!"

Maria comes out with a tray of a hundred small shells, holds it in front of me, and cries out, "Kiss me!"

Ciatta takes one up and sticks it in my mouth, telling me to suck on it, and I obey. Out slides a slippery worm, which I swallow. The others gather around the tray, sucking joyfully on the shells. "They call them 'kiss me' because you have to kiss them to get the meat out," Ciatta says.

The rest of the food comes out. Baked chicken bathed in a spicy sauce, whole grouper with fresh lime, salad, and Irish potatoes. We feast blissfully. Discussion turns to a planned party at Christmas, which is a month away. Each invitee would chip in "fifty U.S. dollars," and it would be decadent! A roasted pig with a red tomato in his mouth. An *orgy* of food. And the attire?

"Nighties and pajamas?" Ciatta suggests.

"G-strings," Maria says to a roar of laughter. They plan every detail of the party, though I know it is a dream of earlier times, when people actually had "fifty U.S." to throw around.

Bob Dylan's "Visions of Johanna" is now streaming from the stereo, and I get up and walk onto the balcony. ("Just Louise and her lover so entwined. And these visions of Johanna that conquer my mind," he sings.) As a teenager, I loved Dylan, and this song gets me sentimental. I am full of delicious food, laughter, and Ciatta's touch. I'm feeling so happy and alive, almost to the point of tears. As "Visions of Johanna" blends with the laughter inside the apartment, I stand alone, peering down into a Monrovia where a boy carries a jug of water from the well and water splashes onto the filthy sidewalk. A teenager pushes a wheelbarrow with a blue-and-white cooler, shouting "Sof'drink ten dollar!" Clothes flutter in the wind on the balconies facing me, and beyond the shells of buildings, beyond the tooting taxis and the wandering salespeople selling rat poison, beyond all of this is an electric storm flashing over the ocean.

Ciatta's arms slip around my waist, gently surprising me. She presses her cheek against my back, and we stare out into the electric storm together. "Y'all right?" she asks.

"Body fine."

Even as I became more integrated into Liberian daily life, there was no escaping my position in the social hierarchy. As I got closer to Ciatta, the voice of that Surf Buddha (*She's only after you for the green card*) remained in my head. As much as Ciatta and I clicked, there was no surmounting the enormous gap between our two worlds, particularly the fact that I was her key to a better life. In other parts of my life, I similarly found it near impossible to break out of the bossman dynamic that I so resisted. Even as I made the rounds of Monrovia's Lebanese businesses to feel out the worsening security situation, I could not get beyond being bossman.

When I entered the Sharif and Sharif hardware store on Randall Street, the Lebanese clerk abandoned the Liberians he was assisting in order to serve me. It was my first time visiting that store, since I normally asked Evans to handle hardware purchases. I pointed to the extension cord I needed and then flipped through the liberty notes in my wallet.

"Bossman! What are you doing?" the clerk asked with a frown.

"The name's Bill, not bossman. And I'm paying you."

"So you want to *pay?*" he asked, his voice rising at the end of the last word.

"Yes. I want to pay for this extension cord. How much do I owe you?"

The Lebanese man's frown melted into a smile as he thrust a plastic bag into my hand and said, "You no pay."

I shifted from one foot to the other. "I don't want to start a line of credit."

"No-no-no." He shook his head vigorously. "You no pay now, you no pay later," he said, and winked and added, "Bossman."

I shot a glance over at the two waiting Liberian customers. "Look," I finally said, removing 150 liberty from my wallet. "Will this do?"

"No! You are my friend, and *you no pay*!" He swiveled around and disappeared behind a curtain into a back room.

I put the money back into my wallet and trod toward the door. The two Liberian men didn't even blink. I thought the shorter man's mouth rose into a slight smirk. The plastic bag felt heavy in my hand, and the walk across the store stretched out into what seemed like an eternity. As I pulled open the door and felt the rush of humid air hit me from outside, one of the Liberians said in a mock Lebanese accent, "You-no-pay-bossman!" A burst of laughter accompanied my exit.

That Lebanese man did not know me personally, but he did know that there were few poor *whitemen* in Liberia. Like other NGO officials, I controlled a hefty budget, some of which I could potentially swing his way. From his perspective, this was venture capital: Throw some to this bossman and that, and eventually you may reel one in.

But, aah! In the commotion of not having to pay, I forgot to probe for information on the conflict. Lebanese merchants like Mr. Sharif had become expert at gauging security after several generations in West Africa. In the 1930s, they immigrated to the French colonies of Guinea and the Ivory Coast and then spread to the neighboring countries, including Liberia. Similar to Jewish, Gujarati, and overseas Chinese diasporas, the Lebanese "merchant minority" class was formed in West Africa. They started out as small traders and gradually cornered the market on knowledge, connections, and capital, dominating economic activity in countries like Liberia. To protect their valuable assets in fickle political climates like that in Liberia, they had honed an acute sense of risk. I was looking for signs: If the Lebanese kept their stocks lower than usual, this was the real level two security; if they sent some family members back to Lebanon, level three; and if they closed up and left themselves, level four was imminent.

As I arrived at Stop-N-Shop, the Lebanese grocer called out to me, "Mr. Powers! How are you?"

"I tryin' small," I said.

"You talking like a real Liberian, bossman!" He laughed, putting his hand on my shoulder and whispering to me, "I've got something you are going to love." He led me through one of the grocery aisles. There were six aisles guarded by six Liberians in their twenties in shorts and flip-flops. It was evidently cheaper to pay them each a dollar a day to stand there and stare down the aisle than to install a videocamera system to monitor theft. I followed the store owner into a dim back room, and then he disappeared for a moment. He came back reverently cradling a blue plastic container. "Ice cream!" he exclaimed.

Sure enough, it was real ice cream. He explained that he had shipped it from Holland in a rare refrigerated vessel. I looked longingly at this comfort food and asked what the half-gallon container cost.

"Only twenty U.S. dollars each!" he said, opening the lid and showing the half-melted ice cream.

"Next time."

I finished my shopping and signed for the purchase. I paid my month's bill with a personal check onto which he would insert the name of a U.S. supplier in order to save on currency transfers. While signing, I asked, "So, how is security shaping up in Liberia? Are you keeping the same levels of stock?"

I bit my tongue after asking this. He winced. The idea was to be subtle.

He finally offered a thin smile and said, "Security . . . it's tryin' small."

"Bossman!" exclaimed the Lebanese owner of the videotape rental store of which I was a member, as he came over to shake my hand. Bluckbuster Video used the same blue-and-yellow insignia as the international chain.

I handed him a couple of tapes, saying, "Sorry, these were due over two weeks ago."

"You know *you* don't pay fines! Don't worry about it." Sure, I knew it. I justified my perpetual lateness in returning tapes to the lack of an after-hours drop slot. I mentioned this deficiency to one of the Liberian clerks in Bluckbuster once time and he replied, "What?! We don't have *that* in Liberia *yet*," as if I had suggested a space exploration initiative.

The sole customer, I browsed the shelves. All of the tapes were copied illegally. In the middle of one film I'd rented, a man with a bucket of popcorn walked across my screen. Someone had recorded it right in a movie theater. The poor quality of the tapes, combined with Monrovia's humidity, left me cleaning my VCR's heads after each use.

Bluckbuster specialized in American action films and East Indian Bollywood musicals, and as usual, I had a hard time finding something I liked. I finally asked the owner, who was trailing me, "Do you have any Woody Allen?"

"Woody . . . Allen," he repeated, testing out the two words for the first time together. "*Woody.* Now let me see." He thumbed weakly across a few action titles before saying that he was sorry, but no Woody Allen.

I settled on a film, and as I checked out the tape, I said, "This country's really heating up."

"Yes," he said, closing his cash register, "it reminds me of 1990, when Taylor first attacked Doe from Côte d'Ivoire. Same feeling."

"You were here in 1990? And this is as bad as *that*?"

"My friend, I was born here. And it bad, I telling you. The thing about Liberia, though, is it all happens so quick! You turn around and—boom!—the small-boy soldiers."

CHAPTER 26

I'M DOWN IN the CRS food warehouse in Buchanan when a security guard runs over to me: "Bossman! Urgent radio message!"

I trail him back to the radio room, snatch the receiver from Boimah, and say, "This is Tibet One, go ahead with your traffic."

"Tibet One, Tibet One, Tibet J and J. Uncle Two in lower Lofa. Guinea pigs heading toward Gbarnga. Please return to Mike Oscar."

What in the world is the Jacket saying? I press the transmitter button. "J and J, could you please repeat your message in plain English. Over."

"Negative. Consult your security manual. Over."

I ask Boimah if we have one.

"Not in the warehouse. But I think I understood the Jacket . . . 'Guinea pigs' are refugees, and he said they are heading toward the CRS-controlled area in Gbarnga because of a rebel attack from Guinea. 'Uncle Two' means rebels from Guinea."

"Guinea pigs from Guinea? Who came up with these codes?" I say to Boimah, and then get back on the radio with Jacket: "J and J, Tibet One. Good copy, I am heading back to your location."

Back in Monrovia, there isn't time to sit around the conference table debating the finer points of the situation. We must act. Internally displaced persons surge into greater Gbarnga, wrested from their farms by an invading rebel force wanting to overthrow Taylor. The IDPs need to be sheltered, fed, and clothed. They need basic medicines. In the rush of activity, I dismiss my aid worker's creed ("Don't just do something, stand there and think") as complete nonsense. I do not have the luxury of reflection. Twenty thousand IDPs have already flooded Gbarnga, and their numbers swell by a thousand more every hour.

In response to the crisis, the government agency responsible for refugees, the Liberian Refugee Resettlement Commission (LRRC), calls a meeting. I gather with my counterparts from Save the Children, Action Contre la Faim, and UNHCR in the LRRC director's office, a large room with paint peeling from the walls. A calendar, several years out of date, adorns the wall. The LRRC director insists that "all resources must be channeled through his agency" in order to "ensure a coordinated response to the crisis." Despite our diplomatic nods, I know that, smelling corruption, none of us will channel a penny through the LRRC.

Back in my office, I hastily arrange $20,000 in emergency funds from the CRS regional office in Ghana and coordinate the purchase of plastic tarps for shelter, medicines, and fifty-five-gallon drums of gasoline for the hospital generator in Gbarnga. I complete the procurement and shipping to Gbarnga in thirty-six sleepless hours. When I finally collapse into my bed, a huge smile covers my face. Not only had I "done no harm," but I had actually done good. I had saved lives!

"I really screwed up," I say to Gabriel over a beer at Kind of Blue. I still haven't quite recovered from the shocking news. Just hours after the supplies I purchased were ware-housed near Gbarnga, rebels sacked the place and marched off with the plastic tarps, drums of gasoline, and medical supplies. Not one item I sent helped a refugee family. Instead of saving refugee lives, I had resupplied the rebels for continued plundering.

Gabriel is lost in thought but finally says, "During the war in Liberia, CRS lost twenty-five large trucks and over a hundred light trucks and motorcycles to rebel factions in Liberia. Have you read Mary Anderson's study on this? She shows how humanitarian interventions often worsen and lengthen conflict."

"But what else can you do when people are starving? Take the Jacket, for instance. He fed people on the brink of death."

"He also kept the warlords fed. As soon as the Jacket left a village after a delivery, the rebels would come and seize most of it in the form of 'taxes.' Then they would sell the food to buy more weapons."

After a silence Gabriel continues, "This is tied in to a larger problem with international development aid. It's the current manifestation of the colonial impulse to control and dominate. You in the West feel you know the right way of doing things. 'Just look at our economies!' you say. So the West defines the problems in Africa—in education, health, agriculture, or emergencies—and then prescribes a response taken from your own context."

The Economist ran an article entitled "The Sins of the Secular Missionaries," which dealt with what Gabriel was talking about: that we development practitioners are missionaries, bringing to the third world a prescribed path to economic heaven. The article bothered me because I felt uncomfortable with the comparison to religious missionaries.

On one occasion, a field officer and I were waiting for a canoe to cross a river in Rivercess County to spot-check a clinic on the other side, when a trio of college-age students in white sneakers appeared as if out of nowhere.

"What brings you here?" I asked.

"Oh, we're just checking it out," one of them said.

"Yeah," another chimed in. "We're learning about the local cultures, talking to the people, you know, like, getting to know them."

"You've sure come a long way."

"Yup, all the way from Kentucky, U.S. of A."

"Anything else you're up to here?"

"Oh, you know, not much. Well . . . I guess we're saving a few heathen souls from the fires of hell."

Dig just below the surface of what looks like a cross-cultural exchange and you often find a hidden agenda. The true motivation of missionaries such as the ones I met in Rivercess is the standardization of souls. They dream of a world with a single Christian religion. I felt differently. In Liberia, the *sande* and *poro* bush schools, the *zoes,* the belief in the sacredness of all of nature held by these so-called animist peoples, all of it enriches our world. As Nobel Prize recipient Rigoberta Menchu said, "We must accept that humanity is a multicolored flower garden." The elimination of cultural diversity has a corollary in the destruction of biological diversity—as we raze the planet of its last stretches of unique ecological habitat, so too do we slash and burn traditional cultures and religions and cultivate a spiritual monoculture in its place.

And here was *The Economist* telling me that I too am a missionary, a secular missionary, bent on transforming traditional economic, social, and political systems into those more closely resembling my own.

"I love Jesse Helms with more fervor every time I come here," John remarks. We have just arrived at the United Nations restaurant, where we are to dine with Gabriel and Liza.

"You just said 'love,' and then you said 'Jesse Helms,'" I reply.

"Look at all of these vehicles!" he says, the arc of his hand taking in what looked to be an auto dealer's lot. "They never leave the city! They're for the exclusive use of these UN leeches, masters of bureaucracy and nothing else."

Walking into the restaurant, we find Gabriel and Liza on the balcony. They stand to greet us, Gabriel towering two heads above John as they shake hands. The African American John is several skin shades lighter than Gabriel. John knows of Gabriel and Liza, but they have not yet met. I let the three get to know one another a bit as I squint across the St. Paul into the lights of Carolina Farm, trying to figure out which is my house.

"I was telling Bill how I like Jesse Helms more every time I come here. It's so decadent."

"Hmmm . . . ," Gabriel muses. "Helms's distaste goes beyond mere inefficiency. I think he feels threatened."

"How so?" I ask.

"Sovereignty. He thinks the U.S. should be able to do what it wants, when it wants, and on whatever terms it wants. A stronger international regime, in his view, threatens that. And yet that is precisely what we need, isn't it?"

"I don't think we need these incompetent and overpaid UN bureaucrats running the planet," John mumbles, sipping his drink.

"The point is not what exists now—this is the hollow shell of a true international regime—but rather what could be."

"So, enlighten me, Gabriel," John rejoins. "What *could be*?"

"We are still at an early stage in our evolution as a species. We are nationalistic, which is just another way of saying 'tribal,' and lack consciousness of suffering in other parts of the planet. We can't yet extend our sense of love beyond our immediate families and friends to the whole earth and her people. We lack empathy."

"Easy does it there! You're definitely losing me now," John says.

"Okay . . . In more concrete terms: Sovereignty needs to be redefined. Predatory regimes like Taylor's exploit the concept to say that because they are a *sovereign* nation they can do *anything* they wish within their own boundaries—destroy rainforests, draft ten-year-olds into combat, hack off infants' arms to control diamond fields. Only a *strong international government* can ensure international human and ecological rights."

Gabriel pauses, and I look over into John's mischievous eyes, his mouth hiding behind his drink. He appears ready to pounce but does not. Gabriel continues, "It's not just authoritarian leaders like Taylor who are violating basic human and ecological rights. We need to look at the other side of the coin: our bubbles in the first world."

John raises an eyebrow.

"It's a metaphor," I jump in. "We drag huge bubbles of all that we consume. OTC's timber and Colonel Bloodshed's diamonds are in our bubbles, so in a direct sense we support Taylor."

"Exactly," Gabriel says. "But as we become conscious of our own role in all of this, we will begin to demand a strong yet caring world government that can truly regulate cross-boundary issues like logging, weapons, and diamond trading. These issues go way beyond what sovereign nations can control on their own."

John shakes his head and drains his Scotch. "You know, you're right, Gabriel. There *is* suddenly going to be a world government based on love! Let's recite mantras together and drop some acid."

"It's a long-term process," Gabriel says, "but we have to begin. I feel like a good place to start is with our inner lives, to see ourselves as loving and loved creatures with the power to realize powerful changes in our institutions. A small circle of conscious individuals around the world can make a huge difference."

"I've had enough," John says, slamming down his drink. "Check, please!"

"Maybe we should switch topics?" Liza suggests.

"Sure," Gabriel says, "but I wonder why John has such strong emotional reactions to this."

"Because this is a load of horseshit!" exclaims John. "People like Taylor are the crooks who need to be brought to their knees. We Americans with our so-called bubbles aren't the crooks! Consumption is a good thing. It fuels the economy and improves our quality of life. I only wish Africans could enjoy our standard of living someday—good highways, rationally managed forests, excellent universities, shopping malls. A kick-ass economy will really change things."

John had had a few drinks before we arrived. His glasses are crooked on his face. "What are you staring at? I'm trying to bring things down-to-earth! I'm tired of ivory tower intellectuals spewing crap."

"I was born and raised on this coast," Gabriel said, "and I work in refugee camps. Is that the ivory tower?"

CHAPTER 27

FRED AND MINNIE are dead.

The two guinea pigs lie in a shoebox-size coffin on the floor of my kayak. I row hard and steady as a drizzle comes down on my head. A lot has happened in the past three months since the argument between John and Gabriel in the UN restaurant.

Low-level tension flared into all-out fighting along the Guinean border. It had seemed the economy could get no worse, but it did. Ciatta remained out of work and moved out of her apartment and in with an aunt to save the little money she had. Then something even graver happened: The military forcibly enlisted her twin brother, Jackolie, and took him to the front.

I had seen him a few days before. He stopped by my house, where Ciatta and I were engrossed in a video. Jackolie's knee moved rapidly and his eyes were shifty as he said, "I need some money."

I looked at him and then over at Ciatta, who avoided my glance and stared at the television. Her brother continued, "You know I got that electronics repair shop, right? But business bad-o. Hard times. They are going to evict me tomorrow if I don't have the money. Hey, man! If I on the street, looking for job, the ATU will get me and take me to the front!"

I was so used to people asking for money that I had become callous. And I had already told Ciatta that I could not be responsible for her entire family. "What will happen when I leave?" I'd asked. For the same reason, I did not lend Ciatta money, and she, possessing a strong pride and individualist streak, never asked.

I paused a long moment and looked at the TV and then back at Jackolie, who was twitching all over. I finally told him that I really sympathized with him but that I couldn't lend him money right now. Ciatta backed me up. "Hey, Jackolie, you'll be all right. Why don't you look for a loan somewhere else and not always be embarrassing Bill?"

When he was taken to the front, I felt responsible and questioned my orthodox approach to eliminating dependency. It would have been so easy to help him. Ciatta reacted by retreating inside herself. She didn't visit me as often, and when she did the previous ease of our relationship, the way we clicked so well as lovers and as friends, had diminished. When she did come by, she seemed distant and numb. Some nights she roamed the streets or just sat on the steps of a bullet-scarred Monrovia building, staring at the sidewalk. I tried everything to comfort her—making her dinner, taking her to the beach, helping her improve the presentation of her résumé, and connecting her with some colleagues in other NGOs who might have jobs—but she hardly responded. She played along with all of this but was only going through the motions. She knew Jackolie was in enormous danger, if indeed he was still alive.

During these months, Gabriel temporarily vanished from my life, spending all of his time either at his far-flung project sites or with his girlfriend, Liza, in Europe. Liza had secretly filmed OTC's illegal logging practices and smuggled out the footage to where it was now being shown at progressive discussion groups in several European countries.

Luckily, moments of lightness punctuated these difficult months, such as the Saturday afternoon when my American colleague Susan said to me: "We're going to the movies."

I eyed her skeptically. I knew only of the Logantown Cinema Ruin, which now appeared under that very name on a recent map of Monrovia. But sure enough, downtown on Broad Street, a former movie theater had been restored to basic functionality. As we flopped onto lumpy seats, Susan exclaimed, "Isn't this great!" Mildew blanketed the walls of the dank theater, which until recently had been home to hundreds of refugees. However, by the time someone pressed PLAY on the VCR and the video image was projected onto about a third of the original screen, I fully shared Susan's excitement. The place was packed with Monrovians thrilled to see Richard Gere, Julia Roberts, and Joan Cusack in *Runaway Bride*. Comments flew from all directions. Laughter kept exploding at moments certainly unforeseen by the film's makers. A bearded man directly next to me repeatedly piped out: "Fine girl gonna run *away*!"

On another occasion, my secretary stuck her head into my office and said, "TURD is here to see you."

"Turd?" I answered vaguely, my mind wrapped up in a proposal. I focused in on her face, which was surprisingly free of irony. She walked over and handed me a letter with the letterhead "TURD: Technocrats United for Reconstruction and Development." In it they had requested a meeting with me, and, yes, I had scribbled to my secretary to set something up.

Two men in cheap suits strode in. We shook hands—with clean snap finishes—and sat down, they on the sofa and I in an armchair. I studied them, and they me. I'd been in Liberia long enough to know what was going on. They were a completely bogus NGO. As unemployment shot up above 80 percent, everyone had been rushing to set them up, particularly current or former government bureaucrats, like these guys sitting in front of me. Some called them GINGOs, or government-initiated nongovernmental organizations.

I asked them what TURD did. One of the men straightened his tie and rattled off a laundry list: health, education, agriculture, environment, food security, peace, and justice.

"But what is your specialty?" I asked.

"What are you funding?" he replied.

I smiled, and a slow smile spread in unison on their faces. Perhaps they discerned right from the snap handshake that they weren't going to have any luck with me. The only reason I had not marked an A, B, or C at the top of their request (shorthand for which generic rejection letter to mail) was that I was intrigued by their name. It was right up there with another fake NGO that had contacted me that week: BAG (Breastfeeding Awareness Group). I asked him why they called themselves technocrats.

"We're technical people," he replied. "Not politicians."

"Technicians of what sort?"

"You name it."

Beyond these lighthearted moments, I found myself increasingly absorbed in fieldwork during these months, particularly in Chief Wah's Vanjahtown outside of Greenville. The program there had made a 180-degree turn. Gone were the massive monthly donations of food to Wah's community. In their place, better food production systems were taking root. His swamp rice paddies had produced more rice than the community had ever seen, and they had not only enough to eat, but a surplus to sell in Greenville. His lowland rice paddies were bordered by agroforestry systems, pigs and chickens, peanuts, and fishponds recently stocked with tilapia fingerlings. Wah's sense of pride increased along with his purchasing power.

These successes rested on a delicate give-and-take between Wah and me. During my visits, we examined why the swamp rice initially failed to take root in his community. It finally occurred to him what was missing: music! Swamp rice was a new innovation that did not yet have its own song. Vanjahtown moved to music. "Talking drums" (drums that communicated messages from one village to the next) often accompanied me to sleep, and I awoke to the pounding of cassava. Women beat out a tempo unique to Vanjahtown, as did their counterparts in neighboring villages. Harvest songs, often accompanied by the pulse of drums, marked each crop and season—except for swamp rice.

The epiphany came to Wah one night during a community meeting. We had been discussing the benefits of swamp rice—it increased yields; it reduced deforestation; it lessened labor after the water control system was in place—when Wah suddenly jumped up and shouted, "What will be the song?" The ensuing debate was lively. They couldn't use the same song as upland rice! Before long, someone just started singing, a beautiful Sapo-language tune that rose and fell, and the rest joined in, the swamp rice song filling the palava hut. We all rose and continued singing and clapping as we marched together through the village.

The next morning a dozen villagers were up to their knees in the swamp, pressing the fresh seedlings into the mud as they sang the new song.

The community forest also took shape through listening and adapting. For hours, Wah led me through the jungle, harvesting plants beneficial for medicines and teas, as well as wild fruits and vegetables. We lugged these samples back to Vanjahtown and inventoried them for use as part of the legal justification for conserving the community forest.

The things that failed were those I stubbornly tried to impose, such as guinea pigs. Even though the community had elected pigs, rabbits, and cane rats as the animals they wanted to raise, I insisted that Wah try guinea pigs. I exclaimed eagerly, "Everyone will love them!"

A number of visits to Greenville later, I saw that the guinea pigs were gone, to which the barely five-foot-tall Wah shrugged and said, "I let them go into the forest!"

When I tried to protest, he piped up, "Guinea pig meat *small*!"

I am rowing out toward the horizon, Fred and Minnie in their balsa-wood coffin at my side. I'm going way out, farther from the shore than I've ever been, thinking of something my mom said when I was little: "Later in life, you'll remember this moment. You'll remember the joy you felt at the birth of precious new life. These guinea pigs are proof of God's life in our home."

When I got home from work today, I found Fred and Minnie stiff in their cage. They were curled up in the corner together, and they didn't stir to greet me as they usually did when I brought them their potato greens. Seeing them there, dead, I felt a sudden acceptance of something I'd felt for a while: I had no first world life to go back to. I had rowed out too far from shore. My engagement had unraveled; I had broken off with most of the expatriates in Liberia; and my family in the United States felt very distant, even foreign. My parents' idea of love had led me on the path to Liberia, but it no longer served, since their map was drawn when the world looked different. This map of the world was born in the urban ethnic neighborhoods of the East Coast, developed in the isolation of the clergy, came to fruition in the idealism of the 1960s, and reached maturity in the comfort of Long Island suburbia. Just as the maps of Liberia that I inherited from my predecessor, Amanda, changed dramatically with time, so too do the mental maps that help us understand the world.

To my mother, guinea pigs were a reflection of the loving God that had bestowed so much safety, comfort, and security on our Long Island home. The Fred and Minnie of my childhood lived long, healthy lives, filling dozens of suburban homes with their offspring; this Fred and Minnie died young, having borne only one offspring, which died at birth. The first Fred died on the Bible on Easter morning after a proud and heroic journey across our home; this Fred died of a nasty tropical disease, shriveled in the corner of a cage.

The world had changed. Globalization was breaking down the walls that separated human beings from one another. Global population growth and migration brought AIDS to our front door; a new age of terrorism brought foreign worldviews into our cities; tropical deforestation was contributing to global warming. Each year, it was becoming more difficult to ignore the third world's problems, because they increasingly came right to us.

I've finally reached a riptide. Just what I wanted. I pick up Fred and Minnie's coffin and launch it into the rip, which will pull it out into the deep Atlantic, back toward the New World from whence they came. With Fred and Minnie I promise to send away my ethnocentrism. I will no longer try to impose guinea pigs, or any of my preconceived notions, on Chief Wah or anyone else. If development is to be useful, it needs to come about through listening, not by speaking yet louder so that the other person will understand.

Floating away from the edge of Africa, I stretch my body flat in the kayak and look up at a cobalt blue sky with wispy white clouds. Water slaps against my boat, salty air fills my lungs, and I fall asleep.

A drizzle awakens me. I'm not sure how long I've been asleep, but the blue sky has turned overcast and the riptide has pulled me far from shore. I feel a tinge of fear as I plunge my paddle into the water.

It is a long, difficult row. After the first hour I am physically exhausted, and after the second I am about to give up. The drizzle had built to a rain, then slowed, and is now beating down harder once again. My arms ache and I think of letting myself just drift. Perhaps a boat will pick me up when the rain stops. But when lightning flashes behind me, I know I must keep going. As I approach the shore, I make out the shapes of people on the beach; and as I get closer, I see that it is a small crowd. Arms wave in my direction.

The waves carry me into the final stretch. Evans wades out into the water to meet me. He slides his strong arm under mine and guides the kayak up onto the beach. A circle forms around me: the Carolina Farm guards, Evans, Ciatta. Hands reach down to lift me out of the kayak and fold me into their circle. Ciatta is crying as she hugs me tightly against her.

CHAPTER 28

ONE OF CIATTA'S late night wanderings in Monrovia led her to the door of Home Sweet Home, a hospice for AIDS and tuberculosis patients. She recognized it as one of the centers she used to monitor when she worked for CRS and fell asleep on the front steps until one of the patients discovered her in the morning and offered her a bed.

"It was so beautiful," Ciatta tells me. "It was like they weren't judging me or asking me if I was sick, just offering me a bed!" She decided right there to dedicate herself to improving the lives of the patients.

Though Home Sweet Home is one of the centers in the CRS institutional feeding program, I've never been there, partly because it is among two hundred others. While I have cut many bogus centers (with so-called ghost beneficiaries on their rolls), this is one of the many that have fulfilled the basic criteria to remain on our lists. Social services such as health clinics and homes for people with mental retardation will always be to a certain extent "dependent" on outside help. I decide to pay an inspection visit to Home Sweet Home, hoping to run into Ciatta, who has been volunteering there nonstop for the past month.

Momo drives me. It's located in the slum called West Point, which took its name from a U.S. military base constructed there during World War II. The road penetrates only so far into West Point, and then Momo and I head off on footpaths lined with women crouched over piles of garlic and onions. We walk between the zinc-and-stick structures, through the swarms of flies, past dogs, the stink of meat gone bad. Ducking overhangs, circumventing naked children, and jumping puddles stocked with mosquito larvae, we finally reach the food storage house.

The CRS food shipment has arrived just an hour before. The fifty-pound bags of bulgur wheat are intact, but someone has tampered with the lentils. The employees on duty insist that the food arrived in that condition. I find the holes that the truck driver or casual laborers had poked in order to siphon off a few kilograms. I jot down a note to follow up on this. Inside the storage room, I observe that the tins of U.S. surplus vegetable oil are on pallets alongside the bulgur but that a crumbling roof and wall would allow moisture inside. "You got rat here?" I ask the Home Sweet Home employee.

"Bossman," he answers, "we try to stop rat-o! We use kill-rat and we use trap. But *everyone* here got rat, and they don't stop their rat. Rat still come."

At the Home Sweet Home main facility, dozens of children press against me. One little boy strokes my exotic blond arm hair. (I have a rule while working: The right hand is dedicated to shaking the inevitable dozens of clammy hands, while the left is reserved for scratching my forehead and such. Adorable as the children are, their hands are disease vectors.) Beyond the bustling crowd of children, I see Ciatta. Dressed in a flowing white cotton dress, she stands before a rainbow-colored sign proclaiming HOME SWEET HOME. She is striking, her flowing braids and dark skin assuming a deep glow, straight white teeth set in a broad smile. I wade through the crowd of children toward her, feeling an overwhelming attraction.

Inside, Ciatta and four Home Sweet Home employees explain that the center assists seriously ill people, providing a roof to sleep under and transportation to clinics. The cramped rooms smell of urine, and a coat of mold covers the walls.

"Ya got AIDS patients here?" Momo asks Ciatta.

"We had four AIDS patients when I got here a month ago, but they are dead now," she answers. "Right now we have two confirmed cases out of the twenty patients here. Others may have it as well. We also have six who are quarantined over at the TB center in Congotown."

As we walk from one cramped room to the next, the sounds of pots banging and rough talk come through the windows. A sense of discomposure gnaws at my insides, though I have seen worse. My anxiety arises from the sensation that *I too can be exposed.* Transported into the Dark Ages, I am some kind of well-dressed physician or merchant among black plague patients.

We walk into one bedroom where a man wasted away to skin and bones lies on the bottom bunk; two other men lie practically lifeless on other mattresses. "Those two got stroke," an attendant explains. "They can't walk." I ask if Home Sweet Home could provide physical therapy for these men or at least have a wheelchair to roll them out into the sun. The attendant replies that there is no money.

Ciatta jumps in: "We working on that! I wrote a proposal for funding, and I'm looking for more volunteers."

As we are leaving Home Sweet Home, I spot one of the hand-sketched posters CRS had printed as part of an AIDS awareness campaign. One poster shows a young, attractive countrywoman with a jug of water on her head pushing away a suitor as she says, "Nooo, don't bring it to me-o! AIDS *kills.*" A bulletin board with photos hangs beside the poster. One is of a gaunt man with all of his ribs standing at attention. "That Roger from Ghana. He lived here with us. Roger, he died of AIDS," an attendant explains.

In front of the rainbow-colored HOME SWEET HOME sign, I kiss Ciatta good-bye. Momo shakes her hand. As we walk away, I glance back over the crowd of children gathering around us, and Ciatta is still there, her posture straight, a white dress blowing in the breeze.

Ciatta is staying at my place, trying to recover from typhoid. She insists on going to work at Home Sweet Home anyway, to continue working, and it takes an hour to convince her to stay put. "Where do you think you got typhoid? It's from those West Point mosquitoes."

"But what about my patients? Who's going to make sure Mrs. Togba takes her medicine? Who will change her diaper?"

"Look, I know you love your work, and I promise you can go back in a few days. But you must rest."

When I come home from work one evening, she is curled up on my sofa watching TV.

"How are you feeling?" I ask.

"Ooohh, she such a fine actor!" Ciatta replies, too engrossed in a Nigerian soap opera for a proper greeting.

I put down my briefcase and slump into a chair. The Nigerian program centers on an upper-class Lagos family embroiled in conflict. At one point, a thick-necked father blurts into the phone: "What do you mean, you are not coming home? You are my daughter! You must come back now!" Growing mildly annoyed with both the program and Ciatta's lack of company, I mope into the kitchen and return with a sandwich. I ask her if we could switch to a program we *both* like. Grudgingly she switches channels to a movie about the Nuremberg trials. "I like this one! They always showing it."

I quickly understand why this film is so popular in Liberia; it's about retribution. The Nazi leaders had committed war crimes and would now pay. Some of the Nazi bossmen come to acknowledge their sins, whereas others, led by a sinister Goebbels, hold out until their hanging at the film's end. One particular moment lingers with me. A Jewish psychiatrist who has been analyzing the Nazi leaders observes that the one thing they all had in common was "an inability to feel empathy for their fellow man."

That quote stimulates a discussion with Ciatta later that evening. We laze together on my couch, talking. "I've got another dream," she says. "I want to stop HIV-AIDS before it spreads here. You know that AIDS thing is crazy in other parts of Africa. How many thousands of Home Sweet Homes they got in Botswana? Hey, man, AIDS still less than five percent here in Liberia, so I want to get the international community interested in stopping it before it gets worse."

We spin out Ciatta's dream together. Sex education in every corner of the country! Family planning that gives women choices! I mention that this would not only slow HIV, but also control the unsustainable population growth that contributes to deforestation in Liberia. Ciatta talks about increasing education for girls, which in the long run gives women greater independence and tends to reduce the risk of AIDS. However, right in the middle of this fantasy I get the image of Home Sweet Home—those patients whose lives mean little to the rest of the world. So much depends upon our ability to feel empathy for our fellow human beings.

I'm lying on my back with my feet in Ciatta's lap, voicing these thoughts, when in the middle of a sentence she takes my big toe into her mouth and trims a piece of my toenail off with her teeth.

"What exactly are you doing?"

"Your nails are long! I'm giving you a manicure," she says, nibbling some more at the toenail and pulling off a sliver.

"You cut toenails with your teeth?"

"Relax, civilized man!" she says, getting up for her purse and fishing out a nail file. "Okay, here's your *Western* manicure."

She spends twenty minutes filing my toenails, while I switch the topic to her intention to enroll in the university to finish her engineering degree, which was interrupted during the war. "You might as well do it now while you are not working. You can still volunteer at Home Sweet Home in your free time. The tuition is on me, you know."

"Taylor closed the University of Liberia yesterday! It's right across from his presidential mansion, and he's worried that the rebels could use it to launch an attack."

"What about the Methodist university?"

"It's up-country. You think I going up near the rebels?" she says, finishing my toenails and standing up. "They already got my brother, and I'm not going to let them get me, too."

A graying older man picks up his saxophone and fumbles with the microphone at Kind of Blue. Ciatta and I are there one night along with a dozen or so others. Finally recovering from her typhoid, she is out for the first time in a long while. The old man says, "This tune is one I wrote myself. It's called 'Twisting Makes Stronger.'" He blows a few tune-up notes into his horn. "It's dedicated to all of us Liberians, and everyone else who is still all right after their pain."

The first note emerges long, melancholic, and clear. The note takes me back a few days to Momo's house and his baby son's funeral. The coffin was the size of a few shoeboxes stacked together. Ciatta, Evans, the Jacket, and dozens of others gathered around it as Momo said, "Until now I thought I could take anything, that nothing could really bring me down to the very bottom." His son had died of malaria or perhaps typhoid; the doctors weren't sure. "But when my little boy died, I couldn't believe it was true. How could it be-o? I want to go back to the hospital to ask the doctor some more questions . . ."

"Better not to go back there to that hospital and ask, Momo," one of his friends said, an older man from Lofa. "We can't ever go back."

The man shared a story from his village, which began, "Brothers and sisters, let me tell you about something that happened a *very* long time ago—before the freed slaves came, before the time of the tribal wars, back when people and animals could speak to each other." He spun out a tale of a python that increased his strength by twisting, just as a rope gets its strength from being woven together. The moral of the story was "Twisting makes stronger."

The saxophonist blows out the final notes of "Twisting Makes Stronger." There is a long pause before we all start clapping. A bassist and congo drummer join him in the front, and they start in on Coltrane's "A Love Supreme." Ciatta has her feet up on a chair. She holds out her cup of Spanish Merlot, and we clink our glasses together. Her toes move to the rhythm, and she closes her eyes and leans her head back slightly, as if to let the jazz wash all over her.

I lived in Santa Fe, New Mexico, for a time, and each year the entire town would pile into a plaza and burn a gigantic effigy of a person in a collective purging ritual. In a sense, I feel like that effigy. It's been a burning season for me. Nietzsche speaks of going through a thousand deaths and a thousand pangs of birth to reach a more authentic existence. In the ashes of my former self, a deeper happiness glows inside like a tiny ember left over from the fire. This happiness pulses with a deep baseline and rises with the highest saxophone riffs. A drumbeat steadies it, but it still moves free. That ember burns mildly, gnaws at me, and acts as a foretaste of *mitgefühl,* the beginnings of what I imagine to be oneness with all people and nature.

The musicians segue into Coltrane's "Ogunde." As they groove into this song, bongo drums are passed around and one is handed to me. I hold it and look at Ciatta. Her braids cascade all around her face and shoulders, tinged with streaks of light and dark blue against black, and I know that, like her hair, we are all kind of blue. We are not blue clay through and through, but the pepper is in us. Life is a struggle to take the pepper out one grain a day.

My hands almost unconsciously start to work over the drum's skin, to move along with "Ogunde." In a dark city of a million people, in candlelit Kind of Blue, I'm playing a drum and saying a vague prayer to no one in particular.

PART IV
Warring Season

A Garden of Trees

We may never, this side of death, drive the invader out of our territory, but we must be in the Resistance, not the Vichy government. And this, so far as I can yet see, must be begun again every day.

—C. S. Lewis, "A Slip of the Tongue"

CHAPTER 29

WHEN MOMO AND I arrive at Chief Wah's farm, I jump down from the Jeep and immediately spot the tiny man among a crowd of villagers, reporters, and other NGO officials and technicians. "Mr. Power!" he exclaims as we shake hands. Wah wears a miniature gap-toothed smile, and his tattered T-shirt announces, IT'S HARD TO BE HUMBLE WHEN YOU'RE FROM PIGEON FORGE, TN.

He leads two dozen of us down a windy dirt path, and when we round a grove of fruit trees, the panorama of his farm opens up. Dozens of paddies thick with kelly green rice shoots are interspersed with rectangular fish ponds. Fruit trees and ground crops form an agroforestry system on the gently sloping banks of the rice paddies. Beyond are rubber trees and then towering rainforest.

"Welcome to my farm!" he exclaims, halting the group midpath. He explains in a lucidity that surprises me and the journalists that he is not doing the usual slash-and-burn anymore. With help from CRS he has created a small farming system that mixes food production with conservation.

We wind our way down the path past women and children bathing in a stream. At the first fishpond, Chief Wah pulls off a piece of rotting bark from a tree and displays it to the group. It is swarming with ants, dozens of which crawl up Wah's arm. "We feed the fish with what we find right here, like ants!" He jiggles the bark and a flurry of ants cascades into the water. The water ripples with fish lips as the tilapia suck up this feast. "The fish come to you like chickens!" Chief Wash says proudly. He then demonstrates the compost system he is using to fertilize the pond. "Compost help the algae grow, and the fish eat it . . . And now," Wah says, the group in rapt attention, "what you have all come so far to see . . . *Vanjahtown first fish harvest!*"

On cue, two teenage boys yank a rag from a bamboo pipe in the fishpond's corner, and water gushes into the main canal. We wait. And wait some more. It soon becomes obvious that it will take a long time for the pond to drain, so one of the journalists suggests a tour of the rest of his farm.

As we walk, a reporter asks Chief Wah if he still hunts. Wah answers that he has "plenty meat" now from the livestock and does not need to look for bushmeat. Another reporter takes me aside and asks how it's possible that a "humble man" like Chief Wah has created this small wonder of an ecological farm. "Education," I answer, explaining that he has received intensive training from both CRS and Gabriel's group for two years.

As the journalist scribbles away, I add, "Chief Wah is a risk taker. When his peanut crop failed, he learned from it and put in eggplant. Guinea pigs weren't accepted, but he diversified with other livestock. Now Wah is one of CRS's five 'master farmers' who provides training to others."

One of the teenage boys who had been draining the pond runs over to us, shouting, "No fish! Pond dry!!" We hustle after him to the now nearly drained fishpond.

Chaos takes hold. Phrases like "Pond dry!" and "Where da fish-o?" ring out among the villagers. But Chief Wah takes charge, shouting, "Save the fingerlings!" He jumps into the mud, scooping up some of the silvery tilapia fingerlings before they suffocate in the mud. A dozen other villagers follow. These tiny offspring of the last pond stocking are the precious stock for future ponds.

"*Fish!!*" someone yells, and sure enough, in the corner where the last of the water is draining out, all of the adult tilapia have gathered and are now flapping to the surface. Dozens of hands reach into the swarm of tilapia, throwing them into buckets or onto the bank. In the emotional chaos of the scene, hundreds of fingerlings suffocate in the mud, while countless tilapia have already escaped through the pipe into the creek. Inefficient as the process is, in the end the crowd hoists four buckets of palm-size tilapia over their heads and parades up to a grove of orange trees for the big sale.

Chief Wah cries out, "Here is our harvest!" waving his hand over the buckets of what to me are miserably small fish. "And now get ready for big sale! Twenty Liberian dollars a pound!" Teenage boys scoop up handfuls of still flapping fish into a scale.

A local government official steps up with eighty liberty, shouting, "Four pounds!"

"Four pounds!" Chief Wah yells joyfully, removing a few fish from the scale and filling the bag. I cry out, "Five pounds!" and he shouts back, "Five pounds for Mr. Power!" and fills a bag for me. Remarkably, there are enough fish to go around, with all of the guests and journalists buying some.

As we head back to our vehicles, I steal one last glance at Master Farmer Wah. His right hand fans a wad of red-and-green liberty bills—his Christmas. In his left hand, he scoops up two cabbage heads, which he gives me, a tremendous warm smile enveloping his face.

*   *   *

The headline in the Monrovia daily paper the *News* is MASTER FARMER CHIEF WAH LAUNCHES FISHPOND HARVEST. Since a "foreign expert" was present, many of the photos also feature me. The article takes note of my speech after the harvest: "The whiteman, who kept smiling as he was speaking, stated that he was impressed by Master Farmer Chief Wah."

A tremendous lesson, perhaps the most important lesson of our time, which Gabriel and other Africans have taught me, is that there is a point called "enough." It is elusive, but it exists, and Chief Wah and many of Liberia's simplest people know where it is, even if they slip below it during the hungry season, during the warring season. Enough is food, water, clean air, and community. Enough is the rhythm of a talking drum under a moon that speaks to you through its light. Enough is listening to nature rather than dominating it. We in the West must relax and ratchet down to the joyful place called enough; many Liberians need to increase their well-being until we meet there, in a sustainable world.

Wah's fish are in my Monrovia sink, looking pitifully small. I finger through the five pounds of virtual minnows, trying to find one big enough to cook, when Evans joins me in the kitchen and puts down his dust mop. "Beautiful fish!" he exclaims. "I will make some palm butter with those fine fish-o!" I help him make the palm butter, and later we eat together. The delicious tilapia slides off the bones and fills us up, leaving plenty to spare.

CHAPTER 30

AFTER THE FISH harvest I return to Vanjahtown, grab a hoe, and jump into the swamp with Wah and a dozen others. We spend all day shoveling out a fishpond while singing a Sapo digging song. My fellow workers begin to call me Kolleh, which means "the brightest-skinned worker in the group." Each work group in Liberia has someone called Kolleh. When Wah tells me what the name means, I look down at my arm and am mildly startled. Having seen nothing but African friends for weeks (and without access to a mirror), I have unconsciously come to see myself as black as those around me. Growing up outside of New York City, I felt white; as an undergraduate at Brown University, I felt white. But in Liberia, despite being called "whiteman" half a dozen times each day, I have come to feel completely unself-conscious about skin color. This puzzles me until the reason hits me: Whiteman is not my race, but rather my tribe. The Kpelles are skilled farmers; the Mandingos are Muslim traders; the whitemen are a well-off tribe from across the sea.

So now that I have sweated in the rice paddies with the men of Vanjahtown, I am no longer Mr. Power, but simply Kolleh. After another day of work, I'm walking with Chief Wah through the Vanjahtown Community Forest, inspecting the baseline and transects that have been cut, and Wah says to me, "Kolleh."

"Hmm?"

"Kolleh, I know this is our forest. We use it for plant, animal, and to teach our children. But what will we do when OTC comes to take our log to their places?"

A sense of anger and helplessness builds up in me, and I have no answer.

I'm racing down the OTC Road between Buchanan and Greenville. Momo is at the wheel and Gabriel sits next to me in the backseat. Smoke enters the Jeep from cleared and burning swaths of Krahn-Bassa National Forest. The single settler family I saw last time has been joined by others. Several wood-and-hatch shacks stand where there had been only one. Children swarm around the houses while shirtless men hack at trees with their cutlasses.

"How can you love both humanity and nature?" Gabriel says, a tear forming in his eye. "Six billion of us walk the planet, and even conservative projections show a few billion more on the way. *We* are the problem."

I reflect for a moment and say, "I thought you were the one who told me it wasn't 'either-or.'"

"Liberia really tests all of your beliefs." He wipes the tear from his eye. I never imagined Gabriel crying. "The average Liberian family has six children, and the population of the country will *double* in fifteen years. Those people need lebensraum and will follow the logging roads into all corners of the Liberian rainforest."

"I never thought I'd hear you blaming the poor! I thought Western consumption was to blame."

"It's linked to *both* wealth and poverty. Wealth and over-consumption cause the logging roads to be built in protected areas. Poverty forces burgeoning populations into colonizing the roadsides. My friend, we need to take a hard look at the carrying capacity of our planet."

"So you're for sterilizing the world's poor?"

"Of course not. We need to give every single person on the planet information and the tools to plan their families. I mean, have you ever seen *any* family planning in Liberia? The world is just sitting back and letting the population double."

We slow at an OTC checkpoint. Soldiers in crisp uniforms hold AK-47s—OTC now has its own armed military faction, sanctioned by Charles Taylor to protect their mutual interest: taking down this last stand of primary rainforest. If communities like Chief Wah's Vanjahtown try to resist their entrance into their forests and Sapo Park, they will be killed.

I know I have to go into the park one last time.

"My wife . . ." Momo says, and then this thought disappears into the fire, where he roasts catfish. I stare into the fire and listen to the low call of the red colobus monkey. Eventually I get up, brush off the seat of my pants, and walk into the jungle alone, stopping along the crude trail to observe the fresh tracks of a red bush hog. Farther along the trail, a giant pangolin has scratched out a hole. A hornbill's throaty call echoes over the Sinoe River, whose distant rushing I can barely hear. The flashy colors of tropical birds break the tyranny of green and brown, their yellows, oranges, and reds like glitches in the rainforest matrix.

When I return to camp, Momo has already put some catfish on a plate for me, along with rice and beans. As I eat, lightning flashes in the distance. Between mouthfuls of catfish, Momo says again, "My wife," and nothing more.

I chew for a moment, looking at Momo's gray-stubbled

cheeks, his tall frame sitting on a log, crouched over his metal plate. The air thickens around us, lightning continues to illuminate the canopy above, and finally the rain comes. I crawl into my tent and sleep, waking up hours later with all of that water falling down through the trees onto the thin membrane of my tent, a wonderful sensation. Some moisture seeps in on the edges, so I pull my legs into a fetal position and drift back into sleep.

When I wake again, the rain has stopped and dawn is breaking. I unzip the tent, grab my towel, and head down to the canoe where Momo is waiting by the riverbank, dressed in the same clothes he has been wearing for the past three days, a navy-and-gray uniform that he has saved from his days as a lead park ranger before the war. We paddle upriver to Wiah Falls. As I soap up in the waterfall, dozens of Diana monkeys crash down from their beds in the high branches. A group of them attempts to cross the river by jumping from one side of the canopy to the other. A few fall short and drop into the river not twenty feet from us, swimming the rest of the way.

"My wife," Momo says. I am now air-drying on a rock beside him. Figuring this will be another aborted attempt to express a thought (and quite content with our mutual solitude over the past three days camping in Sapo Park), I stare off over the rush of water to the forest.

"Remember that ten U.S. you gave me last month?" he says. "M'weekend?"

We both smile, and I nod that I remember.

"That ten dollars paid my sixteen-year-old daughter's school fees for the whole semester. She would have been sitting down without it. Thanks."

"You're welcome."

"But she doesn't like me even though I give everything I

get to her. It never enough, because she holds me responsible for her mother . . . my first wife."

Time slips by. "Rebels took her up to the front in Nimba County years ago. I've never seen her again." He pauses for a moment. "I trusted a man with my wife's ID card. I gave him eight hundred U.S. dollars, everything I had, to go to the front to find her, but he never returned. I only wish I'd made a copy of that photo, the only one I had of her."

Again, just the rushing of the river for a long time, and then Momo says, "If I'd made a copy of that photo, my daughter would forgive me. She blames me for me being too weak to get her mother back. Now she'll never know what her ma looked like."

After a while I say, "Why don't you get under the falls?"

Momo strips off his dirty uniform down to his underwear, wades under the rushing water up to his knees. His dark skin sags, falls away from each joint, and the only hair on his body is on his head and stubbly cheeks. He gets all the way in the water and floats face to sky for a very long time.

We talk very little for the rest of that day and into the next, completely absorbed in the rainforest. I fall into a loose pattern: Walk in the forest; curl up in my tent; bathe in the waterfall; repeat. But mostly I just listen. My ears tilt forward into the holy aliveness of that jungle, past the buzz of a thousand insects, past the rustle of lacewood and makere, past the ibis cries, past the rushing waters, and toward the chimpanzees I want to encounter. I hold in my heart that first moment with those two primates: one black, the other almost ginger, their robust builds, long hands and fingers, expressive faces. Their long teeth flashed when they cried out, and I noticed that one had freckles!

But I see far fewer animals than I had on previous trips to the park, discovering them only through their shells, scat, tools, and diggings. Perhaps they sense the chain saws and fire, the cutting and burning, all around their sanctuary. Momo and I are like Ed Abbey and Ralph Newcome in *Desert Solitaire* when they rafted down a particular stretch of the Colorado River for the last time before they dammed Glen Canyon. Abbey writes:

> To grasp the nature of the crime that was committed imagine the Taj Mahal or Chartres Cathedral buried in mud until only the spires remain visible. With this difference: those man-made celebrations of human aspiration could conceivably be reconstructed while Glen Canyon was a living thing, irreplaceable, which can never be recovered through any human agency.

Decades after Abbey wrote this, the domestication of the planet's wilderness continues, reaching the most remote corners of the earth. The cry for conservation goes well beyond Abbey's argument for the uniqueness of a given wild place. The canopy above my head, the Guinean humid forest, provides vital services to the entire planet, including regulating the hydrologic cycle and absorbing the carbon dioxide that causes global warming. No human technology will provide these ecological services: Witness the $60 million spent on the Biosphere II experiment in Arizona, where a mere eight people could not survive for more than two years without the planet's basic ecosystem services.

Cut this rainforest down for mahogany cabinets? The absurdity of it burns a hole right through me. This shimmering moment in millions of years of evolutionary history can be destroyed in weeks, loaded on ships, gone. Recall that this forest contains the highest concentration of mammals anywhere on earth and has perhaps thousands of unrecorded plant species, any of which could contain the cure for AIDS or cancer. *Cut it down.* Sometimes that which is the richest and most precious is also the most fragile. Rainforests are a delicate web of interconnection among the elements and a million living forms. Once the forest habitat goes, everything dies with it, including, in the long run, ourselves.

Cut it down. Momo's body slipped under the falls, and the river we were in split the canopy above into a pair of open lips. The forest absorbed the pain that Momo harbored over his missing wife, and when he came out of that water, he glowed. For beyond all of the economic reasons for conserving rainforest are aesthetic and spiritual reasons: We need wild nature to be fully human. And wilderness does not survive in minuscule fragments surrounded by cities and soybean plantations. It needs to stretch and breathe as we do.

So I'm sitting on the spongy soil under a centuries-old ironwood tree, wanting to put that next word down in a long letter to myself, but no words flow as I breathe in, breathe out.

CHAPTER 31

"WHERE DO THE chiefs sit?" asks the five-foot-tall Wah. "No special seat for chiefs today!" Gabriel exclaims, towering over Chief Wah as he ushers him into the circle of chairs with everyone else. The workshop is about to begin. First comes two solid hours of introduction. I lead a generic "hopes and fears for the workshop" exercise in small groups. All four groups come up with nearly identical fears: "no transportation home after the workshop," "no food," and "no sitting fees." Hopes include "transportation home," "food," and "sitting fees."

These are vulnerable people (unsalaried teachers, park guards and village chiefs), and their primary concerns are how they will fill their bellies and make it back to their villages. Gabriel assures the group that, yes, there will be food and transportation home and then hands off to me the more difficult issue of sitting fees. I stand up and clear my throat, saying, "This workshop is a learning experience for you! CRS will pay your food, your transportation, and your lodging in Greenville, but *no sitting fees-o!* Let me ask you . . . your children get paid to go to school?"

"Nooo!" the group answers.

"Eh-heh! You brush the teacher's farm to pay him?"

The group agrees that this is how it works.

"Fine!" I say. "This workshop is like school. CRS will not pay you to go to school!"

The next two days flow effortlessly, since Dickson and CRS's education, conservation, and agriculture field officers lead the training. Through interactive games and field exercises, the chiefs, teachers, and park guards learn about environmental education and agroforestry. Gabriel and I begin to feel a bit useless since the CRS staff run the show. I have accomplished a personal goal: to work my way out of a job through training my staff well.

Our programs look different; "tough love" has become our rule of thumb. Instead of doling out free bulgur wheat *weekends* and corn-soy blend *Saturdays*, we emphasize empowerment through participatory approaches. Now instructors who teach that France is the capital of Paris do not participate in the food-for-work program until they receive basic training. Unsustainable food-for-work agriculture has been replaced by integrated systems such as Wah's, where local knowledge is combined with improved, sustainable practices like agroforestry and live barriers.

It was nearly a year ago when I called our logistics officer on the radio as I was taught to do each month.

"Go ahead, Tibet One."

"Don't do it," I said.

"Done," he said, and then, after a pause, "Ahh . . . negative copy, please repeat your traffic."

"Do *not* do it. I am heading your way with some new lists."

I did an analysis and discovered ghost beneficiaries within the institutions we fed. For example, ten of the fourteen orphanages we fed were bogus. Children from the neighborhood were rounded up each month just before the shipment came and declared "orphans." Those ten orphanages were cut from the list.

Of course, everything is not perfect. Dependency has

decreased, but people still expect sitting fees for workshops. However, on the whole an atmosphere of risk taking and "ownership over one's own development" has taken root. Other budding Chief Wahs harvest their new fishponds, grow more rice, save labor and trees by using ecostoves, and feel some of the same pride I saw in Chief Wah at his big sale.

We have a final meal to close the workshop, and I'm sitting around a plastic table with Gabriel, Chief Wah, and some other farmers. Something is bothering Gabriel. "All the good work we've done," he says, "can be destroyed in a matter of days by OTC. They're getting closer to the community forests."

I tell Wah and the others what Gabriel and I saw on the way down: settlers following the new logging roads, and OTC's armed faction. "If the war breaks out," Gabriel says, "OTC will protect its operations through its own firepower and also act as a part of Taylor's army."

There is little we can do to protect the community forests or the park when push comes to shove. Wah puts it his own way: "Ol'Pa Taylor . . . he the law."

That night I'm outside Mississippi Street Blues, looking up at the Greenville sky. Fine points of light prick the coal black dome above. Electicity is not to be found for hundreds of miles in all directions, so there is no light pollution. I've never seen a more vivid sky. Looking up at it with me is a twenty-year-old meat seller from the Mississippi Street Blues, who seems to have a minor crush on me and has been following me around Greenville.

"Look!" I say to her.

"Enh?"

"Mississippi Street was laid out on a perfect north-south line! The Big Dipper and Polaris are over there at the tip of the street, and at the other end"—we pivot around—"is the Southern Cross!"

"The stars so clear, but it will rain tonight," she says, gazing toward the polestar, the direction of Sapo National Park. "It already raining in the bush."

"It the dry season! I'll bet you five liberty that it will not rain tonight."

"Money small!"

"Okay, ten, but you must pay me if it does not rain."

"All right," she says softly.

"But if it rain tiny-tiny, you don't win. It must rain with force!"

My call sign comes over the radio on my belt. Dickson says, "Tibet One, my whiskey has prepared some foxtrot. Over."

His *wife* has prepared some *food*. I have come to love Greenville because of this type of constant, unself-conscious generosity. Of the little there is, all is shared. I am invited every night for dinner in someone's home. But beyond this, in this isolated African town a supreme importance is assigned to the moment, to the now. Stripped of television, advertising, or anything else that tells you you're not good enough unless you have this widget or that doodad, the essential things surface: People gather to play drums and watch the sun go down; form circles to braid each other's hair for hours; exchange warm smiles and spontaneous greetings.

As I stroll along to Dickson's house, folks I recognize from my many trips to Greenville greet me. An older woman exclaims, "Hello, whiteman!" and I answer back, "Hello, ma', how'da body?" to which she replies, "Body fine-o!" Relaxing into a rattan chair on Dickson's porch, Theresa hands me a plastic bowl brimming with potato greens and boni fish. The four-year-old Palo eats from a smaller bowl and asks me with his mouth full, "You wanna speak dialect with me?"

Laughter spills out from all directions, and Theresa tells Palo that I do not speak Sapo. As we all eat, a lively argument erupts in the street, and little Palo says, "They makin' palava!" A big-chested woman yells down Mississippi Street, her hands gesticulating dramatically, "You mother rude! You father rude! *You* rude!"

I wake up late that night and stare at the mosquito net around me. My nightly sweat has dried, and I sense the salty residue on my body. I can hear the crash of waves and rustling of palm, but otherwise a delicious silence reigns. I untuck a corner of the mosquito net and slip under it into my flip-flops, crossing the wood floors to the bathroom, with its cobwebs and paint peeling off in giant swaths. The bitter-sweet scent of urine hits me even before I enter.

A mosquito floats by at head level as I duck back into the safety of my net. I survey the inside for these feathery malaria vectors, finding none. Mosquitoes in West Africa are so nimble that they are almost impossible to swat. My head rests again on my hard pillow, its moldy odor blending with the smell of mosquito repellent. All of this is good; I drift into sleep.

I awake to the lively banter of chickens. The faintest, gentlest light blesses the room. I get up and douse myself with cold pitchers of water, working my way up from my feet to my head, soaping and rinsing each section of my body in turn to avoid the shock of too much cold water at once. After getting dressed, I cross Greenville on foot as the morning light joins and spreads. Shops begin to open. I walk past wetlands alive with frogs, insects, and wading birds hunting among the rippling rice shoots. I pass the ruins of two abandoned gas stations with their antique Texaco and Shell signs still standing.

"Morning-o!" the security guard exclaims when I reach the office. It is still empty except for the office custodian, who has already boiled water for coffee and has laid out fresh bread from the Fullah shop.

I spend the morning with paperwork, and at lunchtime drums echo below. It's Levi Washington and his Greenville Show Artists Group! From the office balcony I watch drummers beat an intricate rhythm while colorfully costumed dancers perform acrobatics. A teenage boy flips his legs over his head and scurries around like a crab, winking up at me. The revitalization of this cultural troupe is something I initiated through CRS; they perform a medley of music and educational drama in a dozen villages around Greenville and the park.

A conservation-focused drama follows the dancing. "*What?!*" shouts one of the actors portraying a community member to another playing the role of a hunter. "You wan' shoot that deer? That meat is *zebra duiker*! You shoot that endangered meat and you arrested-o!"

When they finish, the Greenville performers bow and salute in my direction. Levi Washington shouts up through the applause, "Kolleh, that's just a piece of the pie!"

Still smiling back at my desk, I pick up a monitoring report. As I skim through it, a sentence leaps off the page. I bolt across the office and find the monitoring officer who wrote it. I ask, "Is it true?"

"For true."

As I silently pack up my belongings and move out of Dickson's house, he stands equally silently on the porch and watches me climb into the Jeep on Mississippi Street. Back at the CRS Greenville office, I place a foam mattress in the corner of a storage room; this will be my bedroom for now. It's noisy and lacks Dickson's ocean view, but I can no longer share space with him after receiving the news.

Dickson's first reaction is denial. No one sold CRS food! No one had used CRS trucks to ship supplies to the Freedom Gold mining camp! But after a series of meetings with drivers, monitoring and field officers, and security guards, people started pointing fingers at others and the cover-up unraveled. I call a general meeting of all Greenville staff and express my deep disappointment. "Look at all the progress we made. And then you steal food from schoolchildren to sell for your own profit?"

Dickson approaches me personally after the meeting in my office. He breaks down crying, saying he did not know about the trucks being rented to Freedom Gold. But he does finally admit to having personally sold bags of bulgur wheat to the principal of one of our schools. Two witnesses saw it, so he knows lying about this would be futile. "It was just a few bags! I so sorry for selling your food."

"It's not my food."

"I so sorry. I made a mistake and I will repent. It will never happen again! Please. I need this job. I am responsible for so many people . . . aunts, cousins, nephews . . ."

The hospital generator crashes that night and Greenville's few lights flicker out. CRS pays to share the hospital generator, but others have been illegally tapping into the wire, causing it to overload. I stare up from my mattress at the storage room ceiling. I light a candle and walk to the radio to call Monrovia.

"J and J, Tibet One; J and J, Tibet One."

Not surprisingly, the Jacket has his VHF on even late at night in his house. His voice emerges through the static: "Go ahead, One."

"Good to hear your voice, J and J. I request clearance to leave Greenville tomorrow at daybreak for your location. Over."

"Why are you changing plans, Tibet One? Over."

"It is necessary to return. Problems with staff. I can't say more over the radio. Over."

A long delay, and then: "Roger, One, you are cleared to return. J and J out."

CHAPTER 32

BACK IN MONROVIA, two hundred expatriates and Liberians pack Miami Beach for the Full Moon Feast. The moonlight and dozens of torches illuminate a decadent spread of food. Tables are draped with linen and topped with champagne. Fanti children look on from the fringes, their tiny bodies and faces barely visible.

Still feeling the sting of betrayal from my trip to Greenville, I want to lose myself in an evening of drinking. I also know the Jacket will be here, and need to talk to him about what happened. I find him drinking beer with a British engineer named Joe who works for the aid agency CONCERN and join them at their table. They are discussing Monrovia's hottest topic, the UN economic sanctions against Liberia, which kicked in the day before. "Cheers to the sanctions!" says Joe. "They don't affect us!"

Jacket clinks glasses with him and says, "You're wrong about that, Joe. You see all these people here? Half of them are ghosts, man. This is their big farewell bash! Everyone's reducing staff because of the budget cuts."

"I'm one of the ghosts! Next Tuesday and I'm out of this shithole. Longest three months of my life." He takes a sip of beer and continues, "Anyway, CONCERN isn't accomplishing shit here, so I'm changing the name of CONCERN to DGF."

"Hmm?"

"DGF: Don't Give a Fuck. Christ, every single Liberian you meet is trying to get out of here. Plus all the expats are angling for transfers. I haven't had a good night's sleep in ages with bloody rebels about to sack the place."

I ask the Jacket if we could speak in private, and he raises an eyebrow. I tell him it's important. We each pick up a bottle of Club and walk toward the crashing surf as I recount the details of the past week in Greenville: the whistle-blower, the cover-up, and the unraveling of a web of deceit.

"That's nothing," he says, taking a swig of his bottle. "Talk to Sheryl about her mosquito net program. One million mosquito nets were intended for free distribution by her NGO but her staff sold nine hundred thousand of them to traders on the Côte d'Ivoire border. Everyone was in on it, from the drivers up to the Liberian deputy director, and Sheryl was clueless."

"I trusted these people. Dickson—"

"How much of the food was stolen? Ten percent? Fifteen, maybe? That's the minimal cost of doing business here. You should pat yourself on the back for having traveled down to Greenville so much that you kept graft to that level. Think of it this way: Who are Liberians loyal to? *CRS?* Hell, no! They are loyal to their extended families that sleep on the hard ground because they can't afford a mattress."

The Jacket is right about loyalties. Dickson and the others in Greenville put the well-being of their families before that of CRS. Their children, wives, aunts, and uncles are their legs, arms, liver, and heart, and they will not let those vital organs fail, not when thousands of tons of food pass through their hands. Corruption and graft are sometimes a matter of survival in Africa. But it is more often about amassing power—take Charles Taylor and his cronies—and in any case, there is scant excuse for it. Every culture has its weaknesses, and the enormous corruption that plagues Liberia and much of Africa can be addressed only by Africans themselves. The cultural norm that says "Whatever I can get my hands on belongs to me and my tribe" is so deeply ingrained that it will take nothing less than a revolution of thought to root it out; but if it is not rooted out, no political order larger than the tribe will be legitimate, since such institutions are based on public trust.

We walk along the beach. The band has started playing at the Full Moon Feast above. The Jacket says, "No one knows this yet except John, but I'm leaving CRS in a month."

I stop, shocked. He continues, "There's money in the bush. I've signed a contract to sell chain saws and logging equipment with an international firm." He puts his hand on my shoulder. "Ninety-nine percent of species that have been on this planet are now extinct. The rainforests you see now, that you love so damn much, used to be desert, and before that they were a goddamn ocean. If OTC cuts them down, and I help them out with the equipment, we're just speeding along the process. The forests would have gone anyway."

I know the Jacket is trying to provoke me, but I just don't have the energy to respond. The Atlantic crashes to our left. I finally muster up a response: "When these rainforests were ocean, there weren't humans on the planet. If the rainforests go, they take us with them. They provide us with the oxygen we breathe."

"If there are no more forests to produce oxygen, we'll make a machine to do it. Or we'll colonize some other planet. And if not, so what? The universe would be better off without us."

I turn away from the Jacket and stare out over the waves, which are ablaze with moonlight. He continues, "The only thing I feel sure of, Bill, is evil. So I try to stay as close as possible to its source. The presence of evil makes me feel alive . . . CRS would transfer me sooner or later, and all of the good places to go—Rwanda, Burundi, most of the Congo—are landlocked. Liberia is hell with a beach. It's perfect. I've got my Liberian wives, and I'm settling here with them. Well, if things break loose in some other crazy paradise someday, maybe I'll hitch up the saddle and ride out of here."

"Like a good Surf Buddha. Never take a stand for anything, just *riiide*."

"Do you see me getting rich? Everything I earn gets shared with my wives and their families. Do you know how many damn mattresses I've bought them? Think of how many more mattresses I'll give people when I'm selling chain saws!" He's practically shouting now, blond hair swirling in the wind. "I mean, which Liberia have *you* been living in? Two years here and you still think you can change the world? The only thing you can do is spit back at the devil. All you can do is give mattresses. *Just give mattresses.*"

I've felt the force the Jacket is talking about. A tidal wave ripping through the rainforests, sparing nothing, drowning two million Liberians. They try to surface, they gasp for air, but the wave is not kind. I finally say, "Maybe you can't change the world. But I feel we have the choice to act *as if* we can."

The Jacket looks at me and opens his mouth as if to respond, but then he seems to change his mind. After a moment he says, "The war's as close as it's ever been. Reduce your vulnerability. It's coming, the war."

I was invited to the U.S. military attaché's apartment a few weeks back for a security briefing and buffet dinner for expatriates. His apartment stretched out like a sweeping lawn. My feet sank into the luxurious carpeting as I bit into a cracker smeared with caviar. Everyone tried to elbow closer to the military attaché, or at least to the marines. These were the people who might be able to save you.

"We're lucky to have thirteen thousand UNAMSIL soldiers just up the coast in Freetown," a UN security officer was telling a few marines as we waited in line for the buffet. He was referring to the United Nations Mission Sierra Leone peacekeeping force. "The evacuation window in Liberia is usually just three to six hours, so we're talking about a hunker-down scenario." I scanned the buffet: jollof, rice, potato greens, palm butter with seafood, sirloin, baked grouper, jumbo shrimp. "The window opens and bam! I'm in my armored Jeep combing Monrovia for corridors, avoiding hostile fire."

"You're just itching for this to happen, aren't you," said Bob, the marine who always called me "New York."

"No, but we have to be ready. In no time I can land boats full of Nigerian and Indian UNAMSIL troops right on Poo Poo Beach, securing a corridor to the airport."

"Sure, you *could* work with those piddly-assed Nigerian troops," another U.S. Marine said. "Or you could use the biggest war machine on earth. That's what we would do."

"Shit, yeah," said Bob. "Screw messy beach landings, we'll just helicopter our people out and kill any fucking rebel that tries to touch the embassy . . . You know, my biggest regret is that I'm shipping out of here in twenty-three days without having shot a single rebel."

"Hey, Bill," Jim said, pulling me away, "I got to show you something." Jim was the "administration officer" who I thought at one point was CIA until I realized that he must, indeed, be an "administration officer."

After passing a legion of security guards, we walked through a grove of trees to a shed. I followed Jim inside. A fantastic machine hummed away before us. "Desalinization! Epoxy-lined steel . . . That's the flash chamber. After seawater intake and brine discharge, we're left with pure drinking water for the whole embassy. Just installed this week. Heck, if we get cut off from the rest of Monrovia, we can make our own water!"

"How much did this thing cost?"

"Sorry, can't say."

"What, a hundred thousand?"

"More like two hundred grand!" he whispered.

He took me outside to where the tubing dropped off the cliff into the ocean as he explained more about the machine. "You know, we're not as spoiled as a lot of people think we are. We're sharing. We even donated a generator last week."

"You mean one of the thirty-two that you have for twenty people?"

"Yeah, well, it was one of the older ones."

"Who'd you give it to?"

"The American School."

"Is that what you call *sharing*, Jim? There is more wealth packed into this single embassy fortress than in the rest of Liberia combined. Are you actually proud of donating one measly generator to a school that serves the elite?"

"What are you, some kind of Commie?"

"Look, I'd better get back home. I've got work to do."

"Whoa . . . easy does it. I know what you mean. Look. I've got some stacks of *National Geographic* in my house. I was thinking my wife could send them over in the diplomatic pouch, you know, and you distribute them to the poor."

"That's a start, Jim, but it's going to take more than that."

"Like what? I want to do something, but I just don't have any idea what sometimes."

I could write him off, I thought. *I could write off everyone at the embassy, write off the other expatriates, write off myself.* In that moment, the ocean crashing below us, I realized that every moment was a choice of how we see people. Are we made of blue clay? If we are hardwired to overpopulate the planet, destroy the environment, and make war, then indeed the enterprise of development aid, as well as our individual actions, makes no difference. We might as well just ride the wave.

I looked at Jim. A pudgy guy from Idaho, he had never ventured beyond Monrovia in his two years in Liberia and had hardly even left the embassy. I opened my mouth, then closed it, looking at Jim some more. I finally said, "What about volunteering at Home Sweet Home? It's a center for AIDS patients near here that's short staffed. Or you could volunteer at one of the youth rehab centers, teaching former child soldiers literacy."

"AIDS? Yikes, don't think so, buddy . . . But maybe the teaching."

"Can you start tomorrow?"

He paused and said, "Give me the time and place. I'll do it."

CHAPTER 33

"TIBET ONE. THE Jacket on the radio!" Momo says. I pass Momo and climb the half-dozen steps into the CRS Buchanan radio room. "This is Tibet One, go ahead with your traffic."

"One, One, J and J. We're now on level five security. Repeat, level five."

"The highest level?! What's happened?"

"Coins in the streets in Monrovia. Logs are rolling. J and J, out."

Coins? Logs? "Where's the security manual?"

Boimah jogs over with a copy, and I flip through to the part listing radio codes. Coins are bullets, and logs rolling means that bodies are down. Level five is *Hunker down*: Unsafe to evacuate the area.

"Kebeh and Amos are in the field."

"Please make sure that your staff movement chart is accurate. And radio Kebeh, Amos, and any others in the field to hunker down in their present loc until further notice."

The next half hour lasts an eternity. Boimah and I pace back and forth. I finally radio Monrovia, "Tibet J and J, Tibet J and J, Tibet One."

Static, no response.

"Tibet J and J, *J and J.* This is Tibet One. Do you copy?"

Still nothing. "Boimah, they're not even manning the radio! We need to do something!"

"What?"

"Tibet J and J, Tibet J and J, do you *copy*?" I try one last time and then ask Boimah, "Wouldn't the UN have information?"

Boimah, Momo, and I bolt to the Jeep and motor across Buchanan to the local UN outstation, which is surrounded by a dozen immaculately clean Land Cruisers. I take the steps two at a time into the reception area and ask to speak to the director.

"And you are?"

"Prime Minister Jorn Heigelmesiter of Norway."

"One moment, please."

The receptionist sticks her head into an office and then ushers us inside. A large African man sits behind a desk, oddly, for Buchanan, in a business suit. I question him about the situation.

"Yes, there have been some unpleasantries." He has a francophone accent.

"What is the latest?"

"Allow me," he says, making a production of getting up and walking over to pick up the receiver of one of two satellite phones. He places the call to Monrovia, speaking in French in calm tones, and then hangs up. He walks back across the office and sits again with a small flourish, wiping a speck of dust from his blotter.

"And?"

"Ah yes, *oui, oui*. Not to worry, my colleague. Everything has stabilized and you are clear to proceed to the capital."

He lacks the authority to clear me, but I let it go and ask, "What happened?"

"There was a firefight downtown. It was more of a criminal nature than military." He leans back in his chair and adds, "Though in Leeberia, the two are the same."

"How could you leave the radio unattended for a half hour after issuing level five!? Do you know how stressful it was down there in Buchanan? For all we knew, it was all-out war." I am outraged. Not only did the Jacket leave us in the dark, but when we finally reestablished radio contact, he ordered me back to Monrovia.

The Jacket shrugs and says, "By the way, you are being moved out of Carolina Farm."

"To *where*?"

"To an apartment smack in front of the U.S. embassy. I felt *your person* would be safer in that location since we can piggyback off embassy security."

I am further informed that I have seventy-two hours to pack; in the meantime, I am to be assigned a personal bodyguard. Though I do not want to leave Carolina Farm, I understand why the Jacket is moving me. Along with the firefights breaking out downtown, CRS itself was threatened by a major lawsuit.

When the war burst into Monrovia a few years back, CRS's hundreds of employees scattered, many to Côte d'Ivoire. One group of former Buchanan office staff returned two full years later from an Ivorian refugee camp and demanded two years of back pay. Their lawyer explained that they were owed salary because they never received severance letters. CRS claimed that it was impossible to give severance letters to employees fleeing a sudden flare-up of war. Their lawyer responded by saying that he had the president of the Liberian Senate on his side. The lawsuit against CRS

was in the hundreds of thousands of dollars, and this sena-
tor drooled over the thought of a large cut.

The week before, three CRS national staff were held hostage
in the minister of justice's office. The minister demanded that
CRS pay the ex-employees their back pay. He too smelled
money. We were able to negotiate the release of our hostages
from the Ministry of Justice, but the harassment continued.
Government officials slipped into Carolina Farm almost daily
and knocked on my door, "politely requesting" the back pay
for the ex-employees. Then John received a death threat: We
had to move to someplace more secure.

My Carolina Farm house feels vacant when Evans leaves for
the night. He has packed all of my belongings into neatly
stacked boxes. The yellow kayak is half deflated to fit into
the Jeep the next day. I step out into the moonlight and to
the edge of the St. Paul. The palms swaying above me, I gaze
into the swirling eddies as waves crash against the sandbar
across the bay. I recall my first days in Carolina Farm: typing
letters to Jennifer in the evenings and dancing to Cat Stevens
each new morning. I allow my mind to drift as the water
rushes by, firm earth below, the moon above, and a wall of
succulent vegetation behind me . . . *Behind me?*

Behind me, someone is breathing. I whirl around to a flash
of white teeth and eyes.

"It me-o!" my personal bodyguard exclaims.

"Do you have to get so close!"

"Orders, bossman."

"Sorry, just a little more space. Okay?"

He backtracks, his eyes still glued to me, and slips behind
a palm tree, peeking out every now and then.

*   *   *

Ciatta and I explore my new apartment. While she goes into one of the bedrooms, I walk onto the back balcony and look over the ruins of downtown Monrovia. Refugees have occupied an abandoned building beside mine. Open fires light several rooms. The refugees are using the roof as a laundry and bathing area, and I spot a teenage girl lathering her naked body with soap.

Embarrassed at invading her privacy, I leave the balcony.

"Fifteen Liberian families could live in your apartment. Comfortably!" Ciatta says. "Have you seen the view?" She leads me onto the other balcony. The Atlantic Ocean rolls out before us. "I really think we are going to be happy here, honey."

"We?"

"I teasing-o. But anyway, I've been practically living with you at Carolina Farm."

I look away from Ciatta and down from the balcony. At second glance, there is more than sparkling sea. A field of trash lies directly below the apartment, cassava growing among the debris. Beyond the trash is Poo Poo Beach, and next to it the U.S. ambassador's walled-in mansion stands pure white, an American flag flapping above the rotunda driveway.

"I love you, baby," Ciatta says.

I look at Ciatta, and an unspoken message passes between us.

"Hey, relax!" she says. "You know I'm always telling my friends I love them. We always kissing and hugging and saying small-small things . . . like 'I love you.'"

Outside my new apartment a few days later, I hear someone calling, "Bossman!" I swivel around to see a guy in a wheel-chair. "Y'all right?"

"Tryin'," I say.

"You don't remember me?" I look at his broomstick legs, and it suddenly hits me that he is the beggar who came to Carolina Farm ages ago, asking to be my friend.

"Sure I remember you. But your wheelchair . . ."

"Yeah-o, it fine! Handicap International gave it to me. They teaching me computers, too."

We say good-bye and I continue along to Star Radio, where I am to meet up with Gabriel for a beer. "Hey, *mon*!" he says when I arrive, affecting a Rastafarian lilt. We sit down at a plastic table and order two Clubs.

After the waitress places the beer in front of us, he says in a low voice, "Liza's gone. She's on her way to London, slipped out last night. We feel it's for the best."

"Isn't that a bit abrupt?"

"Liberia's not safe for activists. Look what happened to Amos Sawyer's offices four days ago. Completely sacked by some of Taylor's goons. He's in the hospital nearly dead, they beat him up so badly."

I know what Gabriel is about to say. He looks down at his beer and back at me. "I'm leaving, too. You are one of the only people I am telling."

I study his face. The lines in his forehead etch deeper than when I met him nearly two years before, outside of Greenville. That day he towered above Boss Hog and the villagers, surrounded by a radiant glow. Now the glow has dulled. I finally ask, "When?"

"In the next couple of days I plan to slip out by land to Ghana. This is good-bye, my friend. Groups like Global Witness and Greenpeace are launching a major campaign exposing Liberia's 'conflict timber.' I can't be here when that happens."

"I don't want you to leave." Gabriel has been not only a mentor to me, but also a kind of touchstone. Even in the darkest hours, he was a living testament to our ability to live correctly.

"I'm leaving Liberia physically, but I'll still be with you here. I'll be waging the same war. Look, I'm not trying to discourage you. You've seen you can make some real progress with the communities. But what good is that progress if multinationals like OTC are licensed to take out their community forests? The Chief Wahs of the world are power-less against global market forces."

"OTC's getting closer to the park."

"That's why I'm going to Europe. You and I have been treating symptoms, but the disease is worldwide."

We finish our beer and stand to go. We are both silent for a long moment. My gaze finds its way down a back alley to a sliver of sea, and Gabriel pulls me into a hug.

"Will you e-mail me to let us know you've made it out safely?"

He says he will and vanishes around a corner.

CHAPTER 34

A FEW DAYS LATER, I break into a sweat, my body temperature surges, and my joints begin to ache.

"Malaria," Evans tells me. "You must rest small." I take time off from work and let Evans nurse me with cold towels and palm butter, but I leave most of the food he brings uneaten beside the bed. Waves of fever swell and subside, and mild hallucinations accompany both my sleeping and waking hours. The generator follows its schedule: on for an hour in the morning; off for three; on for the lunch hour; then off all afternoon; and finally on again in the evening. The air-conditioning in my bedroom cools me during these spurts of power.

After two days I find myself out of bed, staring at the abandoned building across the alley where refugees continue to bathe. I let my eyes linger a little too long on a lathered-up woman, and she spots me through my window and crouches to cover herself before disappearing down the stair-well. The roof bathing stops completely after that.

When I am finally strong enough to leave the apartment, I often find myself crossing the street to Poo Poo Beach and walking along the littered shore. At night, escape scenarios play out in my mind. In one dream I frantically paddle my yellow kayak into the ocean from Poo Poo Beach, bullets splitting the water in my wake. In another I slide like Spider-Man along a cord connecting my fourth-floor balcony to the

U.S. ambassador's flagpole across the way. Rebels fire at me as I cross but miss.

As the days slip by, I feel increasingly better. I sit on my balcony, staring across at the U.S. ambassador's mansion, and this somehow reassures me. At one point, the sound of an eerie voice below rises up along with the beeping taxis and cries of orange sellers: "The end is coming!" Then more babbling in a voice that ranges the octaves. I look down to see an old woman flailing a hatchet-size cross in front of her as she rants about the apocalypse. As this woman passes below, Evans comes out on the porch and hands me some receipts. "Please send these to your ol'ma. She has done things for me that even my own family cannot do."

I look at the receipts in my hand. Tuition for the electronics courses Evans was taking. I told my mother about Evans, and she sent the money for the course along with a rain jacket for Evans, which he now wears constantly, even in the dry season heat. Evans says, "She is my mother, too. May the Almighty God bless her."

I look out at the ambassador's mansion and am struck by loneliness. "Evans," I ask, "have you seen Ciatta?"

He says he hasn't but offers to look for her, then returns a few hours later with a shrug. No one has seen her for days. I take a cold bucket shower, get dressed, and head over to the office to get the Jeep and search for her.

At the office John sees me and asks, "How's the invalid?"

"A lot better," I reply. "You?"

"I'm tryin' small."

"*Trying?* Weren't you the one convincing everyone to say *succeeding?*"

"Not anymore. I tried small and failed huge. Anyway, I am out of here in nine days!"

"You have a job?"

"You kidding? I'm being freakin' *headhunted*. Four offers already. The economy is smoking over there, and I'm ready to get back in the private sector. But speaking of which, I've got interesting news for you . . . Baltimore called. They have an opening for you in La Paz, Bolivia."

"What?!"

"Look, you've been here two full years now. You've served your time. I say you grab this opportunity."

"Bolivia?" I say, trying to picture it on the South American map. "I don't know. I'm thinking seriously about extending for a year. There's still so much to do."

"Isn't that the truth. And if you stay here, you'll get a better promotion than if you go to Bolivia. One of the perks of a danger post: You can move up in the ranks wicked fast. But between you, me, and the wall, I'd get the hell out of here now before you're evacuated."

I stand there dumbly for a minute, trying to absorb this news. John continues, "You speak Spanish; doesn't La Paz mean *peace*? Bolivia's got McDonald's for sure, not to mention luxuries like electricity and running water."

Before we part, he tells me I have two weeks to decide.

A few hundred Liberians and expatriate NGO workers fill the long-since-evacuated French embassy for a huge farewell bash for Action Contre la Faim staff who are returning to France.

John finds me and says, "Two more days and I'm out of here."

"Not that you're counting."

"Nope. But, hey, have you decided yet? Taking that ticket to the Andes?"

"I'm still thinking about it."

"Well, you know my opinion on the matter . . . But hey, what do you say we play a round of Empathy for One's Fellow Man? Latest version: Find the Jew Hiders."

I roll my eyes back.

"Okay, it's like this. In Berlin in the 1930s, let's assume that some forty thousand Germans hid Jews. Sounds real noble until you do the math. Berlin had about four million people, so a measly one percent hid Jews! The other ninety-nine percent were presumably Nazis, collaborators, or pussies."

"Okay, so the game is to find the Jew hiders in this party."

"Exactly. There are, what, three hundred people here? So only *three* would have had the moral courage to hide Jews. You can pick only three out of this huge crowd."

We both scan the party. Dozens of couples dance and grind to a downbeat Ivorian song. John asks, "What about you? Would you have been a Jew hider or a Nazi?"

We'd all like to think we're among the most moral, but only one in a hundred was when the cards were down in Berlin. "Got one!" John says. "The new Handicap International bossman. He'd hide Jews."

The Monday after the big ACF party, Momo takes me to inspect projects east of Buchanan. Before leaving, I read an interview with Charles Taylor. What shocks me is this: Taylor sounds American.

When the journalist mentioned accusations about diamond smuggling, Taylor replied, "Where's the beef?" At another point Taylor quipped, "Whoa! Don't go there. Don't go down that road." When asked about the building tension in Liberia, Charles Taylor shook his head and said, "The way things are going, it's like somebody's out to get me."

It's like somebody's out to get me. The phrase echoes in my head as Momo drives under the rainforest canopy until the road widens and is flanked with cut and numbered tropical timber, ready for transport to the Buchanan port. We drive beyond the logs and see more settlers clearing what remains after OTC selects the most valuable logs. Machetes hack, the ground smokes. A makeshift wooden shack appears on the side of the road, and men are busy organizing goods for sale.

"Bushmeat," Momo says.

"Stop," I say, and Momo does. I get out and walk over to the shack, where I find carcasses of zebra duiker, a giant forest hog, pangolin, all fresh. A dozen dried colobus monkey bodies hang from racks before being shipped to the industrial logging camps to feed workers. There's a chimpanzee, too. The body is tossed facedown amid cut bush. I walk over and take hold of its long fingers and with two hands pull the chimp face-up, noticing its chest wound and the dried blood on its fur.

"Some people really love those baboons," a voice booms from behind me, one of the traders. "Other people say 'Get it away from my soup-o! Give you AIDS.'"

In shock, Momo and I get back into the Land Rover and pull away. I imagine long tables of OTC's Indonesian loggers and drivers gnawing bones, silently gnawing, and all you can hear is the chewing. Gnawing, eating, and building up the energy for the home stretch to Sapo National Park. I hear Charles Taylor's voice: *Don't go there. Don't go down that road.* My head swirls as we race along that road, the OTC Road toward Monrovia. Taylor's voice, a lilting echo of the antebellum South mixed with the colloquialisms of his years in New England. *The way things are going, it's like somebody's out to get me.*

I recently talked with a U.S. State Department adviser who swooped into Monrovia for a few days. "We need to tighten the vise on Taylor," he told me. "We need a regime change. He's Saddam. He's MAD—Milošević in Africa with Diamonds." *Where's the beef?* He's evil. Evil is always somewhere else, somewhere very far away, and every one of us thinks we are among the 1 percent who would hide Jews in Nazi Germany. *Somebody's out to get me.* We look in the mirror that is Taylor and we see . . . no, not ourselves, but the opposite of ourselves. We see evil.

Don't go there. Don't go down that road. The U.S. State Department official said to me, "*That man* must be removed from power. He's arming to the teeth." (The United States spends more than $300 billion on defense, making it the most heavily militarized nation on earth. Liberia's military does not have a single airplane.) The State Department official: "Taylor's getting rich off of timber and diamonds, while his own people go hungry." (U.S. consumers purchase half of the world's diamond jewelry; an estimated 10–15 percent of it during the 1990s came from African war zones.) There are certain kinds of interconnections we'd rather not face up to. Charles Taylor may not be made in America, but he's got several component parts. If we cease to consume what he's selling, he ceases to exist.

"Eliminate dependency," a large American aid agency said to me when I came to Liberia. This job description is a Zen koan. Like any good koan, the more you meditate on it, the more it unfolds like a lotus flower and makes sense: Eliminate *your own* dependency. Free yourself from dependency on overconsumption, from associating possessions with self-worth, from buying the stuff that fuels deforestation.

Momo steers through Liberia, a nation burning. He stares

straight ahead, his large hands gripping the wheel, and I look at his profile. A single round tear wells up in his eye (I don't think I've ever seen a tear that big), bumps down along his stubbly cheek, and falls. I trace his gaze down the road, through the smoke, and know Momo is thinking about the same thing I am: the destruction of Sapo National Park.

CHAPTER 35

I HAVE BEGUN TO think Ciatta has been kidnapped or worse when someone finally tips me off to her whereabouts. I drive the Jeep past a sign announcing entry into the Monrovia neighborhood of Congotown (Motto: Liberty, Justice, *Survival*) and then down increasingly narrower dirt roads that end at the bank of a swamp. Not five yards from the swamp stands a cinder-block home. A woman washes clothes in the muddy water and hangs them on the skeleton of what used to be a car.

I ask her, "You Sis Julia?"

She shakes her head.

"Where Sis Julia, ma'?"

She stares at me while wringing out a T-shirt and finally raises her head toward the house. I find Julia outside playing backgammon. I tell her I want to see Ciatta. She stands and enters a dark room, shutting the door behind her. Swatting mosquitoes as I wait, I wish I had brought my repellent. A thought enters my head: *Maybe she has another lover in there.*

Julia finally emerges and beckons me toward the door. It is pitch dark inside. My feet find their way a few steps across the dirt floor, and I make out a fading iridescent Jesus poster on the wall above a dresser covered with nail polish bottles, perfume, and some stuffed animals.

"Come."

I find my way to where Ciatta lies on a few blankets placed over straw on the earth floor. Ciatta leans over and lights a candle stuck in the ground. The light reveals the sea change in her body. The first thing I see is the thin arm lighting the candle, then her bony face, damp with sweat. Her hair has changed; where there were long blue braids is now a shock of matted and knotted hair.

"My God . . . What happened?"

"I'm sick."

"What is it?"

"Malaria."

"Just malaria?"

"Well, they saying it's in the brain."

My thoughts jumped to two expatriates (a priest in Harper and the Liberia director of Doctors of the World) who have recently died of cerebral malaria. It strikes and kills within hours.

"I'm taking you to a doctor."

"I've been to the hospital. Was there for a few days. They said I'm recovering and sent me back. But I feel like I'm dying, Bill."

I touch her hand, which feels like sticks in a rubber glove.

"Lie down next to me," she says, moving over. I untie my shoes, place them next to the blankets, and lie next to her. I feel as if we are sharing a coffin. I stroke and hold her hand, which doesn't respond to my touch. Mosquitoes buzz around our heads.

"You promised you would always use the mosquito net I gave you. Why do you think you got malaria?"

"I tried to put it up, but it kept falling."

"Well, I could have helped you put it up!"

"Anyway, it was so hot and damp under that damn thing."

We are silent for a long moment, and I hear the clicking of backgammon chips outside the door. "Look, I am very low. This country . . . I had so many dreams, but what happened? Everything in this place keeping me down. If this malaria doesn't kill me, the only thing left is to take my own life."

Ciatta's words hang in the air. I've never heard her talk like that before. I tell her in soothing tones that she has a lot to live for; that she is a beautiful person inside and out; that she has a loving daughter who counts on her; that so many friends, myself included, care deeply for her. She talks for a long time, her anxiety spilling out in disconnected images and stories: of the war, her childhood, her broken dreams of a better life. I listen, soaking up her thoughts like the sheets that soak up the sweat in that humid room. After a while, her taut frame loosens and she cuddles up against me.

"Why did you come to this swamp? It's full of mosquitoes. You don't even have a bed here. You know you could have stayed with me."

"I just didn't want to be bothered with anyone. I just wanted to be alone."

She is silent, and I lean over her, wipe some of the sweat from her brow, and look at her eyes, which are staring at the mud wall, following the trail of a beetle. I say, "You know, CRS offered me a transfer. To South America."

Silence.

"Well, anyway, I still haven't decided if I'll take it."

"Hmmpf."

"Listen, you've got to come with me right now to my apartment."

"I can take care of myself . . . I should probably sleep small." Backgammon chips clicking. Mosquitoes buzzing. "It pains me," she finally says, "because I really did fall in love with you."

I stare at the beetle clinging to the wall and listen to a single bird singing outside. As it pipes cheerily away, I ask myself what that bird could possibly be so happy about. "Ciatta, I—"

"Baby, just leave it there."

"Do you wish . . . we never met?"

I lie still for a long moment, waiting for an answer. The question stretches out and disperses into the evening. The candle flickers out, and the clicking of backgammon chips stops. I hold Ciatta, breathing in the earthy smell of her hair, like the forest after a rain.

"Do I wish we never met?" she finally repeats, as if in a dream. "I told you I love you. Isn't that answer enough?"

I think of the Jacket "going native," as he put it, taking on multiple Liberian wives, supporting dozens of their family members. Only on the most fragile edge can he self-actualize; only meters above hell can he spit in the devil's face. His choice is to wrap himself up tightly with a few dozen needy souls, sliding mattresses under them and spooning soup into their mouths. I know then that, for all his posturing, the Jacket lives according to a brave kind of love. I know also that I cannot love like that. Perhaps I just did not fall in love with Ciatta; but I wonder to what extent I did not *let* myself fall in love. As much as I care about her, I resist taking her life into mine, because along with her life come dozens of others: her daughter, Yeanue, her mother, her brother, cousins, aunts, uncles; along with her life comes an entire wounded nation, a crying forest, and streets full of children missing limbs.

Ciatta breathes in a slow rhythm, finally asleep. I rise up and go into the night alone, my first steps away from Liberia.

CHAPTER 36

F IFTY COLLEAGUES FROM Greenville, Gbarnga, Buchanan, and Monrovia gather under a palava hut for my
farewell ceremony. I am "gowned" with four brightly colored
West African suits, one of which is that of a paramount chief.
They dug deeply into their limited financial resources to
purchase these costly gifts for me, in order to make me feel
like one of their own.

The Greenville office presents me with an inlaid wood
portrayal of a map of Africa. An arrow labeled CRS points
to tiny Liberia. As I thank everyone for this beautiful gift, I
scan the crowd and cannot find Dickson. His absence hurts
almost as much as his betrayal. Before the food theft he was
a good friend. I struggled with what to do about him when
I returned from Greenville but did not have the heart to fire
him. I informed John about the incident, but it seemed to
slide into the cracks.

After the gowning ceremony, we walk over to Susan's
apartment for the big bash. As empty Club beer bottles fill
the kitchen, the dancing moves from the floor up onto the
tables. Momo busts out in a 1980-style robot dance, while
Boimah pelvic-thrusts Susan. The building's generator keeps
crashing, leaving us a half-dozen times in the dark and without music. No one minds; we continue to laugh and crack
jokes until the power kicks in ten minutes later. In one of
the blackouts, I accompany Momo out onto the balcony.

"Here's your weekend," I say, passing him an envelope of U.S. dollars.

"M'weekend done arrived!"

"For your daughter's week*days,* actually. It's a gift from my mother for her school fees. If she does well, my mother promises to help pay her way as far as she wants to go in her education."

The power comes back on, and my secretary grabs me away from Momo to dance. NGO budgets are being slashed, and an expat exodus has ensued. One of the few new additions to the NGO rolls is a Handicap International staffer. I have been itching to meet him ever since I saw the miracle performed on my friend with the two broomsticks for legs. When he comes into the party, I introduce myself to him. He has a mop of light brown hair and wears a kind expression as he talks about what his organization is doing: "We're providing crutches, wheelchairs, and synthetic limbs to Liberians with disabilities." His eyes shine with a serenity and energy. I cannot find a note of cynicism in his voice. "Oh, and by the way. Thank you for what you've done for Monrovia's disabled. I mean, who would have thought they could start taking down *the mountain*?"

It began a month ago. Coming out of Stop-N-Shop with my groceries, I was barraged by the usual group of former child soldiers asking for money. I reached into my pocket to hand one of them a five-liberty bill when the nagging thought struck me once again: *It's not sustainable. It encourages dependency.* I thought back to Gabriel's reaction and placed my groceries in the Jeep and began talking to them about their dreams. It felt awkward at first, since I lacked Gabriel's ease with them, but their stories began to entrance me and I soon found myself absorbed in the act of listening.

Driving back to my apartment through Waterside Market, I got out of the Jeep to switch into four-wheel-drive in order to cross *the mountain*. The trash hill had grown since I crossed it on my first day in Monrovia two years back. I thought of the diseases carried by all that trash, the malarial mosquitoes hatched in its bowels, the inconvenience it caused passing pedestrians, bicycles, and vehicles. About to switch into four-wheel-drive, I forged an odd connection: *Child soldiers take down the mountain*. Excited, I did a three-point turn and headed back to Stop-N-Shop.

Over the next few days, I convinced several Lebanese business owners to chip in a monthly contribution that Evans would collect each month. He would pay the ex–child soldiers each week to clean up Waterside Market and the areas around the Lebanese businesses. As the scheme began to show results, the Lebanese saw the benefits of not having their customers attacked by a gang of begging youth; the clean streets also improved their image. The teens now had a weekly stipend, which freed them up to participate in woodworking and mechanics courses in the evenings.

Before long they had taken down a decent chunk of *the mountain*, repeatedly filling a Lebanese-owned truck, each load carted away to a landfill outside of town.

Hope lies within the beautiful tyranny of free choice. We can act as if it were possible to achieve structural change. It is touching that Gabriel has returned to Europe to fight the consumerist root causes of Liberian rainforest destruction. Whether he is merely tilting at windmills Don Quixote style is of no concern; an amazing power lies in personally choosing not to let the invader into our own territory. Gabriel's attempting to convince France to change its consumption habits and vote for a UN embargo on Liberian timber exports reminds me of the Chinese student in Tiananmen Square standing in front of a giant tank; individuals speaking truth to power are inspiring.

We can also look at *the mountains* that exist in our communities, families, and inside of us and with creative passion take them down. While we may not be able to control France's penchant for trading tropical timber, we can choose to personally consume only certified wood. We can choose to consume "enough"; as Africans have shown me, enough is a close neighbor of happiness.

Water slaps against the edge of my kayak as I float offshore from Monrovia for the last time. It's almost midnight. Monrovia's few lights are sharp points against a black sky. I feel my kayak drifting out into the ocean and grasp the paddle. Each slice of Atlantic water is a choice. It is a choice to head back to the shore and struggle, awkwardly but nearly always with a grin, to affirm life in all its forms.

CHAPTER 37

"I HAVE A NEW dream," Ciatta says. She is still weak but has made it through the malaria and is helping me pack. I am to leave the next morning. I look over at her as she folds up one of my shirts and places it in a suitcase. She had shared dozens of dreams over the past two years, from starting up every imaginable business to eliminating AIDS in Liberia to forging a new life in Canada to finishing her engineering degree. All of her dreams proved unreachable.

"What are you dreaming about this time?"

"You won't laugh?"

I tell her I will not. She says: "I'm dreaming of owning a mattress."

We continue to pack in silence. My apartment is nearly empty, as I have given away many of my belongings to Evans, Momo, and Ciatta. I pick up my keys and say, "Let's leave the packing for now."

We drive across town in my Jeep Cherokee without speaking until we come to a warehouse near the Logantown Cinema Ruin. Inside, we find a dozen people cutting foam into full- and queen-size shapes, which they cover with cloth. Ciatta picks one out, and I pay for it while two men load the mattress into the back of the Jeep. We head across Monrovia toward the apartment she picked out; I paid her first six months' rent and security deposit.

We unload the mattress along with her boxes of my leftover

belongings, carrying them inside. The building consists of a single dark hallway lined with a dozen rooms. Each tenant occupies one of the rooms. Ciatta has number seven and shares a single bathroom with the others. The place has the institutional feel of an orphanage.

She opens the door to her room, which is spacious but lit only by a single tiny window. We prop the mattress against the wall since the cement floor needs a good sweeping.

"Are you sure this is enough?" I ask.

"It's more than enough. My own mattress, in my very own place. Thank you for helping me."

"The window is so tiny. It'll be dark."

Ciatta comes over and kisses me and says, "Our light is on the inside." She places one of my hands over her heart and then puts hers over my heart. "Hey, man! My blood is still pulsing through my body. I've got a job now. I'm just thanking God for all that I *do* have."

Before he left, Gabriel set up Ciatta with a job at the Sierra Leonean refugee camp. She helps refugee women reforest areas around the camp and construct ecostoves to cut down on wood consumption. I'm leaving for the airport in a few hours but drive out to the camp to see her one last time.

It's the same refugee camp I visited with Gabriel over a year ago. I park in front of the palava hut where he showed the films and once again am swarmed by tiny bodies whose clammy hands grasp for my hands or pet the hair on my arms. I shake hands with each child and talk to them all, asking about Jonathan, the little boy who had cried after the last film, the one Gabriel had touched and healed; no one knows who Jonathan is.

I spot Ciatta and wade through the crowd to her. Her

hands are covered with dirt, and a red bandanna holds back her one hundred braids. A dozen women and girls encircle her as she demonstrates the transfer of tree seedlings into the ground. She gingerly removes one from its plastic bag, adds a few handfuls of compost to the hole in front of her, and pushes dirt around it. The girls and women dig their own small holes and repeat the procedure.

She leaves the group to talk with me, covered in sweat and smiling. She says she wants to go to the airport with me, but I tell her that this is good-bye, that I want to see her for the last time like this, as a healer of people and nature. She laughs and grabs my hand, covering it with earth, and we walk over to the side of the Jeep and hug for a long moment, knowing it is the last time.

As I drive away from the camp, through the crowd of children, along the road that would lead me out of Liberia and eventually to the Amazon, to the front lines of another vanishing forest, I look in the rearview mirror and see Ciatta: the bright red bandanna, her T-shirt caked with dirt, the flash of her teeth in the sun. I feel a smile spread over my face and sense the presence of Gabriel sitting next to me. In this moment, I don't even know whether he's still alive, but I can sense him there, that strong jawbone and those intelligent eyes, and he's telling me that *just because something is impossible doesn't mean you shouldn't do it.*

POSTSCRIPT

> Like a tide it comes in,
> wave after wave of foliage and fruit
> the nurtured and the wild,
> out of the light to this shore.
> In its extravagance we shape
> the strenuous outline of enough.

> —Wendell Berry

THE AMAZONIAN RAINFOREST across the Paragua River glows as the sun sets in the village of Piso Firme (in English: "Firm Ground"), Bolivia. Freshwater dolphins snort in the water before me, while maned wolves, jaguars, and gamas roam Noel Kempff Mercado National Park just across the river. Beyond the park is the Brazilian state of Rondônia, where landless peasants and large cattle ranches have pushed right up to the park and threaten its eastern boundary. Satellite photos show a completely denuded Brazilian side and a forested Bolivian side, but this is misleading. Fresh waves of Bolivian settlers arrive each day along logging roads, slashing and burning the forests for agriculture and cattle, pushing many species toward extinction.

It's a story we've heard.

I've got a small battery-operated CD player with me by the river, and I click to track two of Coltrane's album *Spiritual*. The bass line begins low and deep. Four notes, four syllables: "a-love-su-preme." A light cymbal and drum falls in over the bass line, then piano. Finally the saxophone, played by Coltrane, breaks the tranquillity. The steady "a-love-su-preme" is absorbed by this wily instrument and thrown all over the place; sped up, slowed down, taken up to the heights and dropped back down.

My mind wanders across the park, across Brazil, across the ocean to Liberia, which I left nearly three years ago. Not long after my departure the war entered Monrovia, forcing CRS to close its offices. As my international colleagues were evacuated, national staff and other ordinary Liberians fended for themselves amid stray bullets, chronic dengue, and hunger. Rebel advances combined with international pressure to send Charles Taylor into exile in Nigeria, and Liberian business-man Claude Bryant—who is widely seen as politically neutral—was chosen to lead an interim government. In the power vacuum following Taylor's departure, a small group of United States Marines entered Monrovia, allowing the United Nations to build up what is now the world's largest peacekeeping force.

The cease-fire casts a silence over Liberia, and within the lull is a question: Where to? Pesimists say that there have been a string of peace deals over the past fourteen years, all of them eventually broken. But optimists note that all sides are exhausted by war and realize that peace is in everyone's best interest. They also point out that the different factions did come to agreement on Claude Bryant during peace talks in Ghana. Meanwhile, the *New York Times* reports that in backcountry towns like Greenville and Voinjama, "nature has reasserted control. Jungles sprout from inside the hollowed houses." Those who have been displaced slowly return to these places from refugee camps and try to reestablish something of a life.

A friend in the States told me that he could never live in a place like Liberia. When I asked him why, he responded, "Because I couldn't live so close to a human and environmental holocaust."

"But you do." He looked puzzled, and I clarified that we all share this tiny planet, so Liberia's agony is our own; just because you're not inside Buchenwald doesn't mean it ceases to exist. He clarified that he could not live where he had to *physically see it* every day.

And that's just it. I know that Liberia's pain is my own, but as the months turned to years, what was Technicolor has turned to black and white. I send the occasional supportive e-mail or cash wire transfer to Liberian friends who ask, but mostly, as Liberia slips into an uncertain future, I hold my friends in my heart. I think of Ciatta, Momo, and Chief Wah. I imagine Gabriel, Dickson, and Evans. I let them move around in my soul. Then I go into each new day looking at every person as a unique being capable of miracles; I look with wonder upon the healthy forests that still remain and draw strength from them; I am conscious of what I consume and try to bring my consumption into harmony with my vision of a just world. I attempt to find joy in living simply so that others (including other species) may simply live. I act as if a sustainable world were possible.

When you act as if the impossible is possible, it sometimes is. Sapo National Park still stands; Gabriel's work with Global Witness and Greenpeace miraculously convinced the UN Security Council to place a global embargo on Liberian timber. This embargo was a huge stride toward saving one of the world's most important rainforests, and also limited Taylor's access to funds for weapons, which may have helped lead to his ouster and the current chance at peace.

Coltrane's riffs are taking me back to Kind of Blue as the orange sun bleeds into rust over the Amazon, and I'm saying good night. Good night to another grain of pepper wrested from my blue clay flesh. It's a daily struggle to escape the musty prison cells of our narrow wills, a struggle to dance to a rhythm of empathy instead of moving awkwardly to songs that are not our own. As I say good night to my African mentor, Gabriel, to my lover Ciatta, and to tiny Chief Wah, I hold them in my heart. I don't know of any other heaven or any other hell except the ones right here; the ones that we choose to make each day all over Africa, in the Amazon, and especially in our own souls.

On the far side of the river a fragile, mighty forest slips into darkness, and a silence reigns at the end of the song, but I'm still humming about a love supreme.

Piso Firme, Bolivia
March 2004

ACKNOWLEDGMENTS

SOME OF THE initial ideas for this book took shape in conversation with Eric O. Morrissey, who encouraged me throughout and critiqued several drafts.

Faith Krinsky, Stanley Crawford, Jack Groves, Beth Cohen, Andrew McMorrow, Janelle Schuler, Lara Schwartz, Paige Fisher, Margaret Enis, Jacques Schillings, Jon Clarebout, Hannah Morris, WFP, DAP, ALP, and T. Nelson Williams generously provided ideas and manuscript comments.

For support in the last stage of the book, I am grateful for a fellowship from the Open Door Foundation, particularly for the spacious studio and house they provided me for four months in central Bolivia.

Special thanks to Gisela Ulloa Vargas, Judy Quinn, John Coyne, Harolyn Enis, Robin Broad, Carol Lancaster, and Jamison Suter.

While the vast majority of this book is based on my personal experience, two classic works—*The Africans* by David Lamb (New York: Vintage, 1984) and *Africa: Dispatches from a Fragile Continent* by Blaine Harden (London: HarperCollins, 1991)—were helpful for the sections on Liberian history (pp. 19ff. and 43ff.). Information from Harden's article "Africa's Gems: Warfare's Best Friend" (*New York Times*, April 6, 2000) and Steve Coll's "The Other War" (*Washington Post Magazine*, January 9, 2000) was peppered into my chapter on conflict diamonds. Jeffery

Bartholet's piece "A Big Man in Africa" (*Newsweek*, May 14, 2001) provided the Charles Taylor quotes in chapter 34.

I hope that my candid portrayal of development aid, as it operates in one African country, might act as fodder for ongoing renewal in CRS, a worthy organization staffed with numerous excellent people who have both taught and inspired me.

I cannot begin to thank the countless Liberians who welcomed me into their lives and shared with me the many lessons that enrich this book, and my life.

Finally, I am extremely grateful to my agent, William Clark, and to my editor, Gillian Blake, and her superb team at Bloomsbury.

A NOTE ON THE AUTHOR

William Powers hails from Long Island and is among
a small group of Westerners to have lived long-term
in Liberia and to have traveled to the nation's most
dangerous corners. For two years, he directed food
distribution, agriculture, and education programs
for the largest nongovernmental relief group in
Liberia. He has also worked at the World Bank, and
holds International Relations degrees from Brown
University and Georgetown's School of Foreign
Service. He is currently on assignment in Bolivia.

A NOTE ON THE TYPE

The text of this book is set in Linotype Sabon, named after the type founder Jacques Sabon. It was designed by Jan Tschichold and jointly developed by Linotype, Monotype, and Stempel, in response to a need for a typeface to be available in identical form for mechanical hot metal composition and hand composition using foundry type. Tschichold based his design for Sabon roman on a font engraved by Garamond, and Sabon italic on a font by Granjon. It was first used in 1966 and has proved an enduring modern classic.